National Council for the Social Studies

Linking Literature
with Life

The NCSS Standards
and Children's Literature
for the Middle Grades

ALEXA L. SANDMANN
JOHN F. AHERN

NCSS BULLETIN 99

National Council for the Social Studies

8555 Sixteenth Street ▸ Suite 500 ▸ Silver Spring, Maryland 20910
301 588-1800 fax 301 588-2049 www.socialstudies.org

Editorial Staff on this Publication: Terri Ackerman, Steve Lapham, Michael Simpson
Art Director: Gene Cowan   Graphic Designer: Kami Renee Price

Library of Congress Control Number: 2002101429
ISBN 0-87986-090-1

Printed in the United States of America
5 4 3 2 1

TO MY PARENTS, WHOSE BELIEF IN ME
STARTED ME ON THIS JOURNEY,
TO MY HUSBAND, WHOSE LOVE FOR ME
SUPPORTED ME IN THIS JOURNEY,
AND TO MY CHILDREN, WHO GAVE ME A
REASON FOR THIS JOURNEY.

—*ALS*

TO MY WIFE, ANNE.

—*JFA*

▶ TABLE OF CONTENTS

PART ONE
Using Literature to Teach Social Studies

CHAPTER ONE

Introduction

Three significant changes have had an impact on the teaching of social studies to the young adolescent in the last decade: (1) the development of the Curriculum Standards for Social Studies[1] by the National Council for the Social Studies (NCSS), (2) the growth in the number of middle schools, which are premised on the integration of content, and (3) the expansion of the use of children's literature in social studies.

This book is a response to these innovations. We seek to answer, in a practical way, three questions:

1. Why should literature be used to teach social studies in the middle grades?
2. What are some general reading comprehension strategies that can readily be used when teaching social studies through literature?
3. What are some recommended trade books and ways to use them?

Consequently, in Part One, we answer the first question by providing a rationale for using trade books in social studies, and address the second question, detailing strategies for nurturing students' reading comprehension. In Part Two, we provide annotations for more than 250 trade books, along with ideas for classroom use; we recommend at least 150 more titles.

The Rationale for Using Literature to Teach Social Studies in the Middle Grades

NCSS Commits to Creating National Standards for Social Studies

In 1990, the National Governors Association recommended the creation of national education goals. Two years later, with the support of President George H.W. Bush, Congress passed "Goals 2000," whose intent was to result in national standards. Although social studies was not included in the original list of disciplines, NCSS made a commitment to create social studies standards. This initiative focused on curriculum design and student performance with the assumption that each discipline, such as civics, geography, economics, and history, would have specific expectations about content details. The result was the publication of *Expectations of Excellence: Curriculum Standards for Social Studies*.[2]

The NCSS Standards, as they have come to be called, identify ten themes:

- ❶ CULTURE
- ❷ TIME, CONTINUITY, AND CHANGE
- ❸ PEOPLE, PLACES, AND ENVIRONMENTS
- ❹ INDIVIDUAL DEVELOPMENT AND IDENTITY
- ❺ INDIVIDUALS, GROUPS, AND INSTITUTIONS
- ❻ POWER, AUTHORITY, AND GOVERNANCE
- ❼ PRODUCTION, DISTRIBUTION, AND CONSUMPTION
- ❽ SCIENCE, TECHNOLOGY, AND SOCIETY
- ❾ GLOBAL CONNECTIONS
- ❿ CIVIC IDEALS AND PRACTICES

Each theme is introduced by a statement that provides "a guiding vision of content and purpose." Performance expectations for these goals or purposes are then identified at three levels: the early grades, middle grades, and high school.

A recurring concept in the standards is integration that is appropriate and predictable. The definition of social studies, as adopted by NCSS and cited in *Expectations of Excellence*, begins, "Social studies is the integrated study of the social sciences and humanities to promote civic competence. . . ."[3] In an extended definition of social studies, the authors note: "[Social studies] is designed to promote civic competence; and it is integrative, incorporating many fields of endeavor."[4] Their further elaboration provides additional support for the concept of integration:

1. Social studies programs have as a major purpose the promotion of civic competence, which is the knowledge, skills, and attitudes that enable students to be able to assume "the office of citizen"...
2. K-12 social studies programs integrate knowledge, skills, and attitudes within and across disciplines.
3. Social studies programs help students construct a knowledge base and attitudes drawn from academic disciplines as specialized ways of viewing reality.
4. Social studies programs reflect the changing nature of knowledge, fostering entirely new and highly integrated approaches to resolving issues of significance to humanity.[5]

They conclude: "This characteristic is the nature and strength of social studies: recognizing the importance of the disciplines and their specific perspectives in understanding topics, issues, and problems, but also recognizing that topics, issues, and problems transcend the boundaries of single disciplines and demand the power of integration within and across them.[6]

Thus, NCSS has explicitly embraced the concept of integrated learning, a philosophy it shares with the National Middle School Association.

The Middle School Philosophy: "This We Believe"

The number of middle schools is growing. National Middle School's "Research Summary 3" cites growth documented in the *Digest of Education Statistics*.[7] In 1973, there were 2,308 public middle schools and 7,878 public junior high schools. Twenty years later, there were approximately three middle schools for every junior high, with 9,573 middle schools and 3,970 junior highs in 1993."[8]

There is growing awareness that young people in grades five to eight are physically, socially, emotionally, and intellectually different from both high school students and young children. Middle school students deserve and need an education that reflects their developmental levels and abilities.

In 1982, the National Middle School Association (NMSA) developed a position paper articulating the common commitments of those who believe in the middle school movement. Revised in the mid-nineties, this booklet, titled *This We Believe*,[9] states that middle schools should be characterized by the following:

► Educators committed to young adolescents
► A shared vision
► High expectations for all
► An adult advocate for every student
► Family and community partnerships
► A positive school climate[10]

Furthermore, the position paper states that developmentally responsive middle schools should provide the following:

► Curriculum that is challenging, integrative, and exploratory
► Varied teaching and learning approaches
► Assessment and evaluation that promote learning
► Flexible organizational structures
► Programs and policies that foster health, wellness, and safety
► Comprehensive guidance and support services[11]

NMSA argues that curriculum must engage young adolescents, and "help them understand themselves and the world around them.[12] One could make the case that this is the central criterion upon which NCSS based its standards. Succinctly, in the preface to the NCSS Standards, Michael Hartoonian, writing for the members of the Curriculum Standards Task Force, states, "The informed social studies student exhibits the habits of mind and behavior of one who respects the relationship between education (i.e., learning) and his or her responsibility to promote the common good."[13]

NMSA's "high expectations for all" envision the curriculum as "challenging, integrative, and exploratory" in order to foster "health, wellness, and safety." This echoes the NCSS hope that in a world that is "diverse, ethically challenged, yet globally interdependent," the vision to "bring the blessing of the American dream to all" does not prove impossible. Indeed, as 1994-95 NCSS President Robert Stahl writes in the Foreword, "Implementation of these standards will require a cooperative effort and commitment."[14] Although Stahl was specifically addressing the NCSS standards, his comment is true of all educational reform; professional standards across organizations unite us for the benefit of students.

Additionally, one could make the case that this same criterion, helping students to understand themselves and the world around them, is what respected editors of children's literature use when determining what books to publish. It certainly was the criterion that we used in selecting texts for this work.

Children's Literature and the Social Studies

The use of children's literature as a means of improving social studies instruction is not a recent phenomena. As early as 1962, and since, writers of social studies methods books, such as Leonard Kenworthy,[15] provided lists of recommended children's books by grade level. In 1991, with two subsequent editions, the California State Department of Education provided classroom teachers with an annotated bibliography of children's books to teach social studies: *Literature for History-Social Science: Kindergarten through Grade Eight*.[16]

Although the use of trade books in social studies has a forty-year history, the practice has experienced enormous momentum in the past decade. Particularly given the growth of middle schools, journal articles focusing on literature and social studies for the preadolescent now appear with regularity in professional publications. "Children's Literature in Middle School Social Studies,"[17] "Dreaming of America: Weaving Literature into Middle-School Social Studies,"[18] "Using Trade Books to Teach Middle Level Social Studies,"[19] "Literature and History: A Focus on the Era of the Great

Depression and World War II,"[20] and "Using Literature to Study the Civil War and Reconstruction"[21] are merely a few examples of this phenomenon.

Accordingly, NCSS has long had a commitment to the use of children's literature and to providing resources for teachers. In 1966, in a revised edition of a 1961 version, NCSS published *Children's Books to Enrich the Social Studies*,[22] which provided teachers with titles and annotations for books appropriate throughout the elementary and middle school years. In 1984, NCSS published Schreiber's *Using Children's Books in Social Studies: Early Childhood through Primary Grades*,[23] which provided teachers of younger children with an excellent resource for using trade books to teach citizenship. In 1986, Levstik's chapter on the teaching of history in *Elementary School Social Studies: Research as a Guide to Practice*[24] devoted particular attention to using children's literature with older children. Silverblank's extensive bibliography[25] of historical fiction for grades five through twelve provided teachers with annotations of books available at that time, grouped by historical era or time period. NCSS Bulletin 91, *Enhancing Social Studies Through Literacy Strategies*,[26] especially chapter four, "Linking History, Literature, and Students," provides further evidence of the efficacy of using literature to develop social studies concepts.

NCSS journal publications also have attempted to assist teachers in finding resources to teach for the standards. In *Social Studies and the Young Learner*, in the article titled "Using Media Resources to Implement the New NCSS Curriculum Standards," Field and Hoge recommend a variety of technological media grouped by theme.[27] A second source, published that same year in *Social Studies and the Young Learner*, was Mitchell-Powell's annotated bibliography[28] of other works that compile resources, particularly children's books. It remains an important reference.

Perhaps the most familiar evidence of NCSS's commitment to children's literature is its annual annotated listing of "Notable Social Studies Trade Books for Young People" formerly known as "Notable Children's Trade Books in the Field of Social Studies." Since 1972, this has appeared in a spring issue of *Social Education*. Up until 1999, the listing appeared in the April/May issue; since 1999, it has appeared in the May/June issue. Although the books are grouped in familiar library classifications (biographies, folktales, poetry), since 1995, each summary concludes with a reference to one or more of the strands.

Published in 1994, *Children's Literature and Social Studies: Selecting and Using Notable Books in the Classroom*[29] gathered these yearly lists of the previous twenty-two years and extended them by providing ideas for using these texts in the classroom. Given the year of this resource, however, it does not sort the literature by strands.

The most recent related publication is Krey's 1998 work, *Children's Literature in Social Studies: Teaching to the Standards*,[30] which does group annotations around the NCSS Standards. Focusing on books written in the 1990s, Krey provides lengthy annotations that include recommended age levels. Her work is helpful to teachers of all grade levels, from preschool to high school. Although each annotation is grouped according to the strand for which it is considered most appropriate, she also includes in her annotation other strands to which the book might apply. In addition, there is, at the conclusion of each strand's annotations, a listing of books "as a second thematic strand." Although it does not focus on middle grade students, the performance expectations, or response activities, as the present book does, Krey's annotated bibliography reflects both the currency of the issue as well as the importance of the NCSS Standards.

Organization of the Book

In Part One, we seek to explain the importance of using literature to teach social studies at the middle grade level. The second chapter provides specific strategies that teachers can use with students to help them understand the literature they are reading, by giving them practical, useful ways of making sense of it, whether it is fiction or nonfiction.

Part Two is the heart of this book. We arranged the ten chapters in the order of the NCSS Standards, from Standard ❶, "Culture," to Standard ❿, "Civic Ideals and Practices." For ease of reference, we included, at the beginning of each chapter, the middle grade performance expectations taken from NCSS's *Expectations of Excellence*.[31]

For each standard, we have annotated twenty-three to twenty-eight books. First, we provide the bibliographic information for each book, including author(s), year of publication, illustrator if appropriate, place of publication, publisher, pages, and ISBN. Next, we list the performance expectations that are most viable for that text. An annotation of the book follows, accompanied by at least two ideas, and sometimes up to six, for how the book might be used in the middle school classroom. Our objective is to show how the books can be used to support teaching that enables students to meet performance expectations that are associated with a particular strand of the standards. Of course, many books include themes that are related to more than one strand of the standards, and our inclusion of a book in the chapter focusing on a particular strand does not imply that it cannot or should not be used in conjunction with teaching that focuses on other strands of the standards.

Within each strand, the books are divided in these sections: picture books; nonfiction books; novels, stories and folk tales; and, finally, poetry, if available.

"Picture books" are fully illustrated books that tend to have a brief text. While such books may be fictional, in the form of picture storybooks, this format also allows for texts whose content is nonfictional or biographical.

In the nonfiction section, books whose topics are the most general or broad are listed first, followed by more specific topics, listed in chronological order, if appropriate. In these and the other sections, we have also tried to group together books with similar themes, if appropriate.

In the section that features novels, stories, and folk tales, books are listed chronologically by the time period addressed. Collections of short stories have been included at the end of the section. When this section includes many books of contemporary fiction, I have tried to group together books by theme or topic where possible.

As is the case with any classification system, it is sometimes difficult to fit a book clearly into a category. One example of such a problem is the teaching of history through a format that is "fictitious," such as the presentation of the history of a civilization in the form of "newspaper stories," even if that civilization did not have newspapers. If books of this kind provide accurate information, and educate students in history rather than transport them into an imaginary world, they are classified as non-fiction.

The titles of all books are listed alphabetically in an index on pages 129-133, and the names of authors are included in the general index on pages 135-142.

Selection Criteria for Trade Books

We selected the books for their timeliness as well as their timelessness. Timeliness is important because books do not necessarily stay in print long—especially nonfiction texts. Consequently, in our initial search for books that supported the strands, we chose primarily "new" books, in hard cover, which we felt were so valuable that the chances were exceedingly good that paperback editions would follow. As this book went to print, every book included in it was available for sale, in either hardcover or paperback; however, even those that go out of print by the time this book is published should be available at the library.

Timelessness was also a consideration. We included books recognized by others as contributing greatly to the field of literature. Therefore, Caldecott winners appropriate for middle grade students are included, as are Newbery winners, Coretta Scott King Author and Illustrator Award winners, and Carter G. Woodson Book Award Winners. However, all are not included here because of limitations of space and because some are easier to use than others in instruction based on the NCSS strands.

Variety of genre was a significant criterion as well. While nonfiction books, including biography, and historical fiction books would be the natural genre, we also sought picture books that nurture the concepts of the strands. In addition, we included, as much as possible, anthologies of poetry, often overlooked in teaching social studies.

Beyond the criteria of whether or not these books are available and are of a particular format, we chose books because of the manner in which situations and people were presented. Using criteria established by Day,[32] we carefully considered both the illustrations and the text. Specifically, we looked for stereotypes (i.e., defined as over-simplified generalizations about a particular group, with implications that are usually negative) as well as tokenism (i.e., whether the presence of a certain character seemed authentic or simply "politically correct"). We looked at the roles characters took, in other words, who was doing what, particularly noting the roles of females in problem-solving situations and who was achieving success in various circumstances. We also strove to find books that honor a variety of life-styles and relationships between people.

Above all, we chose texts in order to have the greatest positive effect on a student's self-image or awareness of the world. This does not mean that we included in this bibliography only books that take a "rosy world" perspective. It means that we chose books that we believe deal with issues fairly; cruelty must be acknowledged as such before students can learn to avoid it. In particular, historical fiction sometimes presents scenes that are difficult for teachers to read and students to hear. We believe such works must be included in our curriculum in order to honor the past—so that we can create a more compassionate future. When students read about brutal historical events in the spare descriptions of a textbook, they might feel emotionally distant from what happened and brush it off as "no big deal." But a detailed and expanded version of the massacre of the Arawak people upon Columbus's arrival or the systematic genocide during World War II in a fictional but historically accurate text provides "the flesh" for the "bare bones of history," says Trelease.[33] The impact of the detail feeds students' learning capacity. Ultimately, the decision about the appropriateness of any text for one's students rests with each educator and the expectations of the community.

Readability was a factor in our selection process, but was not the most significant one. We chose books primarily for their content, which explains why we included picture books in the bibliography as well; however, we need to note that despite their name, all picture books are not designed or are not even suitable for younger students. The novels and informational texts that we selected vary in reading level. Some are close to a fourth grade independent reading level while others are closer to a seventh grade level; we believe this variety is a strength of this text. With at least four hundred recommended texts for both teachers and students to choose from, we believe that there is "something for everyone" in both content and format.

Notes

1. National Council for the Social Studies, *Expectations of Excellence: Curriculum Standards for Social Studies* (Washington, D.C.: Author, 1994).
2. *Ibid.*
3. *Ibid.*, 3.
4. *Ibid.*
5. *Ibid.*, 3-5.
6. *Ibid.*, 5.
7. National Center for Education Statistics, *Digest of Education Statistics* (Washington, D.C.: Author, Department of Education Statistics, 1995).
8. *Ibid.*
9. National Middle School Association, *This We Believe* (Columbus, Ohio: Author, 1995).
10. *Ibid.*, 11.
11. *Ibid.*
12. *Ibid.*, 21.
13. NCSS, *Expectations of Excellence*, xix-xx.
14. *Ibid.*, xviii.
15. Leonard Stout Kenworthy, *Social Studies for the Eighties: In Elementary and Middle Schools* (New York: Macmillan, 1982).
16. Ralph Hansen, ed., *Literature for History-Social Science: Kindergarten through Grade Eight* (Sacramento: California Department of Education, 1995).
17. Marsha K. Savage and Tom V. Savage, "Children's Literature in Middle School Social Studies," *The Social Studies* 84, no. 1 (1993): 32-36.
18. J. Lea Smith and Holly A. Johnson, "Dreaming of America: Weaving Literature into Middle-School Social Studies," *The Social Studies* 86, no. 2 (1995): 60-68.
19. Robert H. Lombard, "Using Trade Books to Teach Middle Level Social Studies," *Social Education* 60, no. 4 (1996): 223-226.
20. John Ahern and Alexa Sandmann, "Literature and History: A Focus on the Era of the Great Depression and World War II," *The Social Studies* 88, no. 6 (1997): 277-282.
21. Alexa Sandmann and John Ahern, "Using Literature to Study the Civil War and Reconstruction," *Middle School Journal* 29, no. 2 (1997): 25-33.
22. Helen Huus, *Children's Books to Enrich the Social Studies* (Washington, D.C.: National Council for the Social Studies, 1966).
23. Joan Schreiber, *Using Children's Books in Social Studies: Early Childhood through Primary Grades* (Washington, D.C.: National Council for the Social Studies, 1984).
24. Linda Levstik, "Teaching History: A Definitional and Developmental Dilemma," in *Elementary School Social Studies: Research as a Guide to Practice*, ed. Virginia A. Atwood (Washington, D.C.: National Council for the Social Studies, 1986), 68-84.
25. Fran Silverbank, *An Annotated Bibliography of Historical Fiction for the Social Studies* (Dubuque, Iowa: Kendall/Hunt, 1992).
26. Judith Irvin, John P. Lunstrum, Carol Lynch-Brown, and Mary F. Shepard, *Enhancing Social Studies through Literacy Strategies* (Washington, D.C.: National Council for the Social Studies, 1995).
27. Sherry Field and John D. Hoge, "Using Media Resources to Implement the New NCSS Standards," *Social Studies & the Young Learner* 8, no. 1 (1995): 26-32.
28. Brenda Mitchell-Powell, "Standards and Practices: Children's Literature and Curricula Reform for the Twenty-first Century," *Social Studies & the Young Learner* 8, no. 1 (1995): 19-21.
29. Myra Zarnowski and Arlene Gallagher, *Children's Literature and Social Studies: Selecting and Using Notable Books in the Classroom* (Dubuque, Iowa: Kendall/Hunt, 1994).
30. DeAn M. Krey, *Children's Literature in Social Studies: Teaching to the Standards* (Washington, D.C.: National Council for the Social Studies, 1998).
31. NCSS, *Expectations of Excellence*.
32. Frances Ann Day, *Multicultural Voices in Contemporary Literature: A Resource for Teachers* (Portsmouth, N.H.: Heinemann, 1994).
33. Jim Trelease, *The New Read Aloud Handbook* (New York: Penguin, 1995).

CHAPTER TWO

Reading Comprehension and Trade Books for Social Studies

"So now, in addition to all the history, economics, and geography, I'm supposed to teach reading, too?"

"Yes," comes the reply, "because you are best prepared to do it."

"How can that be? I have never taken a reading course."

"Easy. You know how a historian, an economist, a geographer thinks, and it is these ways of processing such vast amounts of information that your students need most desperately."

"Okay. Maybe. Are there some techniques that I could easily learn and use with my classes?"

"Absolutely. Naming these reading strategies, describing the strengths of each, and detailing how to implement them is what this chapter is all about. Each social studies teacher must choose the best strategies for the students and content at hand."

A Little Background Information on Reading

Reading and writing are critically important in all subject areas. If students cannot make meaning from the symbols on the page, that is, truly read, not just decode, words, they cannot succeed in school or, more important, in life.

Our world is becoming increasingly print driven, and technology is a major part of this trend. "Where once Americans depended on the vagaries of the post office to communicate in personalized, written messages, now we send 2.2 billion E-mail messages a day, compared with just 293 million pieces of first-class mail… With at least a third of the nation now sending messages over the Internet, E-mail has become second nature to tech savvy Net-Setters and groovy grandmas alike."[1]

Students are an increasing part of this on-line crowd as well. Schools are fostering these technological connections. In 1998, according to the U.S. Department of Education, 78 percent of students in public schools in grades 1-12 used the Internet at school.[2] As of 1999, 95 percent of public schools had access to the Internet, and 63 percent of instructional rooms (classrooms, computer labs and library/media centers) had such access.[3] Because Internet-related activities require the ability to read and write, we may have discovered one of the best motivators yet for refining literacy skills. In many schools, students typically look first to the Internet as they begin research projects. Discerning valuable and reputable sources has become a part of students' standard learning practices across disciplines; thus, students' critical thinking skills are nurtured in authentic ways.

While being able to consult with the reading teacher in your building would be a tremendous resource for you as a social studies teacher, school days are typically not designed to accommodate extensive time for such collaboration. Consequently, it makes the most sense for you to know enough strategies to make your own curriculum attainable for your students so that they can achieve an understanding of social studies concepts. As Thomas Jefferson believed, an educated citizenry is critical to the success of a democracy.

Literature in social studies classrooms energizes and nurtures concept development. We have designed this chapter to give you brief background information on reading comprehension and some ways to use these strategies in your classroom.

Although the primary purpose of this book is to encourage the integration of literature to support the NCSS strands, the strategies we provide may also be helpful with textbooks. "Historically junior and senior high texts have been written with more concern for content than for difficulty level,"[4] all the more reason to use trade books that are student friendly.

Basics of Reading Comprehension

Reading comprehension is enhanced dramatically if three conditions are met: (1) the student is prepared to read and understand the material, (2) the student understands the organization of the material, and (3) the student reflects and extends his or her thinking about the material by understanding parts of the selection, as well as understanding how the parts fit within the whole text. Consequently, reading strategies typically are divided into three categories: (1) before reading (*preparational strategies*), (2) during reading (*organizational strategies*), and (3) after reading (*elaborational strategies*).

The problem with this system of categorization is that strategies are, in fact, flexible and are not meant to be confined to one specific stage of the reading process. As such, depending on the text, students can use strategies at various times during the process of *making meaning*. The phrase "making meaning" is the pivotal one in terms of making choices regarding which strategies to use and when. Once you understand the basics of the strategies, you will be able to adapt and tailor them to fit students' needs with a particular text, whether it is a textbook or a trade book.

Preparational Strategies

Typically, the most underused strategies are preparational ones, especially once students are in middle school. Teachers may expect students to be able, and even to desire, to "dive in" to absorb information. We know from all-too-familiar conversations with students, however, that this is not the case. Motivation is certainly part of the reason. Textbooks in particular are not motivating; they are often overwhelming, in physical weight, design, and length. The advantage of most literature, especially paperback books, is that the books are lighter, are formatted to be easy on the eyes, and are much shorter.

Motivation and Interest

Getting students ready to read is the goal of preparational strategies, and their use greatly increases the odds that students will learn the intended material. For teachers to decide that there is not time to build motivation and interest can be an enormously costly decision; students' lack of achievement may force teachers to circle back and reteach. Therefore, one of the easiest ways to motivate students is simply to allocate the time necessary to "read aloud" a picture book about the topic.

For example, if you were to begin a unit on the Civil War, reading aloud Patricia Polacco's *Pink and Say*[5] would get, probably tearfully, students' attention about the issue of race in the war. *Pink and Say* is the story of two boys, one black and one white, who come to understand the true nature of war, which is death, and the connectedness of humanity, which is love. This

picture book could be followed by Gary Paulsen's diary-like novel, *Soldier's Heart*.[6] Through this book, students' perceptions of the realities of war would similarly be extended and enhanced as students "linked literature with life," recognizing the emotions in their own lives while connecting with the characters.

Alternatively, no picture book needs to precede the reading aloud of a novel like *Soldier's Heart*. A section of the novel could simply be read aloud each day, and class discussions could link the information with previous and future concepts. The literature would provide students with ongoing motivation to learn more. Many classrooms do not engage in reading texts aloud, especially at the middle grade level and higher. Since 1985, however, when *Becoming a Nation of Readers*[7] was published—a study that looked at more than 20,000 pieces of research on reading—we have known that "the single most important activity for building the knowledge required for eventual success in reading is reading aloud to children."[8] In addition, reading is the key ingredient to academic success.

One important advantage of reading aloud a picture book, in terms of specific content, is that everyone is privy to the same information and is prepared for discussion. Reading aloud longer texts can also be particularly effective for nurturing conceptual understanding because students' listening comprehension of text is nearly always at least two years beyond their reading comprehension, and oftentimes more. Thus, students who might struggle to read a text independently would gain the support of hearing the text read aloud and discussed. For example, when a picture book is read aloud, students gain the benefit of being prepared to participate in all class activities related to the text, which may not be possible if students are asked to complete independent assignments and do not finish them. Also, we should note that entire books do not need to be read aloud. Because of their brevity, picture books typically are read cover to cover, but only powerful scenes from a novel or a particular section of an informational book may be needed to build interest and motivation.

If willing to practice, students can also read aloud texts in class. What should be avoided is "round robin reading" (i.e., teachers asking students to read aloud spontaneously). For this method of sharing literature to be effective and enjoyable, preparation is critical. Without it, students may not be able to focus on the content of the book because they may start to fall asleep if the pace is too slow or because they may become confused as words are mispronounced or omitted. Practice also means that all students can take part in this activity, not just those for whom reading aloud is easy.

Asking students to be actively involved in the reading of the picture book or longer work is another way to encourage interest. If at least one copy of the book is available for every two students, students could read the book together. Called paired reading, students would sit side by side and take turns reading aloud to each other. Typically, the student on the left would read the left side of the two-page spread and then the student on the right would read the side in front of himself or herself. Or students could simply take turns reading a page of text, because pictures can make the left-side / right-side design approach difficult to coordinate.

Still another variation on this theme of having students interact with the books in an ongoing way—if enough copies of the book are available for every student to have one—students could *independently read* a class novel. Similarly, if there are only single copies of a variety of texts, students could independently read different texts. Either way, teachers would provide students with time to read the assigned or selected sections of the book silently, allowing students to move along at an individual pace. Oftentimes, teachers could permit students to choose a more conducive place to read other than having them sit upright at a desk. Nestled under desks, tucked into corners, or stretched out on the floor, students may become immersed in the world their book describes. Many middle grade students could easily handle a thirty-minute sustained silent reading (SSR) period.

Another way to create enthusiasm for a topic would be to design an anticipation guide.[9] An anticipation guide is a set of statements, typically five to eight, that asks students to agree or disagree with statements of opinion, thereby recording what they think, or what they think they know, before the topic is actually covered. Students discuss responses as a class, and then they put aside the paper until after they have finished reading. Then, following the reading, students once again decide if they agree or disagree by marking in the appropriate spaces. Anticipation guides work best with information that allows for at least some of the statements to be open ended versus simply factual statements with right and wrong answers.

For example, statements on an anticipation guide for the Great Depression might be the following: "Geography had little to do with how people were affected by the Great Depression" and "The stock market crash of 1929 was the precipitating event of the Great Depression." The first statement is open to more debate than is the second. Who is to say those in the Dust Bowl of Oklahoma were in more distress than were the field laborers in the South or West?

Anticipation guides are usually formatted in one of two ways. On the far left side of the page is a column called "Before Reading," and on the far right side is another column called "After Reading," as shown in Figure 2a. Beneath each are two spaces, one for Agree and another for Disagree. In between is a statement. Alternatively, two columns are created at one side of the page, one for Before Reading and another for After Reading. Students then place an "A" for Agree or a "D" for Disagree in the single spaces allotted, as shown in Figure 2b.

If you decide you are going to teach a social studies unit that uses a novel everyone will read, probably no strategy would be as easy or as effective for motivating or interesting students as would be *predicting*. You could start by looking at the cover on the book. You could ask students to look at the cover, talk about the title, and decide whether the cover seems to fit the title or if the jacket illustration seems more focused on "selling books." At that point, you could ask students to predict, or make an "educated guess," regarding what they believe the book will be about. You could then record the ideas on the blackboard, an overhead transparency, or chart paper. Next, you could read aloud or have students read any information on the back of the book. Students could then consider this additional information and revise their earlier predictions as needed. Finally, you could read the inside flaps of the book jacket, or any supplementary pages if the book is a paperback, and have students add any revisions to their predictions. Then you could note these, and review with students what their expectations are for the book. They may be eager to read to find out how accurate they are.

If you choose to read a nonfiction text with students, an extension of predicting that works particularly well with informational text is called *previewing*. After students have looked at the front and back covers, or the book jacket, you could ask them to preview the text with you: notice the illustrations, photographs, maps, or graphs. Then you could read the table of contents together, looking at the headings and skimming the titles or subtitles. In other words, you could have students "get the feel" for the information they will be

FIGURE 2a ANTICIPATION GUIDE, TYPE A

Before Reading

Agree Disagree

  ○   ○   Geography had little to do with how people were affected by
the Great Depression.

  ○   ○   The stock market crash of 1929 was the precipitating event
of the Great Depression.

After Reading

Agree Disagree

○   ○

○   ○

FIGURE 2b ANTICIPATION GUIDE, TYPE B

Before Reading   **After Reading**

Agree / Disagree   Agree / Disagree

_____   _____ Geography had little to do with how people were affected
by the Great Depression.

_____   _____ The stock market crash of 1929 was the precipitating event
of the Great Depression.

studying. You could ask them which sections look particularly interesting. Perhaps you could respond to their interests by creating either small group or whole-class activities or projects.

Envisioning is another technique geared toward building interest in reading. Before having students read *Amos Fortune: Free Man*[10] by Elizabeth Yates, you could read students a parallel version, as indicated in Figure 2c, of the opening chapter. They might be able to put themselves in the place of a black princess, or her brother, the man who becomes Amos Fortune and who began life in Africa as a prince who is captured by slave traders. If students first listen to an account of a contemporary kidnapping that attempts to heighten their senses, they might more readily relate to the opening events in the novel.

Activating Background Knowledge

As previously discussed, engaging students in the topic is a critical first step toward getting them involved in their learning. Sometimes, however, motivating students occurs simultaneously as we activate their prior knowledge about a particular topic. Students are relieved to realize that they already know something about the topic at hand; they are not starting with nothing. And if they find it reassuring that they already know something about the topic, the topic probably will already have some significance in their lives—another bonus. Finally, activating prior knowledge honors the individuality of each student. Students want to be respected for what they already know. By using strategies to find out what they do know, teachers can sidestep the possibility of boring students with redundant information and invigorate them by planning lessons that link them with previous information.

Graphic organizers are visual representations of information (i.e., a means of looking at information to literally "see" relationships between ideas). One kind of graphic organizer is a semantic map or web that helps students recognize what they know about a topic already or what their feelings are about that topic. Before beginning a unit on economics, you could put that word in the center of the blackboard or on an overhead transparency, circle it, and then ask students what ideas they relate with this word. A diagram like that could be called a "sunshine web" because lines come from the central concept like rays of the sun. It is the simplest kind of semantic map because it accepts all answers (see Figure 2d) and does not attempt to cluster them.

Although there are no absolute definitions for the differences between semantic maps and webs, generally speaking, semantic maps are more detailed and often contain categories or hierarchies. For example, a semantic map also could begin with the word economics in the center of the diagram, but instead of just asking for connections from students, you could supply categories of information you would like from them. Thus, you would impose some organization on students' thinking from the beginning. Categories could

FIGURE 2c   GUIDED IMAGERY FOR *AMOS FORTUNE: FREE MAN*

Close your eyes… tell all your muscles to relax and imagine…

It is night, but it is not quiet. In Toledo, the citizens are gathering for Riverfest, a celebration on the river for the Fourth of July. All around you, hear the people talking and laughing at this festive occasion… You talk with your parents as you anticipate the fireworks, which will be the culminating event of the evening. You think about what the Fourth of July means to you. The word freedom keeps coming to mind…

You have looked forward to this night all week. You knew that you and your little brother or sister would be able to stay up extra late. You look at your brother or sister and are glad that he or she is with you to sample all the food. Taste the possibilities—sweet cotton candy, tangy corn dogs, salty popcorn, or cool ice cream…

See the variety of people around you… people of different cultures… of different neighborhoods… You realize that all are smiling tonight. Past quarrels are forgotten. All are equal tonight, brought together in this celebration of freedom…

Listen to the music rise from one corner of the festival, then fall as applause rises, only to rise again momentarily. . . . People are dancing both on and off the dance floor, feet tapping, arms swinging, bodies moving to the beat of the drums and electronic guitar. Voices lifted in song fill the night air in unpredictable patterns….

Just before the fireworks begin, you take your little brother's or sister's hand in a rare show of emotion. Seeing your sibling's smile, you remember that while having a sibling can certainly be a nuisance, this one, after all, is the only one you have…

You squeeze your little brother's or sister's hand to signal that the fireworks are almost ready to begin. You see your parents talking with some neighbors across the park. In the darkness, in anticipation, you wait….

You see the first fireworks display. Color fills the sky…. First, red streaks. Then another—silver. Then another—blue, and then another, and another, and another…. The explosions begin, coming like rapid fire… filling the night air with a cacophony of sound so that cries of "Help" are lost in the confusion.

Two large men, huge, muscular, carrying guns, surround you and your brother or sister, but they choose only you. In the darkness, in the midst of exploding fireworks, you are quickly gagged, tied, and carried off, away from the celebration.

Imagine your fear, your confusion, your disorientation. You are a prisoner, but at least you are alive.

FIGURE 2d   START OF A SUNSHINE WEB FOR ECONOMICS

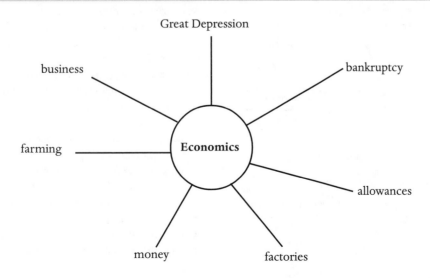

be Economic Theories, Historical Periods, Factors of Production, and Specialized Vocabulary. Accordingly, students could put *macro* and *micro* under "Kinds of." They could put *Great Depression* and *Boom of 1990s* under "Historical Periods." Students could suggest *land* and *labor* for "Factors of Production." "Specialized Vocabulary" could generate *recession, entrepreneur,* and *currency.* Clearly, the more background information students have, the more complex the visual organizer could be initially, as shown in Figure 2e. At that early stage in the unit, don't be afraid of allowing students to place information in the wrong category or to include information that is not technically correct. As with the anticipation guide, these misconceptions will be corrected as the unit progresses. These "creative errors" also map out the most effective route for instruction.

A variation on this theme would be to ask students, before they read, simply to brainstorm ideas they have on the topic; you could cluster the ideas so that a logical order would be imposed on the information. Your modeling of how to group ideas would be an important one. While these webbing/mapping activities are most frequently done as a whole class, they can also be done individually or as a small-group activity, with the students or small groups then reporting back to the whole class.

Building Background Knowledge

Taking the time to build background knowledge is ultimately, and ironically, a great saver of time. Providing students with some specific information before reading text will engender a far greater likelihood that they will understand the text in a deeper, more satisfying way. The question at hand then becomes, "What do students need to know before reading the assigned material?" Sharing a literature excerpt, perhaps by reading a picture book aloud,

FIGURE 2e   START OF A SEMANTIC MAP FOR ECONOMICS

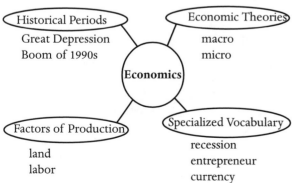

is often the way teachers resolve this question. Reading Margaree King Mitchell's *Uncle Jed's Barbershop*[11] aloud would help students understand readily what race relations were like in the 1920s and 1930s, an invaluable precursor to Mildred Taylor's *Mississippi Bridge.*[12]

In *Uncle Jed's Barbershop,* students learn that most blacks in the South were sharecroppers; that towns had separate public rest rooms, water fountains, and schools for blacks and whites; that black men could have their hair cut only by a black barber; and that hospitals had "colored waiting rooms," that all white patients were seen first, even if a black patient needed immediate care, and that if blacks needed an operation, no matter how quickly, payment was expected first. Students also learn the irony that in the stock market crash of 1929, whites and blacks were suddenly "equal," in that both had the opportunity to lose all of their money. Most important, they learn that black men had dreams of a better society; in the story, Uncle Jed opens his barbershop on his seventy-ninth birthday. In ten minutes or less, this picture book provides both motivation and background information on critical issues to be extended over the course of the unit.

Sometimes, reading an article from the newspaper aloud may be just enough information to provide the link between what students know and what they are going to learn. If the topic is currently in the news, students may become immediately interested because of its relevance to their daily lives.

Vocabulary instruction is another way to build conceptual knowledge. Decisions about its timing, however, can sometimes be challenging. Although traditionally taught before reading is completed, vocabulary lessons are sometimes most effectively taught either during or even after the reading is completed. As surprising as this is, it is true because vocabulary is most easily retained in context. Once students know something about the subject, they begin making connections between new words and their previous knowledge. Those connections are tremendous aids to memory.

Obviously, sometimes several words are critical to understanding from the very beginning. *Concept circles*[13] are an excellent strategy to help students refine their understanding of words. To model this concept with the word *geography,* you could draw a circle with five parts. Concept circles can have as many sections as needed, but four seems to be most typical. Your circle would include the words *place, location, relationships within places, movement,* and *regions,*[14] as shown in

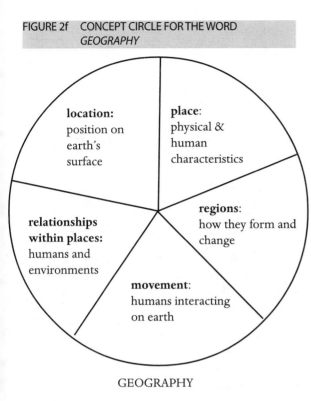

GEOGRAPHY

Figure 2f. Beneath it would be a space for students to write the target word, *geography*. Visually then, students would see the five themes of geography.

As students grow more comfortable with this strategy, you could challenge them a bit more by supplying concept circles that include one word or phrase that does not support the concept. For example, you could select the word *entrepreneur*. In three of these sections, you would write words or phrases that help define *entrepreneur*. These words could be *has good ideas*, *strives to make money*, and *is one's own boss*, as shown in Figure 2g. In the last section, you would write a word or phrase that is not supportive of the concept, such as *needs no customers*. The goal for students, then, would be to cross-out the concept that "does not belong." Again, as students grow more comfortable with the strategy, you could give them a targeted vocabulary word with two sections completed and ask them to supply a third synonym / description as well as one that does not belong.

Another means for vocabulary development is *webbing* or *mapping*, as previously described (i.e., simply writing words as clusters that show associations between and among focal words). This activity provides a broad and supportive schema for retention.

Organizational Strategies

Understanding how information is organized makes a critical difference in students' ability to comprehend. If the material is from a textbook, the fairly consistent presentation of the material means that if students understand how the material is organized, they will be able to pull the most from it. Understanding the format of trade books also enhances students' comprehension. The strategies that follow can be used as students read any text. Because each of the strategies has a focus, students have a purpose for reading, which is critical to their retention of the material. When students understand why they are reading something, they tend to be more motivated and remember information at a higher level because they know their probability for success has improved dramatically.

Text frames are one way to help students visualize information using the structure of the text as the guiding element. Social studies text, both nonfiction and fiction, is often organized around a cause and effect format. With a text frame, teachers could ask students to read a certain section of text that is written in this cause and effect format. Then, teachers could have students complete the frame that explains the relationship, filling in first the cause, or the effect, whichever is first presented in the text, and then filling in the companion information, as shown in Figure 2h for *So Far from the Sea*[15] by Eve Bunting.

Other times, classifying information may be the overriding structural element. Then, students may need to

ENTREPRENEUR

Cause: Japanese bombed Pearl Harbor.	Effect: Americans on West Coast were suddenly scared of having Japanese Americans as neighbors.
Cause: Fear that Japanese Americans might help Japan.	Effect: Japanese Americans were sent to internment camps.
Cause: Japanese Americans could take few possessions to camp.	Effect: Most Japanese Americans lost many of their possessions when they were sent to camps.

keep a list of which generals and other officers are fighting for which side. A *T-chart* can easily be created for students to "sort" people and their positions. For the Civil War, for example, as students are reading *Bull Run*[16] by Paul Fleischman, teachers could help students design a chart like this and have them add names in the appropriate column as each character is introduced (see Figure 2i).

Creating *time lines* of events is particularly useful in understanding certain periods of history, as shown in Figure 2j for the book *Starry Messenger*[17] by Peter Sis. Students could use the visual stimulus of a timeline to place significant events in sequence.

Students could also create parallel timelines to compare multiple perspectives during the same time period, as shown in Figure 2k.

Comparison and contrast might be the critical concept for a particular section of text. Then a *Venn diagram* might be the most suitable. Typically, a Venn diagram is created by two intersecting circles. In the area to the left of the intersection, characteristics are written about one of two entities that are significant but are not true of the other; in the area to the right of the intersection, characteristics are written that are true of the second but not of the first. In the intersection, information is written that is true of both. If students were studying what life was like in the early to middle 1800s for both whites and blacks in the North and the South, students could read the book by Patricia and Fredrick McKissack, *Christmas in the Big House, Christmas in the Quarters,*[18] to compare the life of privileged Southerners with that of their slaves. Teachers could display a brief summary of their reading as shown in Figure 2l.

You could ask your students to become actively involved with a text that presents information in a problem and solution format. You could pose the problem, and students would read to find the solution. A simple visual aid for this centers the problem at the top of the page with various lines extending from it. The multiplicity of lines encourages problem solving by signaling the possibility of more than one answer, removing the traditional single response. Thus, in reading Sharon Draper's *Romiette and Julio,*[19] which is about how a gang wants to discourage interracial dating, you could pose the problem, "How can Romiette and Julio dissuade the gang from harassing them?" as shown in graphic organizer Figure 2m.

About Point Notetaking[20] works particularly well with descriptive text. This strategy first has students name, in a word or two, what the text is "About." Next, you would have your students write a sentence that states what information the writer wants to share about the topic, the "point." Then, students would combine the information recorded in the previous two categories to write a summary statement. Finally, students would reread the section of text—a paragraph, two paragraphs, or section—and add details under the statement, as shown in Figure 2n for Margaret Davidson's biography *I Have a Dream: The Story of Martin Luther King.*[21] This strategy has students first name and understand the topic and second find supporting details. If

FIGURE 2l CLASSIFICATION BY T-CHART FOR *BULL RUN*

Union	Confederate
Lily Malloy	Colonel Oliver Brattle
Gideon Adams	Shem Suggs
James Dacy	Flora Wheelworth
Nathaniel Epp	Toby Boyce

1564	1581	1592	1609	1633	1642
Galileo Galilei born	Entered University of Pisa	Became professor of math at University of Padua	Invented spyglass (telescope)	Condemned for heresy by Catholic church	Galileo dies

1564	1581	1592	1609	1633	1642
Galileo Galilei born	Entered University of Pisa	Became professor of math at University of Padua	Invented spyglass (telescope)	Condemned for heresy by Catholic church	Galileo dies

1564	1589	1595	1606	1667
William Shakespeare born; Michelangelo dies; Vesalius dies (biologist and doctor)	Catherine DeMedici dies (mother of three French kings)	Torquato Tasso dies (great poet of Renaissance)	Rembrandt born	Milton writes "Paradise Lost"

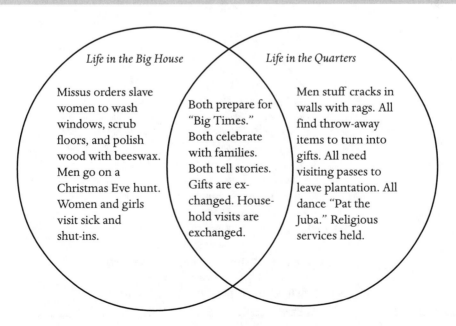

Life in the Big House

Missus orders slave women to wash windows, scrub floors, and polish wood with beeswax. Men go on a Christmas Eve hunt. Women and girls visit sick and shut-ins.

Both prepare for "Big Times." Both celebrate with families. Both tell stories. Gifts are exchanged. Household visits are exchanged.

Life in the Quarters

Men stuff cracks in walls with rags. All find throw-away items to turn into gifts. All need visiting passes to leave plantation. All dance "Pat the Juba." Religious services held.

Problem: How can Romiette and Julio dissuade the gang from harassing them?
Possible solutions: 1. Talk with the school principal.
                      2. Talk with their parents.
                      3. Create a plan of their own.
                      4. Ignore the gang.
                      5. Ask friends to help.

ABOUT: Martin Luther King, Jr.
POINT: Mission was for all people to be treated equally.
STATEMENT: Martin Luther King, Jr.'s, mission was for all people to be treated the same.
DETAILS: 1. King led marches to end segregation.
            2. King gave powerful speeches against segregation.
            3. King won the Nobel Peace Prize in 1964, which honored his lifelong commitment to peace.

SETTING: Big city, probably Los Angeles, in the 1990s
CHARACTERS: Mama, Daniel, Mrs. Kim, firefighter, two cats
STYLE: Story is told from young boy's point of view.
EVENTS: 1. Rioting is occurring.
            2. Building catches fire.
            3. All residents are evacuated to shelter.
            4. Daniel's cat is missing.
            5. A firefighter finds the missing cat with the neighbor's, Mrs. Kim's cat.
            6. Daniel's mom invites Mrs. Kim to her home after things settle down.
THEME: People are more alike than different.

Smoky Night
Title of story
Daniel
Name of main character
caring, questioning
Two words describing the main character
city chaos nighttime
Three words describing the setting
angry rioters burning, stealing
Four words stating the problem
rioters steal anything, set fires
Five words describing one main event
Daniel, Mama have to evacuate apartment
Six words describing a second main event
firefighter finds cats together and rescues them
Seven words describing a third main event
Mama invites Mrs. Kim to apartment as friend
Eight words stating the solution to the problem

you ask students to use this strategy as they read or reread, they would be reading for a purpose, which is crucial to their success in understanding the material.

If the material is fictional, creating a *story map/grammar* can be a most effective strategy. This strategy provides a way for students to summarize a story; the longer the text, the more challenging the task. To get the full effect of a novel, students need to clarify for themselves the setting (including time and place), characters, plot, theme, style, and especially point of view, so that even more specific knowledge can grow from the basics. Students can set up story maps or grammars in a number of ways. One example is shown in Figure 2o for the book *Smoky Night*[22] by Eve Bunting.

A variation on this is called a *story pyramid*,[23] which is like a puzzle, in that students describe the text using a specified number of words on specific lines. Students begin by naming the main character. Next, students describe the character in two words. In three words students then, describe the setting. On the next line, in four words, students state the problem. Next, students describe a significant event in five words, followed by a second significant event in six words, and, finally, a third event in seven words. On the last line, in eight words, students present the solution to the problem, as shown in Figure 2p, again for *Smoky Night*, for ease in comparing this strategy with a more traditional story map/grammar.

Elaborational Strategies

Teachers can use strategies that incorporate writing either while students are reading, in order to monitor their comprehension and reinforce the information students have obtained, or after reading, inorder to reinforce information and provide opportunities for students to extend their learning. *Summarizing* the information is a powerful tool for comprehension. Summarizing, however, can take a variety of forms. In the previous section, many of the strategies—semantic maps, cause/effect text frames, timelines, problem/solution templates, About Point Notetaking, and story maps or pyramids—are forms of summaries and can be used not only during reading but also afterwards. Summaries can also take the form of *learning logs*; this form of a journal can be open ended, with students recording information periodically as they read, or answering specific questions given by the teacher for various sections of the material as they read or when they are finished with the entire selection. The value of learning logs is that they ask the students to conceptualize information, not just repeat simple, knowledge-level concepts. The chance to write more open-ended responses greatly increases the possibility that students will make connections with the book by reflecting on it.

Thus, a teacher might ask students, at the close of a class session, to record what they learned from what they read. When initially using this strategy, teachers could prompt students to write "three new understandings or ideas." Or a teacher who is using *My Brother Sam Is Dead*[24] by James and Christopher Collier could ask one specific question that would help students focus on the most important concept for the day: "Did our ancestors begin fighting with Great Britain because they *wanted* to be a separate country from them? How do you know? Think about whether any of the characters' responses to Great Britain's rules and regulations would be helpful in responding to this question."

Reading guides of varying types also help students integrate their knowledge. Simply stated, reading guides are "teacher-developed devices for helping students understand instructional reading materials.[25] It is important to note that the definition of "reading guide" is "teacher developed." Reading guides are not just the list of questions at the end of the chapter or the lists of questions many teachers write for specific pieces of literature.

Although it is true that reading guides can simply be a list of questions, the kinds of questions teachers ask should be carefully constructed to provide a powerful model for students' reading in the future when such an instructional aid is unavailable. Students need their teachers' help to discern the significant information versus detail that distracts them from the conceptual understandings. Also, reading guides are student-friendly aids to comprehension so that, typically, they include page numbers regarding where responses to questions can be found.

Reading guides can also be formatted as open-ended outlines so that students can visualize the information presented. By the way the spaces are created on the page, the outline helps students see parallel information, as in novels in which alternating chapters honor one character's perspective and then another and so on, as is done in Michael Dorris's *Morning Girl*.[26] In any case, especially if the text is lengthy, reading guides usually include page numbers to the questions or information sections to help students search for answers more efficiently. Teachers can also design reading guides in nearly all of the formats listed in the "organizational" section. Again, the physical form of these text frames helps students visualize the content.

Strategies That Combine Different Approaches

There are also strategies that blend all three ways of tackling text. For example, the *KWL Plus*[27] strategy initially has three parts. First, teachers ask students what they know (the "K" in KWL) about a particular topic. Initially as a class activity, but later on, as an individual task, students could record this information in the K column. Next, teachers ask students what they want to learn, (the "W" in KWL), and record this information in the middle column. After students have read, and perhaps even researched these questions, students then record what they learned (the "L" in KWL) in the L column. In this last column, students also record information they still need to learn, as shown in Figure 2q.

After students complete the chart, they return to what they have written and categorize in order to organize the information before writing about it (which is the "plus" part of the strategy). They can color code the information or use letters to help them sort the information in the "What I Learned" column. In this case, students have used the first letter of each branch of government to label each piece of information: "E" for Executive, "L" for Legislative, and "J" for Judicial.

Alternatively, students could create a semantic map to sort the information in the "L" column. If students are unfamiliar with how to create a map, show them that the topic becomes the center of the map. Next, write the topic categories away from the center to leave room to write the coded information, as shown in Figure 2r. Finally, students add the coded information from the columns.

In further preparation for writing a summary, students consider the items of information in each category and then number them in the order they want to write about them. In this example, the writer has decided to write first about the Executive Branch, next about the Legislative Branch, and, finally, about the Judicial Branch, as shown by the numbers in parentheses before each of the categories.

Before beginning the writing, students also need to think about the order of the information within each category, also numbering these ideas in the order most logical for their topics. For example, the writer has decided to explain first where the "chief" executive of the country lives before explaining how much the president earns or what the protocol is for accepting gifts. Finally, the writer will explain the sequence of power if anything happens to the president. The writer then moves on to the next two categories, following a similar pattern.

This is a particularly effective strategy for all kinds of report writing because it helps students gather and sort information and then, by its design, reminds them

FIGURE 2q BRIEF EXAMPLE OF KWL PLUS FOR THE TOPIC OF AMERICAN GOVERNMENT

K-W-L STRATEGY SHEET

K-What I Know	W-What I Want to Know	L-What I Learned/Still Need to Learn
Legislative deals with laws. Judicial is courts. Executive links with president. Must be 18 to vote. Must be born in America to become president. Each state has senators and representatives. Washington did not live in the White House.	If president and vice-president die, who is next in line? How much does president earn? Can president accept gifts? What are bills? Why does a case go to the Supreme Court? How are the number of representatives figured out? How big is the White House? How are laws passed?	E-Speaker of the House E-$125,000 E-only on behalf of U.S. government L-proposed laws J-final interpretation of constitution L-by population of each state; one per 1,000,000 E-big! 45 rooms L-House of Representatives, then Senate, then president J-Sandra Day O'Connor was first female Supreme Court judge.

to order the information and write each topic as a separate paragraph. Reminding them to use the center topic as their beginning sentence, and a variant as a concluding one, will nurture their ability to create a well-organized paper.

Reciprocal teaching is another strategy that incorporates all three aspects of understanding text, drawing students in, helping them refine understanding, and extending their thinking. Reciprocal teaching[28] is a cooperative learning activity through which students improve their understanding of text, while simultaneously refining their ability to monitor their comprehension levels and building their enthusiasm for doing so. Although this strategy is typically teacher driven initially, students learn to complete all aspects of it independently after practice.

Usually, a session begins with a teacher reading aloud a short segment of text, a paragraph or so. Then, four steps follow: questioning, clarifying, summarizing, and predicting.

For example, a teacher can read aloud the opening three paragraphs of Jim Crow laws from *Having Our Say: The Delaney Sisters' First 100 Years,* by Elizabeth and Sarah Delaney,[29] a stirring autobiographical memoir of Bessie and Sadie Delaney's extraordinary lives. Once the teacher has read the section, students can generate questions for other students to answer. Questions could be, "What were some examples of Jim Crow laws? What was their purpose?"

Next, if an idea needs clarification, teachers can ask questions to accomplish this, such as, "Why were these laws called 'Jim Crow' laws?"

After students answer all the questions and make clarifications as needed, the leader, in order to model the strategy, can summarize what is known so far. "Jim Crow laws were created to keep blacks from having all the privileges of white citizens. In a famous Supreme Court case in 1896, *Plessy v. Ferguson*, the justices sanctioned the idea of 'separate but equal.'"

At that point, students predict the contents in upcoming sections. In this case, they might predict that the final two paragraphs in the section will explain how and when Jim Crow laws legally ended.

What follows will be a repetition of these four steps, always preceded by reading aloud a short section. This interactive dialogue provides constant opportunity for students to focus on the information at hand. Clearly, the leader's role is crucial, especially as students are learning this strategy. With practice, students can take on this important role.

Two strategies that engage students before, during, and after reading are *literature circles* and *Readers Theater*. Literature circles are a particularly good way for students to take ownership and leadership with their reading. Although there are many ways to "do" literature circles in the classroom, the basic tenet is that students have input regarding which piece of literature they will read and then lead the discussions about that

FIGURE 2r SEMANTIC MAP CREATED FROM INFORMATION FROM KWL CHART

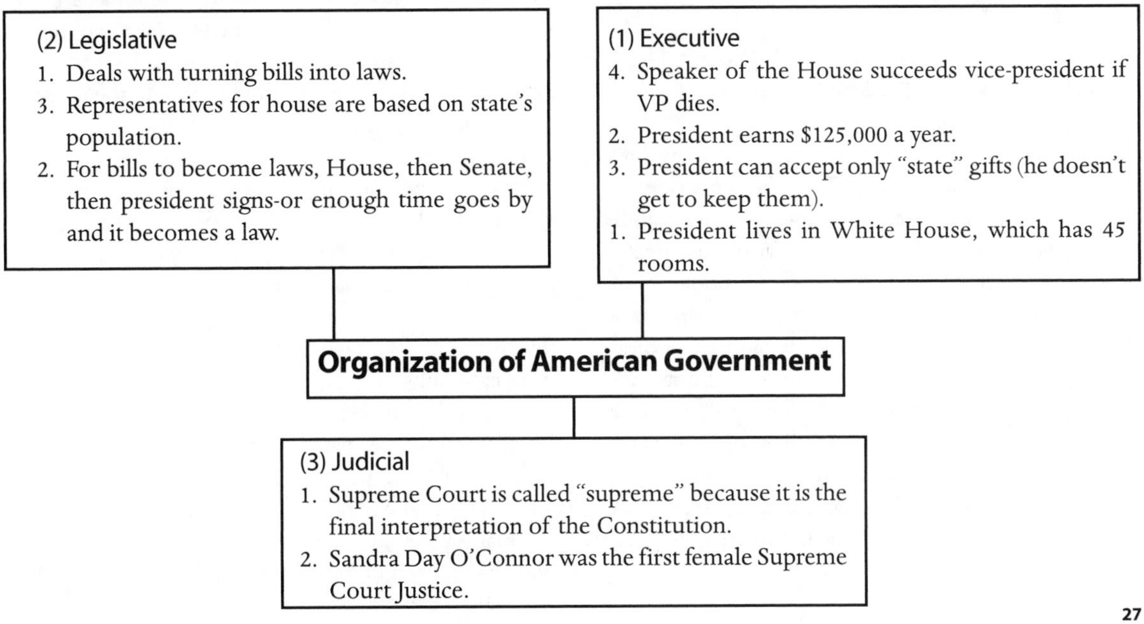

(2) Legislative
1. Deals with turning bills into laws.
3. Representatives for house are based on state's population.
2. For bills to become laws, House, then Senate, then president signs-or enough time goes by and it becomes a law.

(1) Executive
4. Speaker of the House succeeds vice-president if VP dies.
2. President earns $125,000 a year.
3. President can accept only "state" gifts (he doesn't get to keep them).
1. President lives in White House, which has 45 rooms.

Organization of American Government

(3) Judicial
1. Supreme Court is called "supreme" because it is the final interpretation of the Constitution.
2. Sandra Day O'Connor was the first female Supreme Court Justice.

piece of literature. Students can read any type of book in a literature circle, from picture books to novels to informational books. Typically, four or five students form a group, but it is recommended that a group consist of no more than seven. As a group, students decide how many pages or chapters to read before their next scheduled meeting. Students, with each taking this leadership role, always lead the discussions, even if the teacher sometimes participates. Students are encouraged to contribute their responses and listen carefully to others' positions. When students have finished reading and discussing the book, each group is usually responsible for presenting a culminating activity to the class to share what it has learned. This final activity also allows for assessment credit to be given beyond that given for a student's being an active, productive member of the circle. Harvey Daniels' *Literature Circles: Voice and Choice in the Student-Centered Classroom* is an invaluable resource for those interested in learning more about this strategy.[30]

Readers Theater is also organized around small groups of readers. Although it is possible to find scripts already written for certain literature texts, more frequently, students write their own scripts from the texts they read. The difference between Readers Theater and drama is that students simply read the script; they do not memorize it, act it out, or create elaborate scenery or props, which makes it far easier to manage as a classroom activity. The book *Social Studies Readers Theater for Children* is a useful resource for those interested in pursuing this classroom strategy.[31]

Specific Suggestions for Using the Annotated Bibliography in Part Two

For ease in finding a particular kind of book, we have arranged the books within each of the ten strands in the same way. Within each strand, we list the books by genre. If we included picture books within the strand, we list these first. Next, we specify nonfiction or informational books; we conclude this section with biographies. Next, we present novels in chronological order by the period they address. For nearly all the strands, we conclude the list with a book of poetry. Please note, however, that the number of each kind of book is not the same within each strand. We have included what we considered the "best" books for each strand, and while striving for diversity, we did not restrict ourselves to an arbitrary formula.

Although the anticipated primary reading audience for the annotations is social studies educators, students, too, might find them helpful if they are searching for a book within a particular strand. Alternatively, the primary audience for the activities is students. Our hope was that teachers, ever busy, would find this perspective most advantageous.

For example, writing the title of the book at the top of an index card, teachers could photocopy the activities and attach them to the index card. Teachers could then sort the index cards by strand and make them available to students to consult when they are assigned an independent project.

Alternatively, teachers could choose one of the ideas and assign it to the whole class, small groups, or individual students.

Most of the response activities that are included for each book are book specific, meaning that content from that book directly links with the activity. Ideas, however, are also sometimes included that nurture students' understandings across the curriculum, such as reading other books by the author or illustrator. Which activity a teacher chooses may depend on how many copies of the trade book are required and how readily they can be made available.

Ways of Obtaining Multiple Copies of Trade Books

Local libraries can be the best resource for acquiring a class set of books. Once you inform the librarian how many copies you need, he or she will often volunteer to search the system to fulfill your request. The number of copies available is usually related to the number of libraries in your local system.

If the book is unavailable or not available in sufficient numbers, you might want to consider checking with the book clubs that cater specifically to a school market. Scholastic is the oldest of the book clubs. Trumpet, Troll, and Carnival are also possibilities. If you happen to choose a book that is on "special" during a particular month, the savings can be considerable.

Local bookstores typically offer an "educator" discount as well, especially when you order multiple copies. If not, consider asking someone in the central office to speak with your local store about making some kind of mutually beneficial arrangement.

Finally, you may be able to negotiate a "trade" in the way that district dollars are spent. You could ask that money which is typically spent on obtaining new textbooks be spent on purchasing trade books instead—especially if the number of textbooks you have is adequate.

Assessment

In terms of assessment, you could evaluate students—on before/during/after strategies—with particular emphasis on their effort and quantity of information provided (not just on the accuracy of their information), because each strategy's purpose is to engage students' interest. If a student's inference is incorrect, the discussion that results from using a strategy may unearth this misconception—which reveals the value of having a concrete means of assessing comprehension.

More formal kinds of assessment can grow from these process-oriented beginnings. You could ask students to create a certain type of written work in order to "pull the information" together. Some ideas are the following: *letters to the editor or public officials, poems, plays, short stories, children's books, newspaper articles, case studies, reviews, dictionaries, radio scripts, or poster displays.* Any of these projects can incorporate the information students learn through reading literature by transforming the content into another form. The progress of any of these writing projects can readily be monitored and developed through the writing process: prewriting, drafting, revising, editing, and publishing.

Suggested Professional Texts for Additional Reading

This chapter is a "short course" in reading comprehension strategies. We have attempted to provide a beginning set of methods that would work particularly well with social studies content. For more information, either of the following texts would be helpful:

Anthony Manzo and Ula Manzo. *Content Area Reading: A Heuristic Approach.* (Columbus, Ohio: Merrill, 1990).

Richard Vacca and Jo Anne Vacca. *Content Area Reading: Literacy and Learning Across the Curriculum.* (Columbus, Ohio: Addison Wesley, 1998).

Notes

1. Sara Sklaroff, "Science & Ideas: Email," *U.S. News and World Report* 126 (March 22, 1999): 54-55.
2. U.S. Department of Education, "The Condition of Education, Quality of Elementary and Secondary School Environment," found at http://nces.ed.gov/programs/coe/2000/section4/tables/t45-1.html.
3. U.S. Department of Education, *Digest of Education Statistics, 2000.* Chapter 7, "Libraries and Educational Technology," Table 418, found at http://nces.ed.gov/pubs2001/digest/dt418.html.
4. Anthony Manzo and Ula Manzo, *Content Area Reading: A Heuristic Approach* (Columbus, Ohio: Merrill, 1990), 84.
5. Patricia Polacco, *Pink and Say* (New York: Philomel, 1994).
6. Gary Paulsen, *A Soldier's Heart* (New York: Delacorte, 1998).
7. Richard C. Anderson, Elfrieda H. Hiebert, Judith A. Scott, and Ian A. G. Wilkinson, *Becoming A Nation of Readers* (Washington, D.C.: National Institute of Education, 1985).
8. *Ibid.*, 23.
9. Richard Vacca and Jo Anne Vacca, *Content Area Reading: Literacy and Learning Across the Curriculum* (Columbus, Ohio: Addison Wesley, 1998).
10. Elizabeth Yates, *Amos Fortune: Free Man* (New York: Puffin, 1989).
11. Margaree King Mitchell, *Uncle Jed's Barbershop* (New York: Aladdin, 1998).
12. Mildred Taylor, *Mississippi Bridge* (New York: Bantam, 1992).
13. Vacca and Vacca, *Content Area Reading.*
14. Geographic Education National Implementation Project, *K-6 Geography: Themes, Key Ideas, and Learning Opportunities* (Indiana, Penn.: Author, 1987).
15. Eve Bunting, *So Far from the Sea* (New York: Clarion, 1998).
16. Paul Fleischman, *Bull Run* (New York: Harper Trophy, 1995).
17. Peter Sis, *Starry Messenger* (New York: Farrar Straus Giroux, 1996).
18. Patricia McKissack and Fredrick McKissack, *Christmas in the Big House, Christmas in the Quarter* (New York: Scholastic, 1994).
19. Sharon Draper, *Romiette and Julio* (New York: Simon & Schuster, 1999).
20. Eileen Carr, Lovey Aldinger, and Judythe Patberg, *Thinking Works* (Toledo, Ohio: Thinking Works, Ltd.,1999).
21. Margaret Davidson, *I Have a Dream: The Story of Martin Luther King* (New York: Scholastic, 1991).
22. Eve Bunting, *Smoky Night* (San Diego: Harcourt Brace, 1999).
23. James M. Macon, Diane Bewell, and Mary Ellen Vogt, *Responses*
24. James Collier and Christopher Collier, *My Brother Sam Is Dead* (New York: Scholastic, 1989).
25. Karen D. Wood, Diane Lapp, and James Flood, *Guiding Readers Through Text: A Review of Study Guides* (Newark, Del.: International Reading Association,1992), 1.
26. Michael Dorris, *Morning Girl* (New York: Hyperion, 1999).
27. Eileen Carr and Donna Ogle, "K-W-L Plus: A Strategy for Comprehension and Summarization," *Journal of Reading* 30 (1987): 626-631.
28. Annemarie Palincsar and Ann Brown, "Reciprocal Teaching of Comprehension and Monitoring Activities," *Cognition and Instruction 1*, no. 2 (1984): 117-175.
29. Elizabeth Delaney and Sarah Delaney, *Having Our Say: The Delaney Sisters' First 100 Years* (New York: Dell, 1996).
30. Harvey Daniels, *Literature Circles: Voice and Choice in the Student-Centered Classroom*, (York, Minn.: Stenhouse Publishers, 1994).
31. Mildred Knight Laughlin, Peggy Tubbs Black, and Margery Kirby Loberg, *Social Studies Readers Theater for Children.* (Englewood, Colo.: Teachers Ideas Press, 1991).

Suitable Books for Standards-Based Teaching

CHAPTER 3

❶ CULTURE

Performance Expectations

Social studies programs should include experiences that provide for the study of *culture and cultural diversity*, so that the learner can:

a. compare similarities and differences in the ways groups, societies, and cultures meet human needs and concerns;

b. explain how information and experiences may be interpreted by people from diverse cultural perspectives and frames of reference;

c. explain and give examples of how language, literature, the arts, architecture, other artifacts, traditions, beliefs, values, and behaviors contribute to the development and transmission of culture;

d. explain why individuals and groups respond differently to their physical and social environments and/or changes to them on the basis of shared assumptions, values, and beliefs;

e. articulate the implications of cultural diversity, as well as cohesion, within and across groups.[1]

Picture Books

FEATHERS AND FOOLS

Mem Fox. Illustrated by Nicholas Wilton. (San Diego, Calif.: Harcourt Brace & Company, 1996) 36 pages. ISBN 0-15-200473-4. Performance expectations: a, b, d, e.

In this beautifully illustrated fable, Fox reminds us of our foibles as human beings—prejudging others and believing that weapons and warfare are the means to living in peace. The peacocks think it odd that swans swim and fly, and fear their strength: "If they wished, they could turn us out of our gardens, or make us fly, or force us to swim." Gone is their contentment as they build their arsenal; the swans, overhearing these plans, respond in kind. When a reed falls from the mouth of a nest-making swan as she flies over the peacocks, they mistake it for an arrow, and war ensues, with nary a bird remaining alive—until one egg hatches and then another, one peacock, one swan. Their conversation takes a different turn:

> "You're just like me," said the first. "You have feathers and two legs."

> "You're just like me," said the second. "You have a head and two eyes."
> "Shall we be friends?" asked the first.
> "Most certainly," replied the second.

1. Investigate the genre called fables. On a poster, include a short history of famous tellers/writers of fables. Make a list of characteristics of fables and include this page, too. Then, read three or four fables and write short summaries of them and add these to the poster as well.

2. Think of an important concept you think your classmates would benefit from. Write a fable of your own, sharing this lesson.

ROME ANTICS

David Macaulay. (Boston: Houghton Mifflin, 1997) 79 pages. ISBN 0-395-82279-3. Performance expectations: c, d.

The flight of a wayward pigeon sent by a young girl to an artist provides the author/illustrator with an opportunity to provide a variety of perspectives of Roman architecture—from above, then below, even upside down. One senses the flight of the pigeon and almost becomes dizzy! The street scenes contain unexpected "jokes" for those who study them carefully; even the casual observer of the streets and interiors, however, will probably conclude that we are more like people of that era than different.

1. Look carefully at the pictures of the people and their activities. What evidence does the author use to show that we are more alike than different? Using sticky notes, write comments and attach them in the appropriate places on the illustrations.

2. How has the historic architecture of Rome influenced the life-style of contemporary Romans? What is it about the architecture that makes Romans so proud of their city? How would you describe it? Write a travel brochure enticing a traveler to Rome.

3. How is the environment of Rome different from your own community? How important is it to the Romans not to destroy their ancient structures? What is the impact on a culture that is committed to preserving its ancient buildings? Write an article

for a magazine, arguing for preservation of historic buildings.

THE MIDDLE PASSAGE: WHITE SHIPS, BLACK CARGO

Tom Feelings. Illustrated by author. (New York: Dial, 1995) 80 pages. ISBN 0-8037-1804-7. Performance expectations: a, b, c, d, e.

Although this text is all pictures, it is certainly not a "picture book" in a conventional sense. Feelings' black and white drawings chronicle life for those Africans who are sent to America to be slaves. "Powerful" only begins to describe the emotional impact of this work, which won the Coretta Scott King Illustrator Award in 1996.

1. Choose one of the illustrations and write a poem communicating its meaning for you.
2. Read a book such as *The Slave Dancer* (Paula Fox, Laurel Leaf, 1989, 127 pages, ISBN 0-440-96132-7). As you are reading, locate passages for which Feelings' illustrations seem to capture the essence of the prose. As a class presentation, read the passage aloud while showing the picture.
3. Research the history of "the middle passage." What was it? Consulting at least three different sources, write a short report on this topic.

FROM SLAVE SHIP TO FREEDOM ROAD

Julius Lester. Paintings by Ron Brown. (New York: Dial, 1998) 40 pages. ISBN 0-8037-1893-4. Performance expectations: a, b, c.

The uniquely talented author Julius Lester has combined his talents with the equally talented, but less well-known, painter Rod Brown to produce a work that, although brief, tells the story of the African American journey from slavery to freedom. Lester not only tells the story but also, in doing so, raises moral questions that middle school children can and should explore.

1. After reading the book, reflect on Lester's questions and attempt to answer them: Why did these people—and whites in particular—risk freedom and safety to help runaway slaves? Would you risk going to jail to help someone you did not know? Would you risk losing your freedom to help someone not of your race? Create a bulletin board with a summary in the middle. Around it, write these questions and others you create. Leave space for your classmates to respond to them.
2. Read other works by Julius Lester, such as *To Be A Slave* (Scholastic, 1988, 160 pages, ISBN 0-5902-460-2) and *Long Journey Home: Stories from Black History* (Puffin, 1998, 160 pages, ISBN 0-1403-8981-4). In what

ways are they similar to this work? In what ways are they different? For your class, present your findings.

IN THE HOLLOW OF YOUR HAND: SLAVE LULLABIES

Alice McGill. Illustrated by Michael Cummings. (New York: Houghton Mifflin, 2000) 40 pages. ISBN 0-395-85755-4. Performance expectations: a, c.

This collection of songs, chosen and sung by McGill on the accompanying CD, is presented side-by-side, with brief commentaries on the importance of each of the lullabies in McGill's life. Each song is highlighted by quilt collages that visually document the sorrow and pain of that institution called slavery, as well as the love within families and hope for the future. Melodies of each lullaby are included at the end of the book. The importance of the oral tradition is clearly shown. As McGill says in the preface, "These lullabies contain the essence of black survival, a philosophy designed to teach history and to counteract the tribulations of slavery with as many joyous occasions as possible."

1. Choose a song from your childhood, write down the lyrics, and then write a commentary about it, just as McGill does for each song.
2. Create a quilt collage illustration for your song.
3. Explain how either or both of the other activity choices are fitting responses within this strand.

THE INVISIBLE PRINCESS

Faith Ringgold. Illustrated by author. (New York: Crown, 1999) 32 pages. ISBN 0-517-80024-1. Performance expectations: a, c, d, e.

Like Carl Sandburg's *Rootabaga Stories*, this story is an original fairy tale. It has its roots in the African American experience in the early to mid-1800s. Why a traditional tale in a social studies strand? Simply, the theme of the story is a yearning toward a world ruled by peace and love-the goal of this strand. The timelessness of this genre-traditional literature—attests to the power of stories across humankind. Basic human need changes little from person to person, across geography and time; this tale, complemented with vibrant illustrations by the author, emphasizes the need for one of the most basic of all needs—freedom.

1. Using this text as your resource, make two lists, one including information about how the slaves looked at life and another from the master's point of view. Write a statement explaining why an author might choose to present factual information in a fictionalized form instead of in straightforward exposition.

2. What characteristics of this story make it a literary traditional tale? How do you know? (Hint: Relate the similarities to other traditional tales you know.)

THE WAGON

Tony Johnston. Paintings by James E. Ransome. (New York: William Morrow & Company, 1999) 32 pages. ISBN 0-688-16694-6. Performance expectations: a, b, d, e.

A powerful companion to Patricia Polacco's *Pink and Say* (Philomel, 1994, 48 pages, ISBN 0-399-22671-0), this picture book portrays well the connection African Americans have felt toward Lincoln, the "Great Emancipator." Following the master's instructions, the young boy who narrates this story and his father build a wagon that his father likens to a chariot, a glorious one that will be "comin' for to carry me home." The young boy, however, chafes at his lack of freedom as a slave: "I longed to do what free boys do." One day, frustrated beyond reason, he chops away at the wagon, "chariot of false hope," and of course is "striped good for that." "Yours is not the only troubled soul," his grandma tells him. "Mr. Lincoln is sometimes overcome with gloom." He finds comfort in chopping wood, just as Lincoln did when he was young.

1. Find a copy of the Emancipation Proclamation. Make sure you understand what it says, practice reading it aloud, and then present it to your classmates and discuss what it means.
2. Read a biography of Lincoln, perhaps Russell Freedman's Newbery Honor book, *Lincoln: A Photobiography* (Clarion, 1989, 150 pages, ISBN 0-395-51848-2). What additional information can you find about how Lincoln felt toward slaves and slavery? In the persona of Lincoln, write a speech, sharing your perspective.

THE BUTTERFLY

Patricia Polacco. Illustrated by author. (New York: Philomel Books, 2000) 48 pages. ISBN 0-399-23170-6. Performance expectations: a, b, d, e.

Written as a picture book, *The Butterfly* is a story based on Polacco's Aunt Monique, whose mother, Marcel Solliliage, was a part of the French underground and Resistance organized by General Charles de Gaulle during World War II. Polacco's evocative illustrations pull the reader ever more fully into the story of young Monique, who discovers Sevrine, a Jewish girl of her own age, who is being hidden within the basement of her house. Monique, an important part of Sevrine's escape, is clearly an example of how even youth can respond—in an incredibly positive way—in order to meet human needs and concerns.

1. Write a narrative poem, retelling the story of both Marcel and Monique's heroism.
2. With the help of a French-English dictionary, create a glossary, with both pronunciations and definitions, of all of the French words in this text.
3. Find and read other stories of the Resistance movement. Create a "Wall of Heroes" with mini-posters highlighting the courageous actions of others during World War II.

Non-Fiction

CELEBRATIONS! FESTIVALS, CARNIVALS AND FEAST DAYS FROM AROUND THE WORLD

Barnabas Kindersley and Anabel Kindersley. (New York: D.K. Publishing, 1997) 64 pages. ISBN 0-789-42027-9. Performance expectations: a, b, c, d, e.

This work for studying culture and cultural diversity explains more than twenty-five holidays. Each one is given a page or two with photographs of children that may appeal to young people. Some holidays, such as Christmas or Mother's Day, are celebrated in different countries and in different ways, providing an excellent resource for exploring preferences and differences.

1. Make a list of the holidays discussed. Note the country where each takes place. Survey your classmates, putting a check mark next to each holiday that you or your friends have celebrated. Tally your results and present your findings to your class.
2. Are there holidays photographed outside the United States that some Americans celebrate? Name these. Create a poster illustrating your findings in both prose and pictures.
3. Make a chart with a list of the holidays in the left column. At the top, create column headings for characteristics shown in the pictures such as costumes, special foods, special activities, and whatever else you may note that happens in a number of the celebrations. As a result of completing your chart, define celebrations, explaining what all of the events pictured in the book have in common.
4. From your study of how different cultures celebrate seasonal events, report on what it is about the other cultures that results in different ways of celebrating.
5. How do holidays unite people? What national holidays or folk days celebrated in the United States bind us together as a people? Write an essay honoring national holidays.

ONE WORLD, MANY RELIGIONS: THE WAYS WE WORSHIP

Mary Pope Osborne. (New York: Alfred A. Knopf, 1996) 86 pages. ISBN 0-679-83930-5. Performance expectations: a, b, c, d, e.

This fascinating text describes the seven religions most practiced around the world today: Judaism, Christianity, Islam, Hinduism, Buddhism, Confucianism, and Taoism. The author does a masterful job explaining how these faiths are interrelated, how one was born of another, or how one was born halfway around the word but at the same time as another. There is no motivation to persuade the reader to adopt a new religion, but the book helps the reader see how they are similar. As the author states, "They all seek to bring comfort to their followers. They all offer thanks for the world's great beauty and goodness. They all express awe and humility before the mysteries of the universe." The photographs that accompany each religion are exquisite, and the glossary, maps, and graphs at the end of the book provide truly helpful information.

1. Choose one of the photographs and write a story about the character, respecting his or her belief system.
2. Consider the map on pages 74 and 75. Analyze the patterns. Then, write a paper explaining where each of the seven major religions is typically practiced.
3. Choose a novel that includes a character from one of these seven religions. You might choose *Gideon's People* (Carolyn Meyer, Harcourt Brace, 1996, 297 pages, ISBN 0-152-00304-5) for Orthodox Judaism, *Ramsey Scallop* (Frances Temple, Orchard, 1994, 310 pages, ISBN 0-531-08686-0) for Christianity, or *Haveli* (Suzanne Staples, Bullseye, 1995, 276 pages, ISBN 0-679-86569-1) for Islam. Keep a list of religious practices and beliefs as portrayed in the novel. Compare it with the information presented for that religion in this book. Then, write a statement about the authenticity of the material included in the novel.

COBBLESTONE, THE HISTORY MAGAZINE FOR YOUNG PEOPLE AND FACES, THE MAGAZINE ABOUT PEOPLE

Available from Cobblestone Publishing, 30 Grove Street, Suite C, Peterborough, NH 03458. Back issues available for $29.95 for nine-issue annual subscription (March 2002). Performance expectations: a, c, d, e.

Each issue of *Cobblestone* focuses on a theme in U.S. history, while *Faces*, using a similar format, focuses on cultural anthropology. Although *Cobblestone* deals with U.S. history, the immigrant experience relates to the theme of culture. Specific issues that would be particularly helpful would include Greek Americans (December

1997), Japanese Americans (April 1996), and Polish Americans (May 1995). Issues on immigrants tend to include articles on history, food, and a craft activity, as well as resources such as books, videos, and study sites. *Faces* devotes its thematic issues to countries. For example, Ireland was the theme for March 1996, Vietnam for September 1997, and China for January 1996. In addition to stories about families, most issues include a recipe, a craft activity, folk tales, and general information about life-style and culture. Like *Cobblestone*, *Faces* contains a helpful resource section.

1. Plan a class multicultural potluck using recipes from the magazines.
2. Create a classroom museum of student crafts made according to directions in the magazine.
3. Cooperative groups could identify ethnic groups profiled in *Cobblestone*, and using that resource, as well as items in the school resource center, could create a survey instrument. They could then survey classmates, friends, and neighbors of that group in order to report on whether or not, in your sample, aspects of the culture are present.
4. Review the folk tales found in *Faces*. Compare and contrast them by seeking common elements. You might note whether or not the country's folk tales are "place bound," that is, are their settings dependent on the country's geography, climate, flora, or fauna? Write a brief paper revealing your findings.

AZTEC NEWS

Philip Steele. (Cambridge, Mass.: Candlewick, 1997) 32 pages. ISBN 0-7636-0115-2.

AZTEC TIMES, IF YOU WERE THERE

Anthony Mason. (New York: Simon & Schuster, 1997) 32 pages. ISBN 0-689-81199 3. Performance expectation: b.

Aztec News presumes to be a newspaper written in the era. Colorful illustrations and clever "news stories" communicate the history, politics, religion, farming, and trade. It is unique because it is written from the Aztec perspective. *Aztec Times* is not a pseudo newspaper. Rather, using a similarly colorful format with thematic pages and of identical length, it describes the culture from the predictable, European perspective. A game is included at the end, but it is of little help in understanding the reasons for Cortez's victory.

1. Compare the two books. In what ways are they the same? What events or characteristics of the culture consume the most pages? How are they different in the way they treat battles, religion, and explanations

of events? What does this tell you of the perspective of historians?

2. Can you find a book on Egypt or the Middle Ages and create your own newspaper? Attempt to recreate stories similar to those in the book, such as "Throwing The Perfect Party," sporting news, religious news, trade news, and a real estate page.

THEY HAD A DREAM: THE CIVIL RIGHTS STRUGGLE FROM FREDERICK DOUGLASS TO MARCUS GARVEY TO MARTIN LUTHER KING, JR. AND MALCOLM X

Jules Archer. (New York: Puffin, 1996) 272 pages. ISBN 0-14-034954-5. Performance expectations: b, d, e.

The noted author Jules Archer divides his book into four biographies, and while profiling significant events in the lives of these four African American leaders, he explores the issues of separatism and integration that each of these men had to confront. He is not hesitant to acknowledge the personal shortcomings of each man, while effectively communicating the enormous obstacles each man faced.

1. Using an outline map of the United States and the places mentioned in the book, indicate significant places in America's civil rights history. You might choose to do one for each person and then a final one that shows only the five most important places.

2. There are few pictures in this young adult book. Pretend you are the editor and write a memo arguing for the inclusion of more pictures or illustrations for each chapter. If you enter the terms *civil rights* or *African Americans* or *blacks* in your library's computer catalog under "Subject," you should obtain a number of related books, and you could review them for specific photographs to recommend.

3. View the video *Eyes on the Prize*. After reading this book, compare it with the video and prepare a Venn diagram, two circles that overlap. In the intersection of the two circles, indicate what the works have in common. In the left part of the circle, indicate what is unique about the book, and in the right part of the circle, note what is unique about the video.

4. Pick a song with a melody that you are familiar with, such as "Swing Low, Sweet Chariot" or "We Shall Overcome." Create new lyrics honoring one or all of the heroes described in the book.

5. Assume you were on a committee to create a monument for one or more of these men. What would the monument consist of? Describe the monument in a press release.

QUILTED LANDSCAPE: CONVERSATIONS WITH YOUNG IMMIGRANTS

Yale Strom. (New York: Simon & Schuster, 1996) 80 pages, ISBN 0-689-80074-6. Performance expectations: a, b, c, d, e.

From around the world, twenty-six young persons share their viewpoints on coming to America. Their statements honor the promise of this new world, as well as the sense of loss of the worlds they once knew. Many are wise beyond their years as they discuss the irony of speaking negatively about immigrants; these contemporary pilgrims understand that everyone currently living here, except for Native Americans, is descended from somebody who was, at one time, an immigrant. Each "conversation" is accompanied by a sidebar of information about the person's homeland: its size, population, capital, ethnicities, religions, languages, monetary unit, date of independence, "internationally known" persons of that country, traditional foods, and an interesting but unique fact.

1. With which young immigrant do you have the most in common? Write an essay sharing how you are like that young person.

2. For each of the "conversations," pull out a sentence or two that you believe helps you understand what being an immigrant means. Copy these onto index cards and arrange them on a bulletin board. If possible, post a map of the world like the one in the opening pages of the book and, using yarn, connect each of the cards to the homeland of each. Add a title of your own choosing.

3. Imagine you had to leave the United States and move to another country. Write a poem explaining your feelings, like Christian Tico or Ai Hironi does.

Novels, Stories and Folk Tales

HANG A THOUSAND TREES WITH RIBBONS: THE STORY OF PHILLIS WHEATLEY

Ann Rinaldi. (San Diego, Calif.: Harcourt Brace, 1996) 337 pages. ISBN 0-15-200877-2. Performance expectations: a, b, c, d, e.

This fictionalized biography fills an enormous gap in American's literary history, and it is quite appropriate that it was written with middle graders in mind. Phillis Wheatley was the first American Black woman to publish a book of poetry. Phillis was captured in Senegal and sold into slavery in 1761, but her young master, Nathaniel Wheatley, took her under his wing and educated her. When the Wheatleys realize her talent, they have her "perform" for influential guests within Boston society, hoping to have her work published (it was first published in England). While Phillis is accepted in many social circles, she is never a "full partner"; those of her own culture are not quite sure what to make of her and her "white ways," making Phillis's life less peaceful than one would hope given her many accomplishments.

1. This book is a biography of an amazing woman. In the persona of Phillis, write a letter to Nathaniel explaining what troubles you about life and what you wish could change.

2. Find some of Wheatley's poetry (see, e.g., her *Complete Writings*, edited by Vincent Carretta; Penguin Classics, 192 pages, ISBN 0-140-42430-x). Choose at least three poems that appeal to you, copy them, and create a poster highlighting her work. Then, share the poems with your classmates by reading them aloud and explaining why each was significant to you.

3. Phillis's trip to America was grueling. Consult Tom Feelings' *The Middle Passage* (as described earlier in this chapter; Dial, 1995, 80 pages, ISBN 0-803-71804-7). Study the illustrations and then write a poem relaying the misery of such a voyage for those who, unfortunately, were captured. Choose at least three poems that appeal to you, copy them, and create a poster highlighting her work. Then, share the poems with your classmates by reading them aloud and explaining why each was significant to you.

MEET JOSEFINA, AN AMERICAN GIRL
Valerie Tripp. Illustrated by Jean-Paul Tribbes. (Middleton, Wis.: Pleasant Co., 1997) 85 pages. ISBN 1-56247-515-0. Performance expectations: c, d, e.

This book is part of the American Girl series, in which a girl has been identified to personalize events of a historical period, from colonial days to World War II. Josefina is a Mexican girl growing up in the first quarter of the nineteenth century. She lives in a ranchero in New Mexico. This book, the first of six, introduces the main character. She appears to be a bit less mischievous than the main character of the other series, but as in the other books, the reader does get a sense of the past.

1. Create a six-sectioned "family shield" for Josefina's family. In the shield, include pictures related to the family's livelihood, where the family lives, a common characteristic of the family, its heritage, and two other aspects that stand out in your mind. Be sure to include a motto that says something about the family, such as, "We rise through adversity."

2. With five friends, read all six of the books in the series, with each of you drawing a comic strip reflecting on three or more episodes from each book. Create a bulletin board with all six comic strips.

A PICTURE OF FREEDOM: THE DIARY OF CLOTEE, A SLAVE GIRL, BELMONT PLANTATION, VIRGINIA, 1859
Patricia McKissack. (New York: Scholastic, 1997) 195 pages. ISBN 0-590-25988-1. Performance expectations: a, b, c, d, e.

McKissack has done a masterful job of sharing Clotee's thoughts and feelings as a young slave girl. Particularly compelling is Clotee's recognition that literacy is the key to being "free" because no one can enslave her mind. Clotee is an especially endearing character because, while she is slow of speech, her mind is lightning fast, learning to read while pretending not to as she fans her young master during his tutor's lessons. The photographs and information at the end of the novel support the text exceedingly well by reinforcing its horrors—the tiny living quarters, the slave auctions, and the grueling work in the fields.

1. Read Joyce Hansen's *I Thought My Soul Would Rise and Fly: The Diary of Patsy, a Freed Girl, Mars Bluff, South Carolina, 1865* (Scholastic, 1997, 202 pages, ISBN 0-590-84913-1), winner of the Coretta Scott King Author Honor Award in 1998. Compare Clotee with Patsy. How are they alike? How are they different? In a journal format, write a diary entry as if you were either Clotee or Patsy, comparing yourself with the other.

2. Read other books by Patricia McKissack or Joyce Hansen. Share your favorite book by giving a book review before the class.

3. Another book that focuses on the power of literacy is *Nightjohn* by Gary Paulsen (Doubleday, 1995, 92 pages, ISBN 0-440-21936-1). Read it and then decide where you stand on the importance of literacy/education. You could also read the sequel—*Sarny* (Illustrated by Jerry Pinkney; Laurel Leaf, 1999, 192 pages, 0-440-21973-6). Write an editorial for the school or class newspaper.

CHRISTMAS IN THE BIG HOUSE, CHRISTMAS IN THE QUARTERS
Patricia McKissack and Fredrick McKissack. Illustrated by John Thompson. (New York: Scholastic, 1994) 68 pages. ISBN 0-590-43027-0. Performance expectations: a, b, c, d, e.

This 1995 Coretta Scott King Author award-winning book provides a look at slavery on a fictional, but historically accurate, plantation in Virginia in 1859—just before the Civil War began. While the book focuses on differences in how plantation owners celebrated the holiday versus how the slaves did, this focus does not limit the information about the overarching social conditions of the time. The "Notes" at the end of the book provide additional information.

1. As a child of a plantation owner growing up in the Big House, write a letter to a cousin in New York who is an abolitionist. Explain what you think about the lives of the slaves on your plantation. Explain why you think the "slaves don't have it so bad" or why you agree with your cousin's perspective. Be sure to support your position with information from the book.

2. Write a script for a Readers Theater by creating a dialogue of two or more voices presenting a point-by-point comparison of "Life in the Big House" with "Life in the Quarters." Practice and present!

THE PEOPLE COULD FLY

Virginia Hamilton. Illustrated by Leo and Diane Dillon. (New York: Knopf, 1985) 178 pages. ISBN 0-679-84336-1. Performance expectations: a, b, c, d, e.

Winner of the Coretta Scott King Author and Illustrator Awards in 1986, this book is a collection of American Black folk tales. In her introduction, Hamilton comments that it is amazing that a people forced to work as hard as the slaves would have a place for laughter or song in their lives, and yet they did; no amount of hard labor could curb their imaginations. A strength of this book is the commentary that Hamilton provides at the end of many of the tales revealing the origin of that particular tale. These commentaries further connect the reader with "the people [who] could fly," one of the tales in the last section titled "Carrying the Running-Aways and Other Slave Tales of Freedom."

1. Choose the tale you like best from the book. Memorize it and then retell it to the class, indicating why this tale is meaningful to Black culture.

2. Before reading "Carrying the Running-Aways" aloud to the class, research the Rankins' home as a "station" in Raymond Bial's *The Underground Railroad* (Houghton Mifflin, 1999, 48 pages, ISBN 0-395-97915-3). Share what you learned and show the class the photograph of the Rankins' house.

THE GUNS OF EASTER

Gerard Whelan. (Dublin, Ireland: The O'Brien Press, 2000) 176 pages. ISBN 0-86278-449-2. Performance expectations: b, d, e.

This story, about the experience of an adolescent boy during the Easter Week Rebellion in Dublin in 1916, is an exemplar for the use of fiction to teach about culture and history. Like many Dubliners, Jimmy's initial feelings about the rebellion are complex. In order to earn money for food, Jimmy's father has joined the British army. Like many boys, Jimmy is attracted to the pomp and power exhibited by the marching British soldiers, yet his beloved young uncle is a rebel. During the fighting, Jimmy risks his safety by seeking out food for his starving family. In this well-told adventure, Jimmy is befriended by a British solder. The ending is not tragic, and the afterword resolves questions that a young adolescent would want answered.

1. For what would you risk your life? Was it wrong for a boy of Jimmy's age to risk his life? At what age and under what circumstances should a child assume the roles of an adult?

2. When the rebellion was over, Ireland was divided. The south became a free country; the north remained under British control. Northern Ireland became rife with sectarian hatred. Read Carolyn Meyer's young adult work *Voices of Northern Ireland: Growing Up in a Troubled Land* (Harcourt Brace, 1992, 212 pages, ISBN 0-15-2006-362) to appreciate growing up in America.

3. The Irish Republic's flag is a tricolor—three colors of equal proportion, vertically placed. The green stands for Roman Catholics, the orange for the Protestants, and the white for the idea that there might ever be peace between them. After reading this book and conducting other research as well, submit a new design for the Republic's flag and explain the symbolism of your color and design. A more challenging task would be to design a new flag for Northern Ireland.

FIELDS OF HOME

Marita Conlon-McKenna. Illustrated by Donald Teskey. (New York: Holiday House, 1997) 189 pages. ISBN 0-823-41295-4. Performance expectations: a, b, d, e.

This is the last of the trilogy. The first, the widely honored *Under the Hawthorn Tree* (illustrated by Donald Testy; Holiday House, 1990, 153 pages, ISBN 0-823-40838-8), has been published in other languages as well. The series begins with the Irish Famine and tells the powerful story of one family's experiences, which unfortunately were repeated hundreds of thousands of times. In the second book, *Wildflower Girl* (illustrated by Donald Teskey; Puffin, 1994, 172 pages, ISBN 0-140-36292-4), the major character moves to the United States. The last book, set in the time of the land wars, takes place in both Ireland and the United States.

1. This series is quite popular in Ireland. The writer is almost as popular as Judy Blume. Read one of Blume's books and then compare it with one from this series. What could you say of the culture of Ireland as compared to that of the United States by making inferences about the popularity and content of Conlon-McKenna's and Blume's books? Share your findings through a presentation to the class.

2. The story in this book, like the others, tells of oppression of Irish Catholics by rich and powerful forces, as well as the indifference of the middle class, who are prejudiced against them "just for being what we are." After reading this book (and, hopefully, the first two), do you think the experience of the Irish Catholics in Ireland is more like the experience of Native Americans or African Americans? See if you can identify parallel experiences for both groups.

SALSA STORIES

Lulu Delacre. Linocuts by author. (New York: Scholastic, 2000) 105 pages. ISBN 0-590-63118-7. Performance expectations: a, b, c, d, e.

Carmen Teresa receives a blank book, "covered with a red fabric sprinkled with daisies," as a New Year's present, but she is unsure how to fill the pages. She receives many suggestions from her family members about what to do: Keep a journal, retell stories from her childhood, or "collect stories" from everyone attending the celebration. At the book's end, Carmen has discovered her own idea. The concluding section of the book is prefaced with a title page: "Carmen Teresa's Book of Fantastic Family Recipes," followed by seventeen recipes, all of which were tested in Delacre's own kitchen. Many have been favorites of her family for generations. The stories and the recipes give fascinating glimpses into Latin American holidays, customs, beliefs, and values.

1. With a small group, choose foods from the recipe section and create a well-balanced menu. Make the foods, share them with your classmates, and enjoy!

2. Which of the stories that Carmen heard did you find the most compelling? Retell it to your classmates and then explain why, or explain first, and then retell the story.

MANIAC MAGEE

Jerry Spinelli. (Boston: Little Brown & Co., 1999) 192 pages. ISBN 0-316-80906-3. Performance expectations: a, b, d, e.

Maniac Magee is an amazing young man. Although incredibly talented in a variety of sports, he is also committed to reading, as demonstrated by his placing his current choice down just long enough to hit a home run, circle the bases, and scoop it up as he returns to home plate. An orphan now residing in Two Mills, Maniac is "color" blind, and this inability to see difference hurts those who he comes to love as family, and so he leaves, only to find his way "home" once again. Maniac is legendary in his ability to relate to people, not facades—a character most worthy of emulation. The writing is superb; indeed, it won the Newbery in 1991. Without a doubt, it is an incredible read aloud.

1. What do we know about Maniac? Brainstorm lists of physical characteristics, accomplishments, and other behaviors. What traits are portrayed by these actions? For example, if you noted under "accomplishments" that Maniac "hit a home run," the trait might be "athletic." Once you have finished creating the lists, write a character sketch of Maniac.

2. Write a summary of the book explaining what Maniac does or does not understand about differences among peoples. You may want to write your summary using the three parts of the novel as your guide, comparing and contrasting what Maniac initially knows in Part I with what he experiences in Part II, and with what he learns in Part III.

3. In "Before the Story," Spinelli writes, "The history of a kid is one part fact, two parts legend, and three parts snowball." What do you think Spinelli means? What do we know about Maniac that is fact? Legend? Snowball? Is it fact, legend, or snowball that helps us bridge cultures? Discuss in a small group, sharing your conclusions with the class.

FORGED BY FIRE

Sharon Draper. (New York: Aladdin, 1998) 156 pages. ISBN 0-689-818513. Performance expectations: a, b, d, e.

National Teacher of the Year for 1997, Sharon Draper has written an intimate portrait of one boy and his family. A reader cannot help but be moved by Gerald and the misfortunes of his life: a drug-addicted mother, the death of his loving aunt, and an abusive step-father. Such realities are played out daily, particularly in urban settings such as Cincinnati, where this story takes place. Gerald's caring heart is the hope of this book as he learns he has to protect the sister he never knew he had until his sixth birthday.

1. How is this novel a story of "all cultures"? Consider how poverty affects students across cultures. With several friends, answer the following questions or create similar ones on your own. Then, after compiling your findings, present them to your class as a panel. (a) Find out how many students in your school, district, or both are on free breakfast or free lunch plans; (b) Research the effects of nutrition on learning; (c) What are the overall poverty rates in our country?; (d) Can you discern any patterns of the consequences of poverty?; (e) What can each of us do to change these patterns?

2. Read Draper's *Tears of a Tiger* (Aladdin, 1996, 180 pages, ISBN 0-689-80698-1), winner of the Coretta Scott King Genesis Award in 1995. At its core is a story of teenagers who drink and drive. What resolution(s) might you make after reading this novel? Design an action plan for your school and then implement it.

3. Read *Darkness before Dawn* (Atheneum, 2001, 233 pages, ISBN 0-689-83080-7), the last book in the Hazelwood High series begun with *Tears of the Tiger* and continued with *Forged by Fire*. As with Draper's other novels, she knows the issues faced by high school students, and without being heavy-handed, she provides incredibly compelling and important stories that warrant much discussion. Lead a discussion for your classmates that highlights these issues and potential solutions.

Poetry

HARLEM

Walter Dean Myers. Illustrated by Christopher Myers. (New York: Scholastic, 1997) 32 pages. ISBN 0-590-54340-7. Performance expectations: b, c, d.

Winner of the 1999 Coretta Scott King Illustrator Honor Award, *Harlem* is a book-length poem celebrating "a promise / Of a better life, / of a place where a man didn't / Have to know his place / Simply because he was / Black." In striking illustrations, Harlem becomes a place all readers can come to know, complemented by descriptive commentary of its history and its hope for the future: "A journey on the A train / That started on the banks of the Niger / And has not ended / Harlem."

1. On a world map, find as many places as possible that are mentioned in the poem and mark their locations on the map.

2. Choose one of the people mentioned in the poem, Langston Hughes, Countee Cullen, James Baldwin, W. E. B. DuBois, Jack Johnson, Joe Louis, Marcus Garvey, or Malcolm X, and write a paragraph highlighting his achievements.

3. Write a poem, create a song, or make a collage celebrating the history of "your" town.

Notes

1. This section is directly quoted from National Council for the Social Studies, *Expectations of Excellence: Curriculum Standards for Social Studies* (Washington, D.C.: Author, 1994), 79.

CHAPTER FOUR

⓫ TIME, CONTINUITY, AND CHANGE

Performance Expectations

Social studies programs should include experiences that provide for the study of *the ways human beings view themselves in and over time*, so that the learner can:

a. demonstrate an understanding that different scholars may describe the same event or situation in different ways but must provide reasons or evidence for their views;

b. identify and use key concepts such as chronology, causality, change, conflict, and complexity to explain, analyze, and show connections among patterns of historical change and continuity;

c. identify and describe selected historical periods and patterns of change within and across cultures, such as the rise of civilization, the development of transportation systems, the growth and breakdown of colonial systems, and others;

d. identify and use processes important to reconstructing and reinterpreting the past, such as using a variety of sources, providing, validating, and weighing evidence for claims, checking credibility of sources, and searching for causality;

e. develop critical sensitivities such as empathy and skepticism regarding attitudes, values and behaviors of people in different historical contexts;

f. use knowledge of facts and concepts drawn from history, along with methods of historical inquiry, to inform decision-making about and action-taking on public issues.[1]

Picture Books

THE BOSTON TEA PARTY

Steven Kroll. Illustrated by Peter Fiore. (New York: Holiday House, 1998) 32 pages. ISBN 0-8234-13160. Performance expectations: b, c, e, f.

Although this book is in a picture book format, much content is provided about the events leading up to the Boston Tea Party, as well as the event itself, and its consequences. Describing a precipitating event in the Revolutionary War, this book helps make clear the human reactions behind various events—on both sides of the ocean. The "Afterword" and the timeline included at

the end of the book will be useful to middle grade students.

1. Create a list of all of the "Acts": Sugar, Stamp, and Townshend, defining each.

2. Draw a map of Boston, locating all of the significant places during this time in history, noting the role of each.

3. Create a visual aid of some type that explains the cause and effect relationships among events during this period of history.

SLEDS ON THE BOSTON COMMON: A STORY FROM THE AMERICAN REVOLUTION

Louise Borden. Illustrated by Robert Andrew Parker. (New York: McElderry Books, 2000) 40 pages. ISBN 0-689-82812-8. Performance objectives: a, b, c, d, e.

The concept that an enemy is either "all good" or "all bad" is addressed clearly in this story of a young boy who asks General Gage of the British Army to instruct his soldiers to clear a "sledding path" through the Boston Commons. His request is fulfilled because General Gage is reminded that his own children would want to sled down such a hill.

1. Write a letter in the persona of General Gage, recounting to your children the young boy's request and why you fulfilled it.

2. Find out more, and then share with the class, through a newscast, about how the British soldiers behaved on Boston Commons and what significant events occurred there.

DAISY AND THE DOLL

Michael Medearis and Angela Shelf Medearis. Paintings by Larry Johnson. (Middlebury: Vermont Folklife Center, 2000) 32 pages. ISBN 0-916718-15-8. Performance expectations: a, c, d, e.

Part of the Family Heritage Series from the Vermont Folklife Center, *Daisy and the Doll* is a tribute to Daisy Turner, who was born in 1883 in Grafton, Vermont. The middle child of thirteen, she was eight years old when she realized her skin had more color than her classmates' skin and that this characteristic made her different. Carrying a black doll to the center of the stage during the school year's closing program, she chose not to share the poem her teacher had given to her to recite. Instead, she spoke from her heart—and won first prize. This book is truly for all ages. Although Daisy's words were spoken a century ago, each of us needs always to remember to be "original and honest." With or without a ten-dollar gold piece as a prize, we each, then, will always be winners.

1. In the persona of Daisy, recite the poem she shared during the program. Then, explain to the class why this was such a significant event in both Daisy's life and the life of the community in Vermont at the end of the twentieth century.
2. Choose a poem that you think Daisy's teacher might have given her to memorize for the program. Explain why you think she might have chosen it.
3. The last page of the book provides a variety of ways to approach writing a poem. Explore the options and then adapt them so that you write a poem about a time you did or said something that showed how you truly felt about the experience.

JOURNEY TO ELLIS ISLAND: HOW MY FATHER CAME TO AMERICA

Carol Biermann. Illustrated by Laurie McGaw. (New York: Hyperion, 1998) 48 pages. ISBN 0-7868-0377-0. Performance expectations: b, c, e.

Written as a tribute to her father, Biermann describes his experience when he traveled to Ellis Island in 1922. Julius (a boy of eleven), his mother, and his seven-year-old sister Esther board the *Rotterdam* in Rotterdam, Holland for their historic journey to New York. Having escaped from Russia, they intend to join Julius's brother in America, but not before Julius loses a finger to a stray bullet. This accident almost keeps Julius from being permitted to enter America, where strict rules about persons who might become "liabilities" were followed by the doctors and social workers who made decisions on Ellis Island. Beautiful photographs and illustrations of the Island, both then and now, grace the oversized pages of this picture book. They tell the "rest" of Julius and his family's story, including Julius's visit to Ellis Island on the seventy-fifth anniversary of the "run around the Island," which won Julius entry into the "golden country."

1. Read one of the other books about Ellis Island listed at the end of the book.
2. From further reading, create a chart, by decades—1900-1910; 1911-1920; and so forth, listing notable Americans who entered America through Ellis Island.

3. Choose one decade and create a chart that details from which countries people emigrated.
4. Why did so many people come to America at the beginning of the twentieth century? Create a cause and effect chart showing as many different reasons as possible.

Non-Fiction

LIVES OF THE PRESIDENTS: FAME, SHAME (AND WHAT THE NEIGHBORS THOUGHT)

Kathleen Krull. Illustrated by Kathryn Hewitt. (San Diego, Calif.: Harcourt Brace & Co., 1998) 96 pages. ISBN 0-15-200808-X. Performance expectations: a, c.

These short biographies of the presidents should be appealing to the teacher, because they contain significant aspects of each president's term of office, as well as to the students, because the biographies also include insights into the presidents' life-styles, such as favorite foods and music loves.

1. The "Man on the White Horse" is a theory of the causes of historic events, which argues that one individual causes events. Review the information presented on the major presidents and argue that the author of this work believes in and supports that thesis.
2. "Behind every Great Man is a Greater Woman." Review the chapters and argue that the author appears or does not appear to believe in this premise.

LIVES OF EXTRAORDINARY WOMEN: RULERS, REBELS, (AND WHAT THE NEIGHBORS THOUGHT)

Kathleen Krull. Illustrated by Kathryn Hewitt. (San Diego: Harcourt, 2000) 95 pages. ISBN 0-15-200807-1. Performance expectations: a, b, c, e.

In the newest of the "Lives of" series by this dynamic team, Krull and Hewitt have created yet one more collection of short biographies of an amazing group of individuals, this time linked by a common gender. On the heels of *Lives of the Presidents*, in which all of the occupants of that position have been white and male, *Lives of Extraordinary Women* honors women who have also wielded substantial political power: as queen (Cleopatra, Isabella I, Elizabeth I, Nzingha, Catherine the Great, Marie Antoinette, Victoria, Tz'u-hsi), prime minister (Golda Meir, Indira Gandhi), first lady (Eleanor Roosevelt, Eva Peron), Indian chief (Wilma Mankiller), military/revolutionary leader (Joan of Arc, Aung San Suu Kyi), social activist (Harriet Tubman, Rigoberta Menchu), or government official (Gertrude Bell, Jeannette Rankin). This book provides a fascinating look at the lives of these famous (and not-so-famous) women.

1. After reading the whole book, choose one woman in the book. Reread the biography and then do additional research, looking specifically for information that shows what made her a leader at that time and place. Then present the information to your classmates. After all presentations have been given, vote for the "Woman Across the Ages" you believe demonstrates the best example of leadership.

2. After reading the book, choose one woman and create a short biography, with an accompanying drawing, that highlights how that woman influenced either her country's development or the world's or both.

3. Create a timeline for your classroom, highlighting the three major accomplishments of each woman.

WOMEN OF HOPE: AFRICAN AMERICANS WHO MADE A DIFFERENCE

Joyce Hansen. (New York: Scholastic, 1998) 32 pages. ISBN 0-590-93973-4. Performance expectations: b, e, f.

In this beautiful and thoughtful work, which is a recipient of the Carter G. Woodson Secondary Book Award for 1999, Hansen has written the portraits of thirteen African American women who have made a difference in our world. Not one of these women was content to make it better only for "herself" or "her" people. These were women who pursued justice for all. A black and white photograph accompanies each biographical sketch. This book features women such as Ida B. Wells-Barnett, the Delaney Sisters, Septima Poinsette Clark, Ella Josephine Baker, Fannie Lou Hamer, Ruby Dee, Maya Angelou, Toni Morrison, Marian Wright Edelman, Alice Walker, Alexa Canady, and Mae C. Jemison. These women are role models for us all. As Walker states, "It's so clear that you have to cherish everyone . . . every soul is to be cherished."

1. The women whose accomplishments are highlighted in this book made contributions across various disciplines such as medicine, law, theater, literature, and science. More "women of hope" are listed at the end. Choose one and write a portrait of her achievements, just as Hansen has done.

2. Make a list of other noteworthy women in our history, particularly those of other cultures, who have "overcome obstacles of race and gender, and have by their examples and efforts given us courage and hope." Categorize them by achievement, as Hansen does.

3. Choose one person from the list created above and write a portrait. Create a "Hall of Fame," sharing your knowledge with others.

COLONIAL DAYS: DISCOVER THE PAST WITH FUN PROJECTS, GAMES, ACTIVITIES, AND RECIPES

David King. Illustrated by Bobbie Moore. (New York: John Wiley & Sons, 1998) 118 pages. ISBN 0-471-16168-3. Performance expectations: b, c.

"Why didn't I write this book?" may be the reaction of teachers of American history who use projects and arts and crafts in their teaching of the Colonial era. Although new ground is not plowed, this would be an excellent resource for a teacher who is looking for activities reflecting life in that period.

1. The glossary is well done and contains words of this historic era that students should know. Create a word game like "Jeopardy" to help students learn these terms.

2. Review the descriptions of the games in this book, such as Playing Jacks, Quoits, Blindman's Bluff, and Jackstraws, and compare them with contemporary games. In your essay, be sure to include non-electronic games and discuss the changes in children's lives that have taken place which influence the kind of games they play.

WHAT'S THE DEAL? JEFFERSON, NAPOLEON, AND THE LOUISIANA PURCHASE

Rhoda Blumberg. (Washington, D.C.: National Geographic Society, 1998) 160 pages. ISBN 0-7922-7013-4. Performance expectations: b, c, e.

Rhoda Blumberg is a prolific and effective writer of history for early and later adolescents. The massive acquisition of land through the Louisiana Purchase clearly was a turning point in our history. There are as many complex twists and turns in this history as there would be in any murder mystery. This is a good source for studying historical perspective.

1. Who is most responsible for the Louisiana Purchase? Prepare an argument for your choice.

2. Compare the information presented in your textbook with this book. Who is better at telling the story? Why?

TECUMSEH AND THE SHAWNEE CONFEDERATION

Rebecca Stefoff. (New York: Facts on File, 1998) 128 pages. ISBN 0-8160-3648-9. Performance expectations: a, b, c, e.

Few individuals in American history have experienced a life with such a grand plan that ended in such desolation. The author does justice to this story of a man who tried to unite the Indians of the Old North West and return them to their ancient and noble ways. The myths of his ancestry and relationships with "Rebecca" are explored and explained.

1. Stage a mock debate between those who accepted and promoted assimilation and those, like Tecumseh, who argued for confrontation. Cite this book, as well as other sources, for support for your arguments.
2. General St. Clair spent much of his life defending his actions—after the most disastrous defeat of the American Army by a Native American force. Using this source and others, attempt to defend General St. Clair's honor.
3. Using the significant dates in Tecumseh's life, prepare a timeline.
4. Although Tecumseh's grand plan failed, make reference to the cause and effect concept and discuss the proposition that Tecumseh's life was not a failure.

SLAVERY TIME WHEN I WAS CHILLUN
Belinda Hurmence. (New York: G. P. Putnam's Son's, 1997) 144 pages. ISBN 0-399-23048-3. Performance expectations: a, d, e, f.
Hurmence, the talented author of *A Girl Called Boy* (Houghton Mifflin, 1998, ISBN 0-395-5569-88), which uses a travel-through-time experience to allow its major character (and the readers) to understand what it was like to be a slave, uses the oral histories of former slaves in this new work. These narratives were recorded as part of the Federal Writers Project during the Great Depression to help us understand the complexity of slavery. Because these histories were recorded during the Great Depression (a time of particularly abject poverty for many African Americans, when the former slaves were in their eighties), a reader is sometimes confronted with attitudes about slavery that seem hard to believe. The brutality of enslavement and the destruction of families is recorded, but some surprising attitudes are noted by several that reflect what happens when a people are taught to be slaves.

1. There are twelve chapters. Each chapter is the story of one person, told in his or her own words. Identify a group in the class, no larger than six, and have each person select one of the chapters and assume the former slave's identify. Choose a host and create a talk show like "Oprah Winfrey" in which each person reveals memories of slavery.
2. Remember that each person in the book was interviewed by a historian, and those writers, like the author, then took the tape recordings and selected the most important parts. Focus on one of the people

in the book. Assume you were to conduct a follow-up interview. What questions would you ask the person? Remember, you want to find out additional information from the person to gain understanding of slavery. It might be helpful to refer to other slaves' memories as a stimulus to writing the questions.

AMISTAD: A LONG ROAD TO FREEDOM
Walter Dean Myers. (New York: Dutton, 1999) 96 pages. ISBN 0-141-30004-3. Performance expectations: a, b, c, e.
One of the most dramatic events in America's sad history of enslavement of some of her people is well told in this brief work of nonfiction. The timeline and map of the voyages are helpful aids for all readers.

1. Do a Venn diagram comparing the film *Amistad* (available in video stores) with the book. Concentrate on the information provided, as well as perspective-taking.
2. Review each of the transgressions experienced by the four children of the *Amistad*. Then, with three classmates, each choosing one of the children, write a letter of apology to the child for what was done to him or her. In your letter, suggest a way that what that child experienced will not be forgotten. As a group, decide what would be an appropriate way of remembering and preventing this type of experience from occurring again.
3. Select five persons in the book and do a "historical report card," that is, choose five adjectives and write these on the left side of the page. At the top of the page, write the names of the five persons you selected. Then, "grade" each person on the adjectives you have chosen. In the available space at the bottom of each vertical column, be sure to include a "teacher's comment" for each, summarizing his or her role in this historical event.

LINCOLN: A PHOTOBIOGRAPHY
Russell Freedman. (New York: Clarion, 1989) 150 pages. ISBN 0-395-51848-2. Performance expectations: a, b, c, d, e, f.
This Newbery winner's special distinction in 1988 was that it was the first time a biography was ever chosen for this prestigious award. Freedman is masterful in presenting the "man" behind the title of "President." The Civil War comes alive as readers understand the extreme anxiety Lincoln felt as he fervently tried to keep the nation as one. Photographs and prints add still another dimension to the authenticity of the text. Although this book is clearly geared toward middle school

students, Freedman, through his writing style, invites readers of all ages.

1. Make a list of the main issues Lincoln was forced to address when he was running for president. Did these change once he became president? Choose one of the issues, and, in the persona of Lincoln, write a statement revealing your beliefs.

2. Freedman tells us a fair amount about Lincoln as a husband, father, and friend. Using his relationships as support for your perspective, write a description of who Lincoln "really" was.

3. Freedman concludes his text with a listing of Lincoln memorials, monuments, and museums, which attract millions of visitors every year. Each invites an interested reader to write for further information. Choose one and do just that, creating a poster with the materials you receive.

4. Compare this text with a newer one, *In Their Own Words: Abraham Lincoln* (George Sullivan; Scholastic, 2000, 128 pages, ISBN 0-439-09554-9). Which do you like more? Why?

BLACK, BLUE AND GRAY: AFRICAN AMERICANS IN THE CIVIL WAR

James Haskins. (New York: Simon and Schuster, 1998) 96 pages. ISBN 0-689-80655-8. Performance expectations: a, b, c, d, e.

In this clearly written, fascinating work, Haskins explains how the Civil War was not a "white man's war," despite attempts to keep it so. In fact, it was the "efforts of the black soldiers" who "tipped the balance in favor of the Union side." Most astonishing to many readers may be that right after the war, the contributions of black soldiers were widely acknowledged, but by "1928 some white American historians had so thoroughly rewritten history that a man named W. E. Woodward stated in a biography of Ulysses S. Grant, the Union general who later became president, "the American negroes [*sic*] are the only people in the history of the world, so far as I know, that became free without any effort of their own." Haskins's text provides powerful evidence to the contrary. Photographs extend the text, and a timeline helps to accentuate significant events. This book concludes with a list of African American Medal of Honor Recipients in the Civil War.

1. Choose one of the Medal of Honor Recipients and find out why he was given the award. Write a proclamation that includes why he was honored.

2. Using the timeline in the book, create a multiple tier or parallel timelines, dividing the events into three categories: acts of Congress, battles, and "other significant events."

3. After finishing this book, write an essay, citing evidence from this book as well as other sources, such as *Dear Ellen Bee: A Civil War Scrapbook of Two Union Spies* (Mary Lyons and Muriel Branch; Atheneum, 2000, 161 pages, ISBN 0-689-82379-7; both spies were women, and one was black), regarding whether the Civil War was indeed "a white man's war."

JUNETEENTH: FREEDOM DAY

Muriel Branch. Photographs by Willis Branch. (New York: Cobblehill/Dutton, 1998) 64 pages. ISBN 0-525-65222-1. Performance expectations: a, c.

The beginning of Juneteenth is a celebration that black Texans held spontaneously in honor of the news of Lincoln's declaration of the Emancipation Proclamation on January 1, 1865, which finally made its way to slaves in Galveston, Texas on June 19. Now celebrated across the country, this ethnic holiday typically features parades, parties, sporting events, and family reunions that may last a day, a week, or a month. It includes a ceremonial reading of the Emancipation Proclamation and Proclamation #3, both of which announced that slaves were free. It also includes a retelling of how the celebration got its name and why the news was late getting to Texas. Branch includes a short history of the event's origin and its subsequent growth as a special holiday honoring black history.

1. Using the suggestions at the end of the book, design a Juneteenth celebration for your class/school/town.

2. Find a copy of the Emancipation Proclamation and create a poster-size version of it. Read it to the class and then display it.

3. Write a poem describing Juneteenth—its celebration elements and significance.

4. Write an editorial supporting a Juneteenth celebration in your town.

IT IS A GOOD DAY TO DIE: INDIAN EYEWITNESSES TELL THE STORY OF THE BATTLE OF THE LITTLE BIGHORN

Herman Viola. (New York: Crown, 1998) 96 pages. ISBN 0-517-70913-9. Performance expectations: d, e, f.

This unusual work gathers together descriptions of the battle as told by Native Americans. The excerpts are short and are presented in an easy-to-read format for middle school students. They are unique resources because they were written at a time when Native Americans were hesitant to share their feelings with those who could harm them.

1. Native American tribes were often rivals, and this division facilitated their defeat. Prepare a speech to one of the tribes that had members acting as scouts, explaining to them the consequences of their behavior.
2. The worst defeat of the American Army was not at Little Bighorn. Research the defeat of General St. Clair in the Ohio Territory Indian Wars. Then present the facts of each battle to your classmates, comparing and contrasting the two.

LEON'S STORY

Leon Tillage. Pictures by Susan Roth. (New York: Farrar Straus, Giroux, 1997) 112 pages. ISBN 0-374-34379-9. Performance expectations: d, e, f.

Oral history projects are not uncommon in the middle school; this one, however, is special. In this case, a school custodian tells his story to a group of students, noting that the ugly incidents of racism are not that uncommon. A parent, hearing of her child's experience, chose to record Leon's life. This act has given us a particularly accessible resource for middle and senior high school students to learn about racism.

1. Choose one member in your family and begin to record his or her history.
2. Read about how to do a careful oral history project at web site www.americanmemory.gov.

Novels, Stories and Folk Tales

THE JOURNAL OF WILLIAM THOMAS EMERSON, A REVOLUTIONARY WAR PATRIOT, BOSTON, MASSACHUSETTS, 1774

Barry Denenberg. (New York: Scholastic, 1998) 156 pages. ISBN 0-590-31350-9. Performance expectations: a, b, c, e, f.

After great success with its "Dear America" series of books, Scholastic has extended the series to include journals (historical fiction) written by boys at the middle grade level in its "My Name Is America" series. This journal features William Thomas Emerson, who loses his family to a lightning strike when he is ten. He is bound as an indentured servant to a childless neighboring couple, but Will stays only two years before he has had enough of his alcoholic master. He heads to Boston where he finds shelter and a sense of belonging with a woman who owns and runs a tavern. There, Will eventually finds himself a part of the activities of the "Committee." As with the other journals in this series, a historical note concludes the text, along with captioned illustrations.

1. Write an article for the *Gazette*, after doing further research on any of the events referred to in the text.
2. The Fitch sisters are "warned" (see page 30) about continuing to sell British goods. Do they have a right to do so? Write a letter to the editor, either supporting the Fitch sisters' actions or the "Citizens'" position.
3. Using the "historical note" at the end of the text, create a timeline of events.

MY BROTHER SAM IS DEAD

James Collier and Christopher Collier. (New York: Scholastic, 1989) 216 pages. ISBN 0-590-42792-X. Performance expectations: a, d, e.

Written in the aftermath of Vietnam, this 1975 Newbery Honor book depicts a family's struggle during the Revolutionary War. On one level, it is an adventure story, and on a deeper level, it is a book that questions the efficacy of war. The central figure is a thirteen-year-old boy who feels divided between his love for his Tory father and his rebel brother. Ironically, the father dies on a British prison ship and the son is executed by American soldiers.

1. How would you have persuaded young Tim that the American cause was a just one? His brother speaks of principles. What principles do you believe justified the American Revolution? Make a list.
2. Tim discovers that his brother has stolen the family musket. His brother has sworn him to secrecy. What are the conditions under which you would break an oath? Explain your thinking to your class.
3. Esther Forbes' book *Johnny Tremain* (see immediately below) is unequivocal in its support of the American Revolution. Attempt to construct a dialogue between Johnny and Tim, as if they were on a television talk show.

JOHNNY TREMAIN

Esther Forbes. Illustrated by Lynn Ward. (New York: Yearling, 1987) 256 pages. ISBN 0-440-44250-8. Performance expectations: a, b, c.

In this classic novel, a 1944 Newbery award winner, Forbes focuses on an orphan boy of fourteen from mysterious origins who becomes an apprentice for a silversmith in Boston at the start of the American Revolution. Many famous Americans living in Boston who were patriots become characters in the book as Johnny himself becomes involved with the American cause.

1. This book, although fiction, articulates many of the causes of the war. Could the conflict have been avoided? If so, how? If not, why not? Write a paper comparing and contrasting these two positions.

2. Review the discussion between the Boston patriots and James Otis. For what beliefs or principles would you risk your fortune, your family's well-being, or your life? Try to articulate them and describe a scenario in which your beliefs might be tried.

3. *Johnny Tremain* was published during a war, which almost all Americans considered morally just—World War II. On the other hand, *My Brother Sam Is Dead* (see immediately above) was written during the era of the Vietnam War. Some have suggested that both books reflect attitudes of their times. To what extent do you think both writers were products of their experience? Write a paper articulating your perspective.

A GATHERING OF DAYS: A NEW ENGLAND GIRL'S JOURNAL, 1830-1832

Joan Blos. (New York: Aladdin, 1999) 144 pages. ISBN 0-689-82991-4. Performance expectations: b, c, d, e, f.

A 1980 Newbery award winner, this fictional diary reveals the thoughts and times of thirteen-year-old Catherine Hall, who is keeping house for her widowed father and younger sister. Blos's research into life in New England in the 1830s is evident in her descriptions of Catherine's anxiety over having a new mother and brother, Catherine's worry about a runaway slave on his way to freedom, and Catherine's deep sadness when her best friend dies.

1. How does Catherine's teacher view society? How does his position differ from that of the townspeople? Create a "compare and contrast" chart, listing these differing viewpoints.

2. Catherine acts boldly when she leaves the quilt for the runaway slave. Is there an act of kindness, equally bold, that you might be able to take today? Brainstorm options with a small group of your classmates and then evaluate the possibilities for actual completion.

3. Can you find any other stories about runaway slaves in New England in the early 1800s? Share your findings with a brief written and oral report to the class.

STEAL AWAY HOME

Lois Ruby. (New York: Aladdin, 1999) 208 pages. ISBN 0-689-82435-1. Performance expectations: b, c, d, e.

Dana finds a skeleton in the closet, literally, and so begins an investigation of a death that occurred more than 130 years ago. The journal that Dana finds in the same room provides many of the answers. She discovers that her house was once part of the Underground Railroad, and the mysterious "guest" was Lizbet Charles, a conductor and former slave. Ruby skillfully unfolds the past through alternating chapters. The contemporary puzzle of the skeleton's identity and the cause of death that Dana, her friends, and the authorities attempt to solve is juxtaposed with the historical information.

1. Read *Two Tickets to Freedom: The True Story of William and Ellen Craft, Fugitive Slaves* (Florence Freedman, illustrated by Ezra Jack Keats; Peter Bedrick Books, 1989, 96 pages, ISBN 0-872-26221-9), which provides greater detail about the escape of Ellen and William Craft. Then, reread Ruby's version of their escape on pages 83-86. Did Ruby portray their place in history accurately? Write a short paper, verifying or clarifying the details.

2. Do research on the major routes that runaway slaves used, either finding or creating a map. Then, write a paper explaining why these routes would have been the best ones, given current population patterns, possibilities of transportation, and geographical patterns.

SOLDIER'S HEART

Gary Paulsen. (New York: Delacorte, 1998) 106 pages. ISBN 0-385-32498-7. Performance expectations: b, d, e, f.

Subtitled "Being the story of the enlistment and due service of the boy Charley Goddard in the First Minnesota Volunteers," this historical novel chronicles the making of a "soldier's heart." Paulsen describes the evolution of such a concept, which currently might be called post-traumatic stress disorder, and compares it to "shell shock" of World War I and "battle fatigue" of World War II. Fifteen-year-old Charley, eager to enlist in the "shooting war," which seems as enticing as the circus, learns quickly that war is not as exciting and wonderful as all the drums and songs, posters and slogans made it appear.

1. Charley believes that "to be a man," he needs to enlist. How else might he "prove" himself to be a man?

2. Identify at least three cause and effect relationships related to the war, such as "Cause: scarce resources" (such as food) leads to "Effect: coffee is made from burned oats." Create a poster highlighting these ideas, being as specific as possible using details from the text.

3. Choose one of the major events of the book and write a letter in the persona of Charley, relaying the information to loved ones.

4. With fifteen other classmates, read Paul Fleischman's *Bull Run* (illustrated by David Frampton; Harper Trophy, 1995, 104 pages, ISBN 0-0644-0588-5) because it can be read easily in a Readers Theater fashion.

5. Make a timeline of the battles in which young Charley fought.

RETURN TO HAWK'S HILL

Allan Eckert. (Boston, Mass.: Little Brown & Co., 2000) 160 pages. ISBN 0-316-00689-0. Performance expectations: d, e, f.

A seven-time nominee for the Pulitzer Prize, this popular historian returns to the young adult fiction genre to continue his documentation of life in the old North West. A masterful story, this chapter book is a recommended read aloud because of the adventures of a boy fighting the elements, wild animals, and a cruel trader; and because the boy ultimately overcomes his family's prejudice toward Native Americans.

1. The author argues in this work of fiction that if you get to know someone who is different from you, you will learn to appreciate that person. Try to think of a situation in your community or this country where prejudice exists; develop a plan whereby people get to know one another.

2. The setting of this book occurs many years after Tecumseh's death. Using Rebecca Stefoff's *Tecumseh and the Shawnee Confederation* (Facts on File, 1998, 128 pages, ISBN 0-8160-3648-9), compare and contrast Tecumseh's attitude toward whites with that of tribal leader Riel.

3. Ben was not a captive despite his fears that he could become one. Compare his experience with that of Susanna Hutchinson in Kirkpatrick's *Trouble's Daughter* (Delacorte, 1998, 224 pages, ISBN 0-3853-26009) or that of Durrant's characters in *The Beaded Moccasins* (Clarion, 1998, 183 pages, ISBN 0-395-85398-2), which is the story of Mary Campbell.

WEST TO A LAND OF PLENTY: THE DIARY OF TERESA ANGELINO VISCARDI

Jim Murphy. (New York: Scholastic, 1998) 204 pages. ISBN 0-590-73888-7. Performance expectations: b, c, e.

This historical fiction documents the journey of a young girl and her family's trip to settle in Opportunity, Idaho, to begin a community under the leadership of William Keil. From Jersey City, New Jersey, they travel first by train to get to Watertown, Dakota Territory, where they then join a wagon train. As usual with books in the "Dear America" series, a historical note is included at the end of the book, along with photographs and illustrations about life in 1883.

1. As you read the novel, keep a list of all of the cities Teresa passes through on her way to Opportunity. Afterwards, create a map showing her journey.

2. Also, as you are reading, keep a list of the events that affect Teresa and her friends. From this list, write a description of what life was like on the trail.

3. Why would Teresa's family have been eager to settle in Opportunity? What reasons are provided for making such an extensive journey? In the persona of Teresa's father, write to a friend back home, convincing him that he should travel west and join them.

STRUDEL STORIES

Joanne Rocklin. (New York: Delacorte Press, 1999) 131 pages. ISBN 0-385-32602-5. Performance expectations: b, c, e, f.

History is often viewed by middle grade students as something that happens only to "others." This short collection of stories dispels that perception as it tells the "history" of one family through seven generations and more than one hundred years. The reader almost smells the strudel baking as various family members relay the stories they associate with making strudel. Included is an important author's note, as well as, of course, a recipe for strudel!

1. Think of a family story you know and write it down.

2. Share your story with a parent, grandparent, sibling, aunt, uncle, or cousin. Do any of them have a story to tell that is connected with yours? If so, have them tell it while you record it, creating a second chapter.

3. Read another immigration story, such as *Journey to Ellis Island* (Carol Bierman; Hyperion, 1998, 48 pages, ISBN 0-7868-0377-0). Compare Bertha's story with Yehuda's by creating a Venn diagram. In the middle section of the diagram, write ways the two stories are alike. In the area to the left, write how Bertha's experiences are unique. In the right area, write how Yehuda's are unique.

4. One of the stories is called "The Best Gift in America." What are the gifts of being in America? Make a list. Then, choose one gift and write a poem celebrating it.

5. Of course, make strudel, multiplying the recipe ingredients as necessary. Enjoy!

Poetry

HAND IN HAND: AN AMERICAN HISTORY THROUGH POETRY

Lee Bennett Hopkins. Illustrated by Peter Fiore. (New York: Simon & Schuster, 1994) 144 pages. ISBN 0-671-73315-X. Performance expectations: b, c, e, f.

In this amazing collection of poetry, Hopkins has orchestrated a feast, from the landing of the pilgrims to the Revolutionary War, Civil War, and even Vietnam. Interspersed are poems celebrating the growth of our nation, such as "Pioneers," "Nat Love: Black Cowboy" (independence), and "Post Early for Space" (our future as "spacefarers"). The softly vibrant illustrations complement the text well, clearly inviting readers to explore the book with others, reflecting on our history the way it was made—together.

1. What patterns do you see in Hopkins's choices? How do you think he decided which poems to include? What criteria do you think he used? Write up the "rules" you think he followed. Then, reflect on what you have written. Did Hopkins portray U.S. history accurately?

2. Which poem do you like the best? Memorize it and then recite it for the class, prefacing your performance with the reason you chose it.

3. What part of history did Hopkins leave out? Write your own poem commemorating that event. Convince your classmates to do the same and create a class book to supplement *Hand in Hand*.

Notes

1. This section is directly quoted from National Council for the Social Studies, *Expectations of Excellence: Curriculum Standards for Social Studies* (Washington, D.C.: Author, 1994), 82.

CHAPTER FIVE

⦿ PEOPLE, PLACES, AND ENVIRONMENTS

Performance Expectations

Social studies programs should include experiences that provide for the study of *people, places, and environments* so that the learner can:

a. elaborate mental maps of locales, regions, and the world that demonstrate understanding of relative location, direction, size, and shape;

b. create, interpret, use, and distinguish various representations of the earth, such as maps, globes, and photographs;

c. use appropriate resources, data sources, and geographic tools such as aerial photographs, satellite images, geographic information systems (GIS), map projections, and cartography to generate, manipulate, and interpret information such as atlases, data bases, grid systems, charts, graphs, and maps;

d. estimate distance, calculate scale, and distinguish other geographic relationships such as population density and spatial distribution patterns;

e. locate and describe varying landforms and geographic features, such as mountains, plateaus, islands, rain forests, deserts, and oceans, and explain their relationships within the ecosystem;

f. describe physical system changes such as seasons, climate and weather, and the water cycle and identify geographic patterns associated with them;

g. describe how people create places that reflect cultural values and ideals as they build neighborhoods, parks, shopping centers, and the like;

h. examine, interpret, and analyze physical and cultural patterns and their interactions, such as land use, settlement patterns, cultural transmission of customs and ideas, and ecosystem changes;

i. describe ways that historical events have been influenced by, and have influenced, physical and human geographic factors in local, regional, national, and global settings;

j. observe and speculate about social and economic effects of environmental changes and crises resulting from phenomena such as floods, storms, and drought;

k. propose, compare, and evaluate alternative uses of land and resources in communities, regions, nations, and the world.[1]

Picture Books

A PLACE CALLED FREEDOM

Scott Russell Sanders. Illustrated by Thomas B. Allen. (New York: Atheneum, 1997) 32 pages. ISBN 0-689-80470-9. Performance expectations: a, d, g, h, i.

In 1832, in a surprising action, the master of a "big house" sets a family free—Mama, Papa, seven-year-old James, and five-year-old Lettie. Together, family members make their way north, following the "drinking gourd," just as many runaway slaves did, finally settling in Indiana. With help from a Quaker family, they raise enough corn and wheat that first year to buy their own land beside the Wabash River. When the winter makes it impossible to farm, Papa goes south to bring back two aunts, two uncles, and five cousins on his first trip, and after many more trips, many more family members and friends join them in Indiana. Other black people from all over the South come to settle with James's family as well, and when the "place was going to be on a map, it needed a name." And so, the town of Freedom was created.

1. Create a timeline of the evolution of "Freedom."
2. The train that prompted the naming of Freedom would have brought more "progress." Draw two maps of Freedom, one showing the town fifty years after its birth and then another one hundred years later.

RIVER FRIENDLY, RIVER WILD

Jane Kurtz. Illustrated by Neil Brennan. (New York: Simon and Schuster, 2000) 40 pages. ISBN 0-689-82049-6. Performance expectations: a, e, g, h, i, j, k.

Using her own experience during the 1997 flood in Grand Forks, North Dakota, Kurtz has captured vividly those days of watching the flood waters rise, taking ownership of her house and life, and then receding, leaving a muddy mess behind. Told in free verse, Kurtz poetically recounts the goodness of "The Red

River," where "In winter, we walked across the river to touch Minnesota," and "In spring, we sat on her back porch and watched the river ripple." The book ends with "Memories," a poem that celebrates life—despite physical losses, Kurtz and her family are alive, and while some memories are connected with things that were lost, she and her family will make new memories and "hold tight to the old ones that stick."

1. Have you ever survived a natural disaster—a flood, drought, hurricane, or blizzard? If so, write a poem(s) sharing your experience.
2. How do you think Kurtz's family's life was changed by the flood? How were neighbors' lives changed by the flood? Think about daily routines, short-term activities, and long-range plans.
3. The river rises each year. Why do you think people choose to live in a place that could be flooded again? Why would people choose to rebuild in the same place? Write an essay explaining your answers to these questions.

Non-Fiction

ATLAS OF EXPLORATION
Dinah Starkey. (New York: Scholastic, 1993) 64 pages. ISBN 0-590-27548-8. Performance expectations: a, b, c, d, e, h, i.
Starkey fully "explores" the concept of "exploration" by considering it both historically and futuristically. This information-packed book is divided into four major sections: "Early Explorers," "The First Great Age of Exploration," "The Second Great Age of Exploration," and, finally, "The Third Great Age of Exploration." While maps of explorers' routes are the most prevalent, as would be expected, other kinds of maps, drawings, and photographs add to the depth of the information presented.

1. Choose one of the explorers and find out more about him. Write a report.
2. Did certain countries have more explorers than others? Create a map showing the countries of origin for all of the explorers listed in this book. Figure out a way to indicate that there are multiple explorers from one country. Alternatively, or additionally, create a graph to show the same information.

SCHOLASTIC ENCYCLOPEDIA OF THE UNITED STATES
Judy Bock and Rachel Kranz. (New York: Scholastic, 1997) 144 pages. ISBN 0-590-94747-8. Performance expectations: a, b, c, d, e.
In a reader friendly format, the authors present a great variety of information about the fifty states, the District of Columbia, American Samoa, Guam, Puerto Rico, and the U.S. Virgin Islands. For each location, "The Basics" are given, such as population, area, capital, bird, flower, tree, song, landmarks, parks, sites, festivals, and a locator map, as well as "Fascinating Facts" in blue-shaded sidebars on either side of the two-page spread. In the middle is a description tailored to the significant information for each topic, including interesting photographs. This book is a gem for middle graders researching these topics.

1. Choose a state and create a "Top Ten Facts" list about the state, that is, the "top ten" most meaningful pieces of information. Present them to the class, justifying why they are significant.
2. Draw a map of the United States freehand (no tracing allowed!) and all its territories, labeling each.
3. Given a map of the continental United States, color code the seven regions into which the country is typically divided: New England, Mid-Atlantic, Midwest, South, Plains, Northwest, and West.

WISH YOU WERE HERE: EMILY'S GUIDE TO THE 50 STATES
Kathleen Krull. Illustrated by Amy Schwartz. (New York: Bantam, 1997) 128 pages. ISBN 0-385-31146-X. Performance expectations: a, b, c, d, g.
In an equally reader friendly style, Krull uses the trip that Emily and her grandmother take across country to introduce readers to the fifty states. In each two-page spread, along with the name of the capital city and motto, a map of each state is presented, including major cities and significant natural landmarks. A locator map is also included, as well as various small pictures of important features, such as the Statue of Liberty, Niagara Falls, and a street vendor in front of the Manhattan skyline for New York City. Each commentary is unique to the state described, which makes for varied and interesting reading. Two extensive charts of "State Facts" and "When Each State Became a State" provide a ready means of comparing states.

1. Suppose you were going on a trip. What states would you like to visit? Write a letter to your parents with trip options for three states: focus on natural land features for one choice, cultural experiences for the second choice, and "just sounds like fun" for your third choice. Try to convince them to take you to one of them!
2. Choose a state and learn as much as you can. Then, write a "postcard home," sharing at least three facts about your location.

3. Using the list of addresses in the "How to Get More Information" section in the back of the book, choose one state and write a letter requesting any materials it might have. Create a poster after the information arrives, sharing your new discoveries. Through the appeal of your poster and a persuasive "letter" mounted on it, try to convince your classmates that "your" state would be a very interesting place to visit.

EVERYTHING YOU NEED TO KNOW ABOUT GEOGRAPHY HOMEWORK: A DESK REFERENCE FOR STUDENTS AND PARENTS

Anne Zeman and Kate Kelly. (New York: Scholastic, 1997) 133 pages. ISBN 0-590-34172-3. Performance expectations: a, b, c, d, e, f, i.

What a book! Beginning with a definition and the five themes of geography—place, location, human and environmental interaction, human movement, and regions—the book continues with a section on globes, projections, and maps, followed by the physical world, plants and animals, and, finally, people on land and water. The appendix includes a glossary of terms, an atlas, and two final sections, "The World in Focus" and "The U.S. in Focus"; these are charts that include a wealth of information, such as area, population, capital, and date of independence of countries. Major language, form of government and leader, literacy rate, life expectancy, and per capita gross domestic product are included in the chart for foreign countries. State nicknames and origins of state names, as well as a separate chart on economic issues, are provided for the fifty states.

1. Choose one of the kinds of maps presented in Part Two and then create one for your school. Post it in the hallway.
2. Choose land, water, or air and summarize the information found in this text. Find two friends to choose the other two topics. As a news team, present your new understandings to your classmates.
3. Choose one of the ten biomes listed on pages 50-51 after reading its description on pages 51-56. Then, find two additional texts and create a mini-unit, complete with activities, so that your classmates can learn about this kind of natural region.
4. Choose a country and a group of people within that country. Then, research its belief system; that is, (a) find out what its religion is and what that means in terms of the group's daily lives, (b) find out what its customs and manners are that may not be linked directly to its religious practices, and, finally, (c) find out about the group's arts and crafts, clothing, music, arts, architecture, tools, and other practices. Share your final report with your class.

POSTCARDS FROM MEXICO (POSTCARDS SERIES)

Helen Arnold. (Austin, Tex.: Raintree Steck-Vaughn, 1996) 32 pages. ISBN 0-8172-4233-3. Performance expectations: a, b, c, d, e, g.

This book is part of a series on different countries, such as Kenya, France and the West Indies, which could be used starting with fourth graders. Following an introductory abridged map, the author selects twelve scenes and writes about them as if she were a tourist sending a postcard home. The index and glossary make one appreciate that this is not just "tourist geography."

1. Using the *World Book* encyclopedia or another reference source, draft a book like this on a country that has not been included in the series. Select eight photographs from your reference work that you think would be included by the author, and write the accompanying text.
2. Or create a similar book highlighting your state.
3. Write a book review that compares and contrasts this book with another book about Mexico.

TIBET (ENCHANTMENT OF THE WORLD SERIES)

Ann Heinrichs. (New York: Children's Press, 1996) 172 pages. ISBN 0-516-20155-7. Performance expectations: a, b, c, d, e, g.

More than one hundred countries have been described in the Enchantment of the World series, including Tibet and the Ivory Coast. The books are thorough, typically more than 150 pages each. They cover all aspects of the country (e.g., geography, history, economics). The index includes one thousand topics. The writing is crisp, the photographs excellent, the timelines helpful, and the "Mini-facts at a glance" useful.

1. Using the important dates from the section on history, create three timelines: the first with only ten entries, the second with twenty entries, and the last with thirty entries. Justify your choices of "important" dates.
2. The author notes and pictures support the statement that Tibetans are often smiling. Assume that you are going to write a book for this series on America. What facial expression do you think would be most common? Why?

JAPAN (FACES AND PLACES SERIES)

Elma Schemenauer. (New York: Children's World, 1997) 32 pages, ISBN 1-56766-371-0. Performance expectations: a, b, c, d, e, g, h.

This new series on countries is appropriate for grades four and up. This author is particularly effective in demonstrating that people from different countries are more alike than different, but that there are differences. For example, children are shown in kimonos, which are worn on holidays, but there are many pictures of children and adults wearing western style clothing—including one of a Little League Baseball team.

1. Select another country from the series, such as China, and assume the identity of a child from that country. Then write a letter to a child in Japan. Next, using what you have learned from this book, assume the identity of the person receiving the letter and write a reply to the child in China.

2. Review all of the books in the series. Assume your parent was going to become a diplomat in one of the countries. Write a letter to your parent telling him or her which country you would like to live in and provide lots of detail to support your choice.

CAIRO (CITIES OF THE WORLD SERIES)
Conrad Stein. (New York: Children's Press, 1996) 64 pages. ISBN 0-516-20024-0. Performance expectations: a, b, c, d, e, g, h.

More than a dozen cities have been described in this series. The book is organized to provide information about each city's history and important sites, as well as people's life-style there. Each work includes a timeline, a section on basic facts, a city map, a glossary, and an index of one hundred entries. Another recent work is *Athens*, which would be an important resource to have available because it shows children wearing sneakers and people working and living in skyscrapers and driving automobiles, images that dispel the idea that certain cities are trapped in time or have not become contemporary.

1. Using a map of Egypt, plan a five-day vacation that would allow you to visit a number of places described in the book.

2. Prepare a half-page advertisement for a local newspaper, encouraging people to visit Egypt.

IN THE FOREST WITH THE ELEPHANTS
Roland Smith and Michael Schmidt. (San Diego, Calif.: Harcourt Brace, 1998) 56 pages. ISBN 0-15-201289-3. Performance expectations: a, e, g, h, j, k.

This fascinating nonfiction book reveals the working partnership of man and an endangered species, the Asian elephant. A century ago, there were more than one hundred thousand elephants in Asia. Today, there are probably only thirty-five thousand. A third of these live in Myanmar—formerly Burma. While thousands roam freely, many are trained as timber elephants,

important to both the economy and environment of Myanmar. Photographs increase the appeal of this important book, which describes the unique partnership between man and animal that may save these creatures from extinction.

1. Research the topography of Myanmar. Draw a map, locating natural features. Write a description of the land where the wild elephants tend to live. Draw a second map, focusing on populations of people and timber camps. Compare and contrast the two maps, sharing your findings with your classmates through an oral presentation.

2. Consider the normal weather patterns of Myanmar. What if something changed? The monsoon season were extended? The dry season were particularly long? How would these changes affect the elephants in particular and the economy of Myanmar in general?

3. Near the end of the book, marauding elephants are captured. Four are retained, while two are set free away from the village. Write an essay supporting or arguing against the decisions made about their fates.

TALKING WALLS: THE STORIES CONTINUE
Margy Burns Knight. Illustrated by A. S. O'Brien. (Gardiner, Maine: Tilbury House, 1997) 40 pages. ISBN 0-88448-165-4. Performance expectations: a, b, c, d, e, g, j.

This book is a sequel to *Talking Walls* (Margy Burns Knight; Tilbury House, 1995, 40 pages, ISBN 0-8884-48154-9). In this unusual work, Knight continues to examine walls as a means of gaining insight into other countries and cultures. The cover was done by sixth graders responding to the message in the first book. It is a great read aloud work that includes not only well-known walls such as the dikes of Holland and Hadrian's Wall, but also contemporary ones that tell us about places and people. For example, the "Peace Lines" of Northern Ireland are designed to separate people of different religions, and Angel Island in San Francisco Bay is comparable to Ellis Island. On the walls of Angel Island is graffiti that tells the story of people who were forced to wait here before entering America. The teacher's guide for this work, *Who Belongs Here?*, written by Knight and Thomas B. Chan (Tilbury House, 1994, 40 pages, ISBN 0-88448-111-5), is well worth its cost. The activities in it include recommended response activities for specific walls, as well as generic activities.

1. After reading about all of the walls, write an essay titled "What Is a Wall?"

2. Become travel agents; create tourist brochures, including information about climate. Use *USA Today's* weather page to report on weather in your chosen area.

3. Using papier-mâché, recreate some of the walls. A recipe is included in the teacher's guide.

4. Create rice flour paintings on exterior walls. The rice flour paint will fade in wind and rain.

MAYEROS: A YUCATEC MAYA FAMILY

George Ancona. (New York: Lothrop, Lee and Shepherd, 1997) 40 pages. ISBN 0-688-13465-3. Performance expectations: e, f, g, h, i, j, k.

An American author tells the story of the land of his ancestors, the Maya of Mexico. Large, colorful photographs depict the life-style of individuals who continue to practice many of the traditions of the past. However, it is interesting to note the changes that modern technology has caused in the people of the Yucatan.

1. Carefully study the photographs, as well as the text, and identify changes in the lives of the Yucatec Maya.

2. What products do you notice being prepared for export? Which ones do you think might be attractive to American buyers? As a worker in a produce store, write a letter to your boss explaining the link between availability and export desirability. Be persuasive that your plan is economically sound for the store.

WHY DO THEY CALL IT TOPEKA? HOW PLACES GOT THEIR NAMES

John Pursell. (New York: Citadel, 1995) 241 pages. ISBN 0-8065-1588-0. Performance expectations: a, b, e, i.

This reference book is a book of trivia divided into ten chapters focusing on names of nations, states, cities, bodies of water, mountains, islands, and continents. The explanations vary in length from a sentence to a couple of paragraphs. Like surfing the Internet, this book should appeal to young minds.

1. Create a matching card game. On one side, give the explanation of the name of the geographic place, and on the other, the name we know.

2. There is a chapter on U.S. states. Do an analysis of the names, seeing if you can make any generalizations about the characteristics of names. For example, you might head one column "Indian origins," another "geographic characteristics," and still another "someone's name." Use a chart to tally your data. Consider doing this for the chapter on rivers, countries, lakes, or mountains.

3. Cluster the U.S. names geographically. See if there are any commonalities of names of certain places in different regions of America, such as New England or the southern states.

THE SANTA FE TRAIL

David Sievert Lavender. (New York: Holiday House, 1995) 64 pages. ISBN 0-823-41153-2. Performance expectations: a, b, e, f, i.

In a story less frequently told than that of the Oregon Trail, Lavender recounts how the Santa Fe Trail became popular. The Santa Fe Trail was a major route for moving goods from the east to the west. The photographs and drawings included in the book are excellent companions to the text.

1. Although this book contains a great deal of information, it might be "easier" to read if the contents were divided into sections. If you were the editor, how would you divide the text? Create chapter titles and subtitles.

2. What economic forces sustained the Santa Fe Trail? Choose one of the men who frequented this route and describe his actions and reasons for following this way of life.

MIST OVER THE MOUNTAINS, APPALACHIA AND ITS PEOPLE

Raymond Bial. (Boston: Houghton Mifflin, 1997) 48 pages. ISBN 0-395-73569-6. Performance expectations: g, h, i.

This talented author and photographer helps the reader appreciate a place that has often been misunderstood and under-appreciated. He recognizes the harshness and beauty of the land, as well as the consequences of the exploitation of the people and the land by mine owners. He presents an honest but sympathetic view of people with a strong sense of tradition and values.

1. Report on the culture of the Appalachians. What is it that the people value? Be sure to describe appreciated art forms.

2. On a U.S. map outline, draw the Appalachian Mountains.

3. Families are important in Appalachia. What evidence do you find in the book that Appalachians have and have had a commitment to family that might be more than or different from your own experience?

GROWING UP IN COAL COUNTRY

Susan Campbell Bartoletti. (Boston, Mass.: Houghton Mifflin, 1999) 128 pages. ISBN 0-395-97914-5. Performance expectations: e, h, i, k.

Carefully chosen photographs are a powerful addition to this record of what life was like for children in the coal country in northeastern Pennsylvania one hundred years ago. In addition to describing different jobs that boys had, the author focuses on defining moments such as strikes and tragedies, as well as on the life-style of residents in a coal company town.

1. Compare and contrast your life with the life of the children in coal country. Write a journal entry for a typical Monday in your life, and then write one in the persona of a "breaker boy."

2. Assume the perspective of a mine owner, perhaps the one living in the home pictured on page 66. Assume his identity and write a letter to the editor of a newspaper explaining why you cannot provide housing for your workers that is better than that pictured on page 65.

3. The 1902 strike described in the book was a turning point for labor. It lasted 165 days. People were removed from their homes; families were sometimes divided over whether to strike or to be a "scab." Find someone who belongs to a labor union and ask him or her about the work of that union today.

Novels, Stories and Folk Tales

SIGN OF THE BEAVER

Elizabeth Speare. (New York: Bantam, 1999) 144 pages. ISBN 0-440-22830-1. Performance expectations: a, d, e, f, g, h, i, j, k.
A 1984 Newbery Honor book, this story takes place in 1768 in the Maine wilderness. This is ostensibly a coming-of-age story about Matt, a thirteen-year-old white boy, but it is also about the grandson of a Penobscot chief, Attean. The chief knows that the hope for his people is for them to know the white man's language so that they can negotiate with them on equal terms, especially about the land. When Matt needs help while waiting for his father to return to the cabin with the rest of his family, the chief makes a treaty with Matt to teach his grandson to read "white man's signs" in return for providing food for his table.

1. Draw a picture of Attean's village. Then write a commentary describing how the village is organized.

2. Research the treaties the government has made with Native American tribes in Maine. What patterns can you discern? Make a chart, recording your findings.

SACAJAWEA

Joseph Bruchac. (New York: Scholastic, 2000) 200 pages. ISBN 0-439-28068-0. Performance expectations: a, d, e, f, h, i, j, k.
Subtitled "The Story of Bird Woman and the Lewis and Clark Expedition," this amazing historical novel comprehensively portrays the journey commissioned by President Jefferson, who was anxious to gather botanical, physical, and social data from the Mississippi to the Pacific. Lewis, Clark, and the rest of their Corps of Discovery were confronted with more challenges than they expected, but they reaped more than they anticipated as well. Bruchac framed this book as a story told to Sacajawea's son, Jean Baptiste Charbonneau, also known as "Pomp," by his mother Sacajawea and his "Uncle" William Clark. Consequently, one perspective reinforces or extends the other, so that a more complete picture is created. Each of Sacajawea's chapters is preceded by a native tale, each of Clark's chapters by a journal entry, although not always his own.

1. The expedition encounters many tribes in its travels. Draw a map that indicates the territory of each tribe, including its central village. Then, speculate why the location of each central village was chosen.

2. The geography of the trail made travel treacherous. On a map of the western United States, flag some of the most hazardous places of Lewis and Clark's journey.

3. Create a timeline of their journey, noting the length of time the expedition stayed in each place, specifically noting why.

4. Read about the travels of Lewis and Clark from a twelve-year-old boy's perspective, *The Journal of Augustus Pelletier, The Lewis and Clark Expedition, 1804* (Kathryn Lasky; Scholastic, 2000, 171 pages, ISBN 0-590-68489-2). Create a three-way Venn diagram comparing Augustus's perspective with that of Captain Clark and Sacajawea.

WEASEL

Cynthia DeFelice. (New York: Camelot, 1991) 119 pages. ISBN 0-380-71358-6. Performance expectations: a, b, c, d.
Set in 1839 in Ohio, *Weasel* is a compelling read, whether silently or aloud. At the core of the novel is the removal of the Shawnees to Kansas and Oklahoma as a result of the Removal Act. One particular Shawnee woman, with her white husband, chose not to be removed. This created conflict in the town, with one man, Weasel, determined to take care of the "savage" and her husband. Discussions about the possibility for unity among peoples of different backgrounds would find rich source material here, as well as issues of power and governance.

1. At one point, a character in the novel is determined to take the law into his own hands. Argue for or

against his decision. Be sure to address whether or not any individual is or should be above the law.

2. Research the history of Native Americans living in Ohio. Draw a map to show which tribes lived in Ohio in the 1830s. Write a commentary to accompany your drawings.

3. At the close of the novel, Nathan says, "If I could fiddle like Eli, I could tell the story better than with words, maybe, 'cause it seems to me life's like Eli's playing. There's everything in it. Without the sad parts, the rest wouldn't sound so sweet." Write a ballad telling Ezra's story.

ACROSS THE WIDE AND LONESOME PRAIRIE: THE OREGON TRAIL DIARY OF HATTIE CAMPBELL, 1847

Kristiana Gregory. (New York: Scholastic, 1997) 161 pages. ISBN 0-590-22651-7. Performance expectations: a, d, e, f, g, h, i, j.

Part of the Dear America series, this novel, written as a diary, documents thirteen-year-old Hattie's journey from "Booneville, Missoura" in early March to her arrival in Oregon City in mid-October. The difficulties of travel are relayed authentically. The struggles of traveling across country were real. The epilog, endnotes, diagrams, and photographs contained in the "Life in America in 1847" section add to the usefulness of the book.

1. Compare the "typical" journey on the Santa Fe Trail with that of the Oregon Trail, including comments on who normally traveled on each and why, what provisions were typically taken, the conditions of travel, and final destination. Find out how much it cost to travel from the east or midwest to the west.

2. Gregory tells us that almost five hundred thousand people used the Oregon Trail between 1836 and 1870. Find out more about what groups of people went in what year, and create a graph that shows which years the trail was used the most.

WALKING UP A RAINBOW

Theodore Taylor. (New York: Avon, 1996) 256 pages. ISBN 0-380-72592-4. Performance expectations: a, d, e, f, g, h, i, j.

In this text for older middle graders, feisty Susan Carlisle finds herself needing to pay off her father's debts by going on an overland sheep drive, an unusual journey for a fourteen-year-old girl in 1852. Almost a "tall tale," this story is definitely "about an adventuresome girl," but one equally appealing to boys because of its adventure and survival issues.

1. Draw a map of the entire journey Susan followed, from Kanesville, Iowa, to California, including the boat trip home by way of the Isthmus of Panama. Make sure to include and label all of the stops along the way.

2. The journey is a difficult one for everyone—humans, sheep, and mules alike. As you read, note the natural features along the way, such as the availability of water, mountains, and sand that make the journey either easier or more difficult. Then, make a map of the journey and write an accompanying "trail book," noting good places to stop or camp for the night.

HIDING MR. McMULTY

Berniece Rabe. (San Diego, Calif.: Harcourt, 1997) 256 pages. ISBN 0-15-201330-X. Performance expectations: a, b, f, h, i, j.

This story of natural disaster and human drama is told against the backdrop of the Great Depression. Set in rural Missouri, the story is told through the eyes of eleven-year-old Rass, son of a proud sharecropper. Rass's father says, "Obeying the rules society sets don't have a blame thing to do with what we think, nor what's right nor wrong. We mind the rules if'n we want to survive" (p. 63). Rass chafes at such a belief, and proves his mettle when he hides Mr. McMulty, an elderly black man, from the rage of the Ku Klux Klan. A flood troubles all of the residents of this area, but it is with Mr. McMulty's land that the "solution" is found.

1. What precautions should residents of flood plains take to protect themselves from flooding? Is flood insurance available to anyone today? How much does it cost? What does it cover? Find out what you can, and then write a position paper to inform future residents of any riverside communities of options open to them.

2. What areas of your state, if any, are especially prone to flooding? What should residents know if they live in such areas? Create a pamphlet for them providing information about evacuation procedures, supplies they should have on hand, and information sources for updates on the situation.

3. What areas of the country are particularly prone to flooding? Choose an area that was ravaged by this natural phenomenon and write a paper cataloguing the consequences. Address geographic, economic, and psychological/sociological consequences.

4. Write a short history of the Ku Klux Klan. When did it start? Who started it? Does it still exist? If so, where are groups thought to be the most active?

OUT OF THE DUST

Karen Hesse. (New York: Scholastic, 1999) 227 pages. ISBN 0-590-37125-8. Performance expectations: b, d, e, i, j.

A 1998 Newbery winner, *Out of the Dust* is an unusual book. Hesse has written this "novel" as a series of poems. Each is titled and tells the life of fifteen-year-old Billie Jo, who lives in the Oklahoma Dust Bowl. Using poetry as her medium, Hesse uses "brushstrokes" that are alternatively soft and bold. She allows the reader to feel deeply the consequences of the drought—both economically and psychologically. This is a story of one family and its survival, although in many ways, it is the story of all families.

1. In "The Path of Our Sorrow" (pp. 83-84), Billie Jo's teacher explains how America created its "dust bowl." After doing some research, write a more detailed prose explanation for this occurrence.

2. Create a timeline of pivotal personal events in Billie Jo's life. In parallel fashion, create another timeline that highlights national events. Then write a short narrative noting any similarities in national events and Billie Jo's life.

3. Forgiveness is a key issue in Billie Jo's life. In the persona of Billie Jo, write a journal entry about your feelings after the accident involving her mother.

JULIE OF THE WOLVES

Jean Craighead George. Illustrated by John Schoenherr. (New York: Harper, 1974) 170 pages. ISBN 0-640-41158-1. Performance expectations: e, f, h.

This 1973 Newbery winner features the unrelenting environment of the North Slope of Alaska and Julie's ability to survive in it. Known as Miyax in her Eskimo home, thirteen-year-old Julie runs away to avoid an arranged marriage. Losing her way to San Francisco on her way to her pen pal's home, Julie survives only because a family of wolves adopts her as one of their own. This compelling story shows how humans' existence depends on nature.

1. Research the climate of Alaska. In chart form, compare aspects of climate in Alaska with those of your state.

2. Using a map of Alaska, note where population centers are in relation to the state's geographic characteristics. Write about your findings.

3. Read the two sequels: *Julie* (illustrated by Wendell Minor; Harper Trophy, 1996, 226 pages, ISBN 0-064-40573-7) and *Julie's Wolf Pack* (illustrated by Wendell Minor; Harper Collins, 1999, 193 pages, ISBN 0-064-40721-7).

Poetry

THIS LAND IS YOUR LAND

Woody Guthrie. Paintings by Kathy Jakobsen. (Boston, Mass.: Little Brown, 1998) 32 pages. ISBN 0-316-39215-4. Performance expectations: g, h, i, j.

Woody Guthrie's classic folk song "This Land Is Your Land" has been given another tribute by the illustrator Kathy Jakobsen. The book includes three verses that are less known, some of which describe poverty during the Great Depression.

1. The artist varies the size of her paintings. Sometimes she uses both sides of the page—a full page spread for one picture; sometimes there is a painting on one page, and sometimes she includes eight separate pictures on a page. Write her a letter telling her what you think of this approach.

2. When Guthrie recorded this song in 1949, the producer omitted some of the verses. Some songbooks also omit them. Do you think the verses add to the theme? Why or why not? Can you add any verses of your own?

3. Sing the whole song together.

Notes

1. This section is directly quoted from National Council for the Social Studies, *Expectations of Excellence: Curriculum Standards for Social Studies* (Washington, D.C.: Author, 1994), 85.

► CHAPTER SIX

ⓘⓥ INDIVIDUAL DEVELOPMENT AND IDENTITY

Performance Expectations

Social studies programs should include experiences that provide for the study of *individual development and identity*, so that the learner can:

a. relate personal changes to social, cultural, and historical contexts;

b. describe personal connections to place—as associated with community, nation, and world;

c. describe the ways family, gender, ethnicity, nationality, and institutional affiliations contribute to personal identity;

d. relate such factors as physical endowment and capabilities, learning, motivation, personality, perception, and behavior to individual development;

e. identify and describe ways regional, ethnic, and national cultures influence individuals' daily lives;

f. identify and describe the influence of perception, attitudes, values, and beliefs on personal identity;

g. identify and interpret examples of stereotyping, conformity, and altruism;

h. work independently and cooperatively to accomplish goals.[1]

Picture Books

THE STRAIGHT LINE WONDER

Mem Fox. Pictures by Marc Rosenthal. (Greenvale, N.Y.: Mondo Publishing, 1997) 32 pages. ISBN 1-57255-206-9. Performance expectations: d, f, g.

In a "straight-forward" manner, this picture book reminds its readers to be true to themselves, a lesson young adults too often forget under the pressure of social conformity. When the first straight line begins to "jump in humps, twirling in whirls, pointing his joints and creeping in heaps, his friend the second straight line tells him to 'Stay straight, silly!' while the third straight line reminds him 'People will stare!' and finally, they run off and leave him. A famous movie director then sees the first straight line and tells him, 'You're a wonder. I just love the way you move,' and invites him to star in his latest movie. The other straight lines quickly claim him as their 'best' friend."

1. Although this picture book was probably intended for primary grade students, its message is appropriate for people of all ages. What other "lessons" help forge one's identity? With your class, brainstorm some other ideas, choose one, and write your own book. If possible, team up with someone to do the illustrations, and then share your story with as many people as you can!

2. How would you define "friend"? Write an essay, poem, or short story that reveals the characteristics most important to you.

COMING TO AMERICA: THE STORY OF IMMIGRATION

Betsy Maestro. (New York: Scholastic, 1996) 40 pages. ISBN 0-590-44151-5. Performance expectations: b, c, e, f, g.

The economic reasons for many immigrants' journey to the United States are clearly evident in this brightly colored and information-filled book, which begins by stating, "America is a country of immigrants." The book credits the Native Americans with being the "first immigrants to arrive in what was truly a new world." Maestro acknowledges other reasons immigrants came as well, helping middle graders to see how factors such as race and religion interplay with economic concerns.

1. Using the Table of Dates in the back of the book, draw a map that shows where immigrants have come from over the years. Write a short paragraph, sharing your results.

2. Research the problem of illegal immigration in this country today, especially in California, Florida, and Texas. With two partners, research these states and then compare notes, creating a three part Venn diagram to show your results (each student learning about one state). Present your conclusions to the class. Make sure to explain how illegal immigration is an "economic" issue.

WHEN JESSIE CAME ACROSS THE SEA

Amy Hest. Illustrated by P. J. Lynch. (Cambridge, Mass.: Candlewick Press, 1997) 40 pages. ISBN 0-7636-0094-6. Performance expectations: a, b, c, d, e, f, g, h.

Thirteen-year-old Jessie is sent to America from her beloved home in eastern Europe. Her skill in dressmaking is her "ticket," the talent that allows her to earn enough money to send for her grandmother three years later. In this book, industry is tied with both pragmatic obligation and personal satisfaction.

1. Onboard ship, Jessie and her companions talk of "Dreams of America, where the streets were paved with gold. America, land of plenty." Where did the immigrants get such an idea? Why would they believe such dreams? Find out why most immigrants came to the United States in the early twentieth century. Then, write a poem expressing their hopes.

2. Read *If Your Name Was Changed at Ellis Island* (Ellen Levine; Scholastic, 1994, 80 pages, ISBN 0-590-43829-8). Then write a detailed summary of what could have happened to Jessie once the ship docked.

3. See what resources you can find about Ellis Island on the Internet. Find out what you can about your family's background and write a short report.

HEROES
Ken Mochizuki. Illustrated by Dom Lee. (New York: Lee & Low Books, 1995) 34 pages. ISBN 1-880000-50-4. Performance expectations: a, b, c, d, e, f, g, h.

In this powerful picture book, Mochizuki helps his reader define "hero" and the actions that make for a hero. Donnie, a boy of Japanese ancestry, always has to be the "enemy" when he and his friends "play war" because he looks "like them." Donnie would rather play football, but because his friends want to play war, it is either that or have no one to play with at all. Donnie's dad and uncle both served in the U.S. military, but are reluctant to "prove" to Donnie's friends their roles in it; they believe the boys should be "playing something else besides war." Still, the day the "friends" push too hard, Donnie's dad and uncle come to the rescue. They pick Donnie up from school wearing their numerous medals, his uncle in full military dress and officer's cap. When Uncle Yosh throws Donnie a pass, all the boys head off to play football.

1. Donnie's dad says that "real heroes don't brag," that "they just do what they are supposed to do." Do you agree? Decide on your own definition of a hero and write a description of someone you know who fits your ideas.

2. The author's note at the beginning of the book briefly describes the all-Japanese American Army regiment that fought in Europe. Write a short report on how this regiment was formed and about its incredible achievements as a military unit.

3. Is the idea of a politician being a "hero" possible? Should politicians be "Heroes of Civic Practice"? Why or why not? Find someone who agrees with you and two classmates who do not, and prepare for a debate. Then present the debate for the class.

4. Read *Baseball Saved Us*, also by Mochizuki and Lee (Lee & Low, 1995, 32 pages, ISBN 1-880-00019-9). Then read another book such as *The Children of Topaz* (Michael Tunnell and George Chilcoat; Holiday House, 1996, 74 pages, ISBN 0-823-41239-3) to find out other pastimes of children in the internment camps for Japanese Americans.

Non-Fiction

WHEN I WAS YOUR AGE
Amy Ehrlich (Editor). Illustrated by Christine Rodin. (Cambridge, Mass.: Candlewick Press, 1996) 160 pages. ISBN 1-56402-306-0. Performance expectations: a, b, c, d, e, f, g.

For this special collection, authors Mary Pope Osborne, Laurence Yep, James Howe, Katherine Paterson, Walter Dean Myers, Susan Cooper, Nicholasa Mohr, Reeve Lindbergh, Avi, and Francesca Lia Block each wrote an original story about growing up. In addition, the authors include notes about the inspiration for their stories, "why they chose a particular memory to write about," and "what in their lives led them to become writers." Adolescents will find these stories comforting in content and nurturing in process; "published" authors fight the same battles with their texts that "classroom" authors fight.

1. Choose one of the authors and read a book by him or her. See if you can find a bit of the author's life in the book you read. Do a book talk for your classmates.

2. Write a story about your own childhood. Then, add the "Notes from" just as each author does in this collection.

3. Choose one of the authors and look at the kinds of writing that author does. Can you categorize the work by genre, such as historical fiction, fantasy, realistic fiction, myths, and so forth? Create a poster for your author, highlighting his or her texts in any way you think is most suitable.

THE SAFE ZONE: A KID'S GUIDE TO PERSONAL SAFETY
Donna Chaiest and Francine Russell. Photographs by Lillian Gee. (New York: Beech Tree, 1998) 160 pages. ISBN 0-688-15308-9. Performance expectations: b, e, g.

It is unfortunate that this book had to be written. Although some of the problems addressed in the book are timeless, such as bullies and getting help, the contemporary awareness of child molesters, burglars, and strangers at the door makes this a strongly recommended book for young adolescents. Some parents may have concerns about the anxiety that this book may raise, but ignorance can be costly. The format is appealing, and the advice is direct and to the point. Although of value to all adolescents, the pictures appear to be of fifth graders.

1. Chapters in the book begin with "What if" situations and conclude with "Answers to what if." Select those problems of interest to you, write a response that is not recommended, and suggest what the consequences might be.

2. Two other recent books also deal with individual identity: Miriam Stoppard's *Every Girl's Life Guide* (DK Publishing, 1999, 96 pages, ISBN 0-7894-3758-9) and Jeremy Daldry's *The Teenage Guy's Survival Guide* (Little Brown, 1999, 176 pages, ISBN 0-316-17824-1). Read both and compare the quality of information and advice in those books with The Safe Zone. For what age level would you recommend these books? Are they too mature for middle school students?

HARD TIME: A REAL LIFE LOOK AT JUVENILE CRIME AND VIOLENCE

Janet Bode and Stan Mack. (New York: Bantam Books, 1998) 218 pages. ISBN 0-440-219531-1. Performance expectations: a, b, c, d, e, f, g.

The power of this nonfiction text comes from the bold stories expressed in the teenagers' own voices. In no uncertain terms, the stories reveal how the teenagers came to be in trouble with the law and how the law finally held them. Becky, seventeen, explains that she helped murder her cousin because she believed her cousin wanted to steal her boyfriend. Sean, also seventeen, tells how he shot his mom and took her car. James, fourteen, says in the treatment facility, "I'm an alcoholic," and "Everybody in my family except my grandma has been shot at. This is no way to live. I don't want other kids to have to go through this. And that's why I'm talking to you" (p. 49). Indeed, this first part of the collection of stories comes from eighteen months of research with incarcerated teenagers, those on the "inside." The last part comes from the viewpoints of teenagers on the "outside" and their perceptions of crime and violence; the middle section, called "The Go-Betweens," provides perspectives of those who work with or who are concerned about these teenagers at risk. The writers hope that this book will be a "wake-up call" and that teens and adults will work together to decrease the violence and "keep the peace."

1. Read *Scorpions* (Walter Dean Myers; Harper & Row, 1990, 216 pages, ISBN 0-064-47066-0). The need to belong to a gang, to honor a brother's word, and to handle a gun are all factors in Jamal's downfall. What would you have done if you were Jamal? In the persona of Jamal, write a letter to your brother explaining whether or not the Scorpions are going to be a part of your life.

2. Consult the current crime statistics of your local community for the past month. How many incidents involved teenagers? How does this number compare with incidents committed by adults? Analyze the statistics for the past two years, considering the same questions.

3. Select several of the "stories" told in this book, and then write and perform, with several of your friends, a Readers Theater for your class. Afterwards, as a group, write a class pledge that commits each of you to "keeping the peace." Select someone to copy it onto a poster board and have everyone sign it—each student's signature a bond with the beliefs revealed in the pledge.

Novels, Stories and Folk Tales

History
TRUE NORTH: A NOVEL OF THE UNDERGROUND RAILROAD

Kathryn Lasky. (New York: Scholastic, 1998) 208 pages. ISBN 0-590-20524-2. Performance expectations: a, b, c, d, e, f, g.

This thoroughly researched novel relates the story of Boston-born and bred fourteen-year-old Lucy Bradford, contrasting her life with that of Afrika, a young woman of the same age who is fleeing the South via the Underground Railroad. Lasky deftly weaves the experiences of the two girls, alternating their stories chapter by chapter, making it easier for the reader to follow by including dates and places at the beginning of each.

1. Was it courage that sustained both Afrika and Lucy, or something else? Write a journal entry in the persona of a friend to either one, encouraging or discouraging her actions.

2. Read another historical novel of a runaway's trip north by the Underground Railroad, such as *Steal Away* (Jennifer Armstrong; Fawcett Books, 1999, 206 pages, ISBN 0-449-00319-1) or *Brady* (Jean Fritz; Viking, 1987, 223 pages, ISBN 0-140-32258-2). Compare and contrast the two accounts.

WHEN WILL THIS CRUEL WAR BE OVER?: THE CIVIL WAR DIARY OF EMMA SIMPSON, GORDONSVILLE, VIRGINIA, 1864

Barry Denenberg. (New York: Scholastic, 1996) 156 pages. ISBN 0-590-22862-5. Performance expectations: a, b, c, d, e, f, g, h

This unique and probably controversial fictionalized diary is one from the Dear America series. Emma's diary entries portray the suffering of a white, slave-owning family in Virginia. The language is appropriately archaic: the term "Negroes" is used throughout. It is unfortunate that the author could not give life to any African Americans other than those slaves who remained loyal to their masters.

1. Nelson is a young slave, a leader who encourages other slaves to run away. The book ends with an epilogue telling what happened to the major characters. In a similar fashion, write what you think might have been Nelson's life story.

2. An excellent book that would give insight into African Americans of the period would be any in the Addy series, especially the first work, *Meet Addy* (Connie Porter; illustrated by Melodye Rosales, Pleasant Company, 1993, 69 pages, ISBN 1-56247-075-2), from the very popular American Girls Collection. More information about the collection, as well as recommended further reading, can be found at AmericanGirl.com. These books are written for younger children than is Denenberg's novel; a review of them, however, and especially the post script, "A Peek into the Past," which provides historical information related to the setting and plot of the book, would be enlightening to students of any age.

3. Create a Venn diagram by comparing this novel with Mary Lyons' *Letters from a Slave Girl* (Atheneum, 1992, 146 pages, ISBN 0-684-19446-5). This work is based on the autobiography of an African American woman who uses letters as a means of telling the story. Much of the story predates the Civil War, and it dramatically portrays the life of those enslaved.

EMMA EILEEN GROVE, MISSISSIPPI, 1865

Kathleen Duey. (New York: Aladdin, 1996) 140 pages. ISBN 0-689-80385-0. Performance expectations: a, b, c, d, e, f, g, h.

In this work from the American Diaries series, the daughter of a middle class southern farmer, who does not approve of slavery, joins her brother and younger sister on a steamboat journey to St. Louis to find family to care for them. Disaster strikes and the boat sinks, but not until the author has introduced a number of characters: a forgiving Yankee who was a former prisoner of war, a racist gambler, a pampered, middle-aged southern woman, and a caring slave.

1. Do a report card on each character's courage. List all the major characters and rate each character on courage, honesty, compassion, tolerance, self-respect, and responsibility. After you grade each character on these virtues, write "recommendations for improvement" (as teachers often do).

2. Write a letter to the author (c/o the publisher: Kathleen Duey, First Aladdin Paperbacks, Simon & Schuster, Children's Publishing Division, 1230 Avenue of the Americas, New York, NY 10020) suggesting adventures or plots that could be included in her next book about Emma Eileen Grove.

SHANNON, A CHINATOWN ADVENTURE, SAN FRANCISCO, 1880, BOOK ONE

Kathleen Kudlinski. Illustrated by Bill Farnsworth. (New York: Aladdin, 1996) 71 pages, ISBN 0-689-80984-0 . Performance expectations: a, b, c, d, e, f, g, h.

This appealing book is briefer and perhaps more appealing to younger middle school-age children than are many similar works of this genre. Part of the Girlhood Journeys Collection, this novel tells the story of an affluent Irish family that moves to San Francisco. Shannon strikes up a friendship with an American-born girl, and together they rescue a Chinese girl who has been enslaved.

1. Reflect on Shannon's character. Write her name in a circle and extend from the circle dotted lines. At the end of each, write a positive character trait that she exhibits in the story. Draw straight lines in a similar fashion and write words that describe her physically. From this pre-writing strategy, write a character sketch.

2. Few Irish immigrants were as wealthy as Shannon. Read one of Ireland's most popular children's books, *Wildflower Girl* (Marita Conlon-McKenna; Puffin, 1994, 172 pages, ISBN 0-140-36292-4), which depicts a more typical experience of an Irish girl.

LITTLE JIM'S DREAMS

Gloria Houston. Illustrations by Thomas B. Allen. (San Diego, Calif.: Harcourt Brace & Company, 1997) 128 pages. ISBN 0-152-015094. Performance expectations: a, b, c, d, e, f, g.

In this touching sequel to *Littlejim* (illustrated by Thomas B. Allen; Beech Tree Books, 1993, 176 pages, ISBN 0-688-12112-8), the challenges of now fourteen-year-old Littlejim's day-to-day life are even greater than before when Littlejim sets out to earn his father's respect by winning an essay contest on "What it means to be an American." Set in rural North Carolina during World War I, Houston's characters portray the prejudices that outsiders held toward Appalachian people. Littlejim's mother encourages him to "Dream your dreams. Dreams are what guide you in life." Littlejim's needing to be true to himself, however, sets up a conflict with Littlejim's father throughout much of this novel. This coming-of-age story reveals how complex one's responsibilities are—to oneself, surely, but also to one's family and community.

1. All of Gloria Houston's books are inspired by her family's stories from Spruce Pine, North Carolina. What are your family's stories? Talk with a grandparent, aunt, uncle, or cousin, and see if you can find a story from your past that resonates with who you are now. Write it down.

2. Read Houston's *Mountain Valor* (Paper Star Publishing, 1994, 239 pages, ISBN 0-698-11383-7), which has a female protagonist. Then think about how Valor and Littlejim are alike and different. Next, create a Venn diagram by drawing two intersecting circles. In the space where they intersect, write how the two characters are alike. Then, in the circle to the left, write how Valor is different from Littlejim. In the circle on the right, write how Littlejim is different from Valor.

FIRE IN THE HILLS
Anna Myers. (New York: Puffin, 1998) 176 pages. ISBN 0-141-30074-4. Performance expectations: a, b, c, d, e, f, g.

Although living during World War I, sixteen-year-old Hallie has little time to worry about the war itself; she has been given the new responsibility of caring for seven siblings because her mother has died recently. The war, however, intrudes anyway; Hallie's brother Starlin is drafted, and a mysterious draft dodger comes to live in Hallie's neighborhood. Hallie worries about the growing hate festering in town toward a local German family. Before the war, the Heidens were considered a stalwart family of the community; now, simply because of their heritage, they are suspect—as are all who defend them. In this finely written novel set in Oklahoma, characters define themselves successfully despite trying times.

1. Throughout time, public sentiment has always been a powerful influence on national events. Why do you think that is? Why do groups seem to make illogical decisions sometimes? Write an editorial encouraging people to think for themselves, not to just go along with a group.

2. Hallie and Johnny Childres are compassionate, thoughtful young adults. In the persona of Hallie or Johnny, explain how you feel about things by writing a poem. Or write a poem about either one as a tribute.

THE JAZZ KID
James Collier. (New York: Puffin, 1996) 216 pages. ISBN 0-14-037778-6. Performance expectations: a, b, c, d, e, f, g.

For the first time in his life, twelve-year-old Paulie Horvath is committed to being good at something—playing the cornet. Paulie's devotion does not take the path his mother wishes—excelling in school—or the path his father expects—going into his plumbing business. Instead, Paulie ventures into the black jazz clubs. Not only does he pursue his dream, but he also comes to understand the nature of prejudice in the tough underworld of Chicago in the 1920s.

1. What makes jazz a unique form of music? Who were the significant people in this country who played jazz in the 1920s? With a friend or two, write your own Readers Theater, honoring the people and history of jazz.

2. Paulie says he is never going to be good at school or at the plumbing trade. Is it because he is just not trying hard enough or is it because he really cannot do those things well—but has other special abilities? In the persona of Paulie, write a letter to either his Mom or Dad explaining how he feels about being "pushed" into doing things he feels uncomfortable doing. Or write a letter to your own parent(s) or guardian(s) explaining how you and Paulie are alike or thanking them for supporting what is most important to you.

ROLL OF THUNDER, HEAR MY CRY
Mildred Taylor. (New York: Puffin, 1997) 276 pages. ISBN 0-140-38451-0. Performance expectations: a, b, c, d, e, f, g.

Winner of a 1997 Newbery award, this book chronicles the survival of one black family during the Great Depression as seen through the eyes of Cassie. As a young person, she struggles to comprehend the importance of the land her family owns. Her father tells her, "You ain't never had to live on nobody's place but your own and long as I live and the family survives, you'll never have to." When she is humiliated by a white girl in public simply because she is black, Cassie begins to understand the reality of the world her family tried so hard to protect her from, a world that also includes night riders and the violence they caused.

1. Cassie is forced to learn how to be a young black woman in a world powered by white men. At what point in the novel do you think she feels the most powerful? Write an essay, first naming and retelling the event, followed by why you believe this is a pivotal event in Cassie's life.

2. Various events happen throughout the novel, both directly to Cassie and to those Cassie knows in the community. Make a list of these events in one column. In a column to the right of it, explain what Cassie learns from each.

3. In the persona of Cassie's father, write a letter to Cassie explaining precisely why the land is so important and what it represents to their family. Use incidents in the story to strengthen your argument.

4. Stacey, Cassie's brother, also is learning to negotiate his role as a young black man in these times. How is Stacey's life different from Jeremy's, a white contemporary's? How are both boys constrained by the times in which they live?

5. Read the sequels to this story, *The Road to Memphis* (Puffin, 1992, 290 pages, ISBN 0-140-36077-8) and *Let the Circle Be Unbroken* (Puffin, 1991, 394 pages, ISBN 0-140-34892-1). How does Cassie change over the years? Make a timeline of significant events in her life.

Personal Growth and Challenges
GIDEON'S PEOPLE

Carolyn Meyer. (San Diego, Calif.: Gulliver Books, 1996) 297 pages. ISBN 0-15-200304-5. Performance expectations: a, b, c, d, e, f, g.

Cultures collide when twelve-year-old Isaac Litvak, who is an Orthodox Jew, wakes up in the home of an Amish family. Taken in by the family after a wagon accident, Isaac is alone; his father has to hurry back to his wife who is expecting to deliver a baby soon. Language and customs prove not to be insurmountable barriers as the Amish children, Gideon and his little sister Annie, nurse Isaac back to health; they become friends. Questioning his own heritage, Gideon runs to his uncle's farm where he can be away from his father's rules and beliefs. There he finds a version of being Amish that is meaningful and satisfying to him.

1. Research the day-to-day practices of both Orthodox Jews and the Amish people. How are they alike? How are they different? What are their belief systems? Create a chart, recording how they are similar or different.

2. Create a tourist poster for contemporary Lancaster County. The Internet or the Tourist Center might be good places to start looking for information.

JUBILEE JOURNEY

Carolyn Meyer. (San Diego, Calif.: Harcourt Brace & Company, 1997) 256 pages. ISBN 0-152-01591-4. Performance expectations: a, b, c, d, e, f, g.

In a surprising and most satisfying sequel to the historical novel *White Lilacs* (Gulliver Books, 1993, 242 pages, ISBN 0-152-95876-2), Meyer begins the "Jubilee" journey in present-day New England and then takes her reader, through the experience of her great-granddaughter Emmy, back in time to the beginning of the story in Dillon, Texas. There, Emmy confronts another perspective on being a "double," having always felt before that it was a privilege to belong to both white and black cultures. In Texas, though, being black is not considered a position of privilege, a startling lesson for her. A spirited yet thoughtful character, Emmy completes her journey far wiser than she began it. She is a role model for all teenagers, not just those whose history embraces more than one heritage.

1. If you made a "Jubilee Journey" for yourself, what would be your final destination? What would the occasion be that called you there? When would be the appropriate time for you to go? Map out how you would get from here to there, including estimates of mileage, costs of transportation, food, lodging, and so forth for your journey.

2. Steven, Emmy's brother, has to address the same issues as Emmy. How are they alike in the way they act and think? How are they different? In the persona of Steven or Emmy, write home to your Dad explaining how confusing life can be for a biracial person in the South.

DEAR MR. HENSHAW

Beverly Cleary. Illustrated by Paul Zelinsky. (New York: Camelot, 1994) 134 pages. ISBN 0-380-70958-9. Performance expectations: a, b, c, f.

Winner of the 1984 Newbery Award, *Dear Mr. Henshaw* is a boy's story told in a diary format. Not necessarily a writer at the beginning of the novel, Leigh Botts feels a kinship with Mr. Henshaw, the author of his favorite book. With Mr. Henshaw's guidance, Leigh eventually realizes that he does not have to write everything to Mr. Henshaw, because Mr. Henshaw cannot possibly respond so frequently. He finds he can simply continue to use the format "Dear Mr. Henshaw" as a way to sort out the issues of his life: being the new boy in school, having the "goodies" in his lunch stolen, and dealing with his parents' divorce.

1. Do a character timeline for Leigh. How is he feeling about his parents' divorce at the beginning of the novel? How do his feelings change over the course of the story? As you read the novel, keep track of the questions Leigh has about his mother, his father, and their relationship. Make a timeline describing how Leigh's perceptions change over time.

2. Read the sequel to this novel, *Strider* (illustrated by Paul Zelinksy; Harper, 1996, 176 pages, ISBN 0-380-72802-8). How has Leigh changed since the end of *Dear Mr. Henshaw*? Continue the character timeline as suggested previously, or create one for this book.

3. As Leigh Botts does, write a letter to the author of your favorite book. Be specific in relating the reasons the book is so important to you.

FRINDLE

Andrew Clements. Pictures by Brian Selznick. (New York: Aladdin, 1998) 105 pages. ISBN 0-689-81876-9. Performance expectations: d, e, f.

Nicholas, a very bright young man, after doing an assignment on dictionaries, decides to organize his class, and later the school, to create a new word: *frindle*. This term would be a substitute for the word *pen*. The school administrators consider this a challenge to their authority, and the national media become involved. Nicholas achieves his goal and becomes rich, but, more important, he learns about others and matures in the process.

1. Write a letter, as was done in the book, to be opened in the future, but address it to your teacher. Tell him or her the letter should not be opened for a year.

2. Nicholas gave away much of his fortune to family members. They were reluctant to accept the money. Just as the character did, decide who you would distribute parts of your fortune to and explain why they should get it.

A REGULAR GUY

Sarah Weeks. (New York: Harper Collins, 1999) 120 pages. ISBN 0-06-028367-X. Performance expectations: a, b, c, d, f, g, h.

Guy is sure he is a "regular guy," but knows that his parents are not. Consequently, Guy decides that he and another sixth grader were switched at birth. Once convinced of this "truth," in a light-hearted but logical manner, Guy and his best friend Buzz methodically create and carry out a plan to convince not only Robert Smith, the kid who shares Guy's birth date, but also both sets of parents. At the heart of this book is the need for all pre-adolescents and adolescents to "know who they really are."

1. How have you changed over time? This story takes place just during Guy's sixth grade year. How have you changed since first grade? Create a timeline. On the far left, put a dot on your line, label it "First Grade," and describe yourself. Then think about how you changed between first and second grades; two inches or so to the right of the first grade dot, make a second one. Describe yourself as a second grader. Then, in the space between first and second, make a list of the factors that caused these changes in you. Continue the timeline in this manner, year by year, finishing the timeline with the grade you are currently in.

2. Create a credo, or "I Believe" statement for yourself. In other words, if someone asked you what you stood for, what would you say? What factors have influenced who you say you are? Your family? Your faith? Your local community? Your education? After you have finished writing it, type it up, decorate it in some way, and frame it, showcasing it in your classroom.

3. Read the sequel, *Guy Time* (Harper Collins, 2000, 176 pages, ISBN 0-060-28365-3). Enjoy!

THE JANITOR'S BOY

Andrew Clements. (New York: Simon & Schuster, 2000) 140 pages. ISBN 0-689-81818-1. Performance expectations: a, b, c, d, f, h.

When the old high school becomes the middle school, Jack's dad becomes the janitor—much to Jack's dismay. For the first month, Jack manages to keep their relationship a secret, but then his dad's "Hi, son" blows his cover. Jack gets revenge, but his resulting punishment is to work with his dad for three weeks after school. This is a story with which many adolescents may identify because they, too, may not want to be like or associated with their parents. The ending is both touching and realistic.

1. What do you think was the most important lesson Jack learned? Why? Does knowing Jack's story help you as a person struggling to make good decisions? Write at least one example and explain how that part of the story helped you.

2. What was the most important idea you pulled from this story? Why? How has it changed you as a person? Is it an idea you can put into an action plan? If so, do so. If not, try to remember this lesson in your daily life.

3. Whose "son" or "daughter" are you? Even if you don't want to admit it, you may have inherited or picked up some of your father's or mother's habits or characteristics, perhaps positive ones as well as negative ones. How can identifying these characteristics help you grow into the person you want to be? See if you can write an essay explaining who you are and who you are striving to be without sharing private information about your family.

DEATH AT DEVIL'S BRIDGE

Cynthia DeFelice. (New York: Farrar Straus Giroux, 2000) 181 pages. ISBN 0-374-31723-2. Performance expectations: a, b, c, d, e, f, g.

This book, the sequel to *Devil's Bridge* (reading that book, however, is not necessary to understand this one), is a suspenseful novel that reveals how easy it is to get caught up with the wrong friends. Thirteen-year-old Ben Daggett never expects to find himself caught up in criminal activity, and yet he does, small step by small step. Wanting to look "cool," wanting to be part of the most popular crowd, Ben edges away from his family's values as well as his own, and finds himself in real danger. Although the book is set on Martha's Vineyard, the possibility of any teenager finding himself or herself in similar circumstances is all too real.

1. Describe Ben at the beginning of the novel. List adjectives that describe him, and then next to each word (at least five), write down the actions that support these adjectives. Repeat this activity at the end of the novel. Did your five key descriptors change? Is this good or bad?
2. Consider "Performance Expectation c" of this strand of the curriculum standards for social studies (p. 61, above). For the three major characters of the novel, Ben, Jeff, and Donny, "describe the ways family, gender, ethnicity, nationality, and institutional affiliations" contribute to each of their personal identities. How are they similar? How are they different? Make a chart to document your ideas, and then write a final paragraph or two explaining what conclusions you reach.
3. Read *Devil's Bridge* (Camelot, 1997, 96 pages, ISBN 0-380-721117-1). What does Ben learn about himself in this novel? How does this compare with what he learns about himself in *Death at Devil's Bridge*? Create a Venn diagram comparing Ben's character in both novels.

STEP BY WICKED STEP

Anne Fine. (New York: Bantam Books, 1997) 144 pages. ISBN 0-440-41329-X. Performance expectations: a, c, f.

Borrowing the form of Chaucer's *Canterbury Tales* (Penguin, 2000, 504 pages, ISBN 0-140-44022-4), the author enables five young people on an overnight study tour to share their stories of divided families. This is an excellent source for bibliotherapy for children who are not living in traditional families. The reader will learn that children need to share their feelings and suggest solutions their parents can accept.

1. Write an editorial for the school newspaper emphasizing the importance of communication between children and parents. Acknowledge that communication is a responsibility of both parent and child.
2. Using the author's style, add a story about your family as an additional chapter.

HEAVEN

Angela Johnson. (New York: Simon and Schuster, 1998) 144 pages. ISBN 0-689-82229-4. Performance expectations: a, b, c, d.

Winner of the 1999 Coretta Scott King Author Award, Heaven is the name of a town in Ohio, a place teenage Marley, her brother, and their parents reside. Marley is happy and content there until she discovers the identity of her biological parents. Not having known until she was fourteen that she was being raised by her aunt and uncle, she feels betrayed. Resolving the conflicting emotions, especially since her father is alive, creates tension for Marley and her family, but results in a most satisfying ending.

1. What do you think? Should children be told they are adopted? Or that the persons raising them are not their "real" parents? Or should children be shielded from this information, no matter how old they are? Find someone who disagrees with you, research the issue, discuss your findings together, and then each write a position paper—unless one of you convinces the other. Then write a joint position paper.
2. How does the town of Heaven contribute to who Marley has grown to be? What details about it have influenced her growth and development?
3. Who do you think has influenced Marley's growth the most? Write a persuasive essay supporting your choice.
4. Johnson notes at the beginning of Part II that black churches are being burned again in the South as they were in the 1960s. What can you find out about this crime in both the 1960s and 1990s? With a friend,

research the burnings in both decades and then write a joint paper about your findings.

SLAVE DAY

Rob Thomas. Illustrated by Aaron Meshon. (New York: Aladdin, 1998) 192 pages. ISBN 0-689-82193-X. Performance expectations: a, b, c, e.

The talented author of *Rats Saw God* (Aladdin, 1996, 219 pages, ISBN 0-689-80777-5) sets his story in a small-town, integrated school: Robert E. Lee High School. Although most of the students are white, the first African American student government president sees no harm in the annual auctioning of teachers and student government representatives as slaves. The story is told from eight characters' points of view, and each chapter is written using a stream of consciousness style. It works. There are enough turns and subplots in the book to hold the reader's interest. Gender and racial consciousness of the characters is raised, and most of the characters experience personal growth.

1. Suggestions are made in the book regarding the future of the characters. Select one character and assume that person is writing his or her autobiography for the twenty-fifth high school reunion. Tell that person's story.
2. Although geared toward young adults, the language is not difficult. This publication would make an excellent Readers Theater play. Students would be assigned a character and read from that person's chapter in the book.
3. Do a story board as if you were making a television documentary about the end of "slave day." Draw pictures to suggest your visuals, and under them, write your narrative.

THE GRADUATION OF JAKE MOON

Barbara Park. (New York: Atheneum, 2000) 116 pages. ISBN 0-689-83912-X. Performance expectations: a, b, c, d, f, h.

The trap of Alzheimer's disease—for the person suffering from the disease and his or her family—is poignantly portrayed in this gem of a book. The dignity with which Jake and his family members treat Skelly, Jake's grandfather, as the disease takes an increasing hold, is evident and commendable. Jake tries to keep his friends away because he fears they will not understand. He's right; neither he nor his friends are good about discussing the situation, so Jake avoids the subject and his friends find it easier to stay away. Strong support from Jake's mom makes the situation with Skelly just bearable for Jake. When Jake understands that it is his turn to "be there for Skelly," however, he truly "graduates."

1. Create a timeline that chronicles events between Jake and Skelly throughout the novel, giving a brief description of the event below the timeline. Then choose the incident you think shows the lowest point in how Jake handles life with Skelly, and briefly explain why, writing your commentary about that incident above the timeline. Finally, decide at which point you think Jake changes, understanding that loving Skelly means accepting the changes in Skelly's life and taking on more responsibility. Explain why you chose this point by writing a brief commentary above that event on the timeline.
2. Some resources for finding out more about Alzheimer's disease are provided at the end of the book. Do some research and report your findings to the class, explaining how this disease seems to "erase" one's identity.
3. Read another of Park's books, *Mick Harte Was Here* (Random House, 1996, 89 pages, ISBN 0-679-88203-0), about Mick, who was "here" for only a short time because he was riding his bicycle without wearing a helmet and was hit by a truck, leaving behind a devastated family. After reading this novel, consider how your "individual development and identity" can be influenced by even "literary" acquaintances.

THE HEART IS BIG ENOUGH

Michael Rosen. Illustrated by Matthew Veliquette. (San Diego, Calif.: Harcourt Brace & Company, 1997) 208 pages. ISBN 0-15-201402. Performance expectations: a, b, c, d, e, f, g.

This quintet of stories provides ample evidence that the heart, indeed, "is big enough." In each story, a young adult finds a way to push past ambivalence, prejudice, or fear to caring communication with a grandmother, a neighbor, residents of a group home, or even a dolphin. Through poignant stories, Rosen reveals how young adults struggle to "come to know," a suitable reminder for adults who work with (or try to raise!) people at this stage of development. Without being preachy, and oftentimes with prose that is nearly poetry, Rosen reveals the understandings that nurture healthy growth and development.

1. As Matthew makes a discovery about himself in "The Trust of a Dolphin," and Dillon does so in "Mastering the Art," think about what it is that you have recently discovered that makes a difference in the way you look at the world. Write your story.

2. In "Juggling," Jonathan finds that he likes working with his neighbor "Sam," Mrs. Edna Sams, in her greenhouse, even if he does not get paid. What does this reveal about Jonathan's character? What "work" does not seem like "work" to you either? How do you account for this? Write a personal essay explaining this seeming irony.

3. At the beginning of "The Walkers of Hawthorn Park," Frayda is fearful of her Nana Clara's neighbors, residents of a group home. Do some research about how people in your community have responded to the need to have group homes in their neighborhoods. Present the information to the class and then lead a discussion. Do you agree or disagree with your own community's stance? Why?

4. Decker's Grandma Rose, in "The Remembering Movies," has Alzheimer's disease. What else can you find out about this disease? Take some notes, report to the class, and then look into how you might help someone in your community who has it.

Poetry

THE OTHER SIDE: SHORTER POEMS
Angela Johnson. (New York: Orchard, 1998) 60 pages. ISBN 0-531-30114-1. Performance expectations: a, b, c, d, e, f, g.

Having grown up in Shorter, Alabama, Angela Johnson recounts the significance of this town for her through the thirty-three poems in this 1999 Coretta Scott King Author Honor book. Johnson retells her childhood through poetry, some fond remembrances, others not. The volume documents individual development and identity incredibly well, enticing readers to want to explore poetry as a way to document their own evolution.

1. In the preface, also a poem, Johnson writes, "My poetry doesn't sing the song of sonnets, but then / I sing a different kind of music— / which is what it's all about anyway." Think about where you lived when you were born or the first place you remember living. Write a poem based on these earliest memories. Then write a poem of today, relating some aspect of where you live now with what you know about yourself. Ask your classmates to do the same, and then compile the poems into a class book titled "I Sing a Different Kind of Music."

2. As Johnson reflects on these earlier days of her life, what does she realize she understands now that she did not understand then? In the persona of Johnson,

write a letter to your grandmother explaining what you learned when you returned "home."

3. With three friends, choose your favorite sixteen poems. Each of you choose four and practice; then read them aloud for your class as a Readers Theater production.

Notes
1. This section is directly quoted from National Council for the Social Studies, *Expectations of Excellence: Curriculum Standards for Social Studies* (Washington, D.C.: Author, 1994), 88.

CHAPTER SEVEN

ⓥ INDIVIDUALS, GROUPS AND INSTITUTIONS

Performance Expectations

Social studies programs should include experiences that provide for the study of *interactions among individuals, groups, and institutions,* so that the learner can:

a. demonstrate an understanding of concepts such as role, status, and social class in describing the interactions of individuals and social groups;

b. analyze group and institutional influences on people, events, and elements of culture;

c. describe the various forms institutions take and the interactions of people with institutions;

d. identify and analyze examples of tensions between expressions of individuality and group or institutional efforts to promote social conformity;

e. identify and describe examples of tensions between belief systems and government policies and laws;

f. describe the role of institutions in furthering both continuity and change;

g. apply knowledge of how groups and institutions work to meet individual needs and promote the common good.[1]

Picture Books

AN AMISH YEAR

Richard Ammon. Illustrated by Pamela Patrick. (New York: Atheneum, 2000) 32 pages. ISBN 0-689-82622-2. Performance expectations: a, b, d, e, g.

Following *An Amish Christmas* and *An Amish Wedding, An Amish Year* chronicles the events of Anna and her family throughout the seasons. From early spring planting and housecleaning, to bundling hay during the summer, to returning to school in the fall, to celebrating the wedding season in November, as well as Thanksgiving and Christmas, the life of this Amish family is vividly portrayed. Ammon's thoughtful and informational text is warmly and accurately illustrated through Patrick's use of pastels, the perfect medium for the content of this book. The author's note provides additional information about the Amish people.

1. Read the other books in this series: *An Amish Christmas* (illustrated by Pamela Patrick; Atheneum, 1996,

40 pages, ISBN 0-689-80377-X), *An Amish Wedding* (illustrated by Pamela Patrick; Atheneum, 1998, 32 pages, ISBN 0-689-81677-4), and the newest, *Amish Horses* (illustrated by Pamela Patrick; 2001, 40 pages, ISBN 0-689-82623-0). How do the Amish, as a people "promote the common good"?

2. Which of the characteristics of an Amish community do you find particularly appealing? Which of the characteristics would you, as an individual, find difficult to accept? Make a two-column chart, listing appealing characteristics on the left and challenges on the right. Lead a discussion with your class, sharing your list and drawing out your classmates' views.

3. Some Amish people refuse to adopt "English ways," such as placing slow-moving vehicle signs on their buggies, even though such a law is meant for their protection. Is enforcing this law a violation of their rights to practice freedom of religion? Research this issue, carefully considering both sides. Present your conclusions to the class.

A KNOCK AT THE DOOR

Eric Sonderling. Illustrated by Wendy Wassink Ackison. (Austin, Tex.: Steck-Vaughn, 1997) 32 pages. ISBN 0-8172-4434-4. Performance expectations: b, c, d, e.

Perhaps because it was written by a ten-year-old boy, this story of the Holocaust is particularly memorable. Young Eric retells a story his grandmother told him. Not knowing anything about a starving young woman who knocks at their door, a kind farmer and his wife take her in. Although the Schmidts have many questions, the young woman is unwilling to share her past until the day when a Nazi soldier also knocks at the door looking for a young woman who escaped from a concentration camp. As they promised to do from the beginning, the Schmidts protect eighteen-year-old Berta, who is never caught by the Nazis.

1. A eulogy is a speech read at a funeral praising the person who has died. Write a eulogy for Mr. and Mrs. Schmidt.

2. Rewrite the story assuming that either Mr. or Mrs. Schmidt or both assumed that the young woman had

escaped from a prison camp. How might their actions have changed?

3. Eric was ten when he won the Raintree/Steck-Vaughn *Publish a Book Contest* in 1996. Eric wrote the narrative, and the publishers selected the illustrator. Organize your own contest. Name it. Every entrant is to write a book of this length. Set a deadline for submitting the finished stories. Contact the Newspaper in Education Coordinator of your local city newspaper or the editors of your weekly paper and ask them to select the winner. You might also ask them to consider furnishing a prize!

4. Publish all of the stories generated through the contest as a class or school book.

SO FAR FROM THE SEA
Eve Bunting. Illustrated by Chris Soentpiet. (New York: Clarion, 1998) 32 pages. ISBN 0-395-72095. Performance expectations: b, e.

This picture book memorializes Laura Iwasaki and her family's last visit to Laura's grandfather's grave at the Manzanar War Relocation Camp before the family moves to Massachusetts. Illustrations done in black and white pay tribute to Laura's grandfather's life in the camp, while the intervening full-color illustrations relate Laura's family's story. With the illustrations juxtaposed as they are, this book compels all who read it to reflect on the impact that the war has had on each of us—the generation that lived it and those who live with its consequences in later years.

1. Draw a mural tracing the history of your family, your ethnic group, or an ethnic group you feel has been persecuted. You might find Sheila Hamanaka's *The Journey* (Orchard, 1995, 40 pages, ISBN 0-531-07060-3) a helpful resource. This book is based on the mural Hamanaka created to tell the story of Japanese Americans, racism and renewal.

2. Compare the photographs in Jerry Stanley's *I Am an American* (Crown Publishers, 1994, 120 pages, ISBN 0-517-59786-1) or those in a book of your choice with the illustrations in *So Far from the Sea*. Which are more effective, photographs or pictures, in depicting the tragedy of the event? Explain your choice.

3. Read Michael O. Tunnell and George W. Chilcoat's work *The Children of Topaz: The Story of a Japanese-American Internment Camp Based on a Classroom Diary* (Holiday House, 1996, 74 pages, ISBN 0-823-41239-3). How does this book extend what you learned about the camp in Bunting's book? Write a report explaining what life would have been like for you if

you had been required to live in Manzanar or Topaz.

YOUR MOVE
Eve Bunting. Illustrated by James Ransome. (San Diego, Calif.: Harcourt Brace, 1998) 32 pages. ISBN 0-15-200181-6. Performance expectations: a, b, d, e, g.

With each new book Bunting creates, she seems to fill a void that readers did not know was there. With a need to belong growing increasingly strong in the youth of our society, Bunting's text and Ransome's illustrations team up to create a powerful story of how belonging to the wrong group can be disastrous. Ten-year-old James thinks he wants to belong to the K-Bones gang, but when his six-year-old brother is almost shot on the night James has to "prove" himself, he says, "Thanks. But no thanks," to the invitation to join. Both brothers learn that it is always "your move," and each has the courage to say, "Thanks. But no thanks."

1. What gangs are operating in your city or town? Talk with the police and find out, reporting back to the class the information that the police believe will protect you and your classmates and prevent you from getting involved.

2. Read *The Outsiders* (Susan Hinton; Puffin, 1997, 180 pages, ISBN 0-140-38572-X) or *Scorpions* (Walter Dean Myers; Harper & Row, 1990, 216 pages, ISBN 0-064-47066-0). Find a friend to read the other one. Afterwards, make a poster to answer this question: How are the gangs portrayed in these books similar to or different from each other or from the gang portrayed in *Your Move*?

3. What do all gangs have in common? Why would anyone want to be in a gang? Write a script with a cast of characters of your choosing but whose message is to "stay out of gangs."

Non-Fiction

A YOUNG PERSON'S GUIDE TO PHILOSOPHY
Jeremy Weate. Illustrated by Peter Lawman. (New York: DK Publishing, 1998) 64 pages. ISBN 0-7894-3074-6. Performance expectations: d, e, f.

Philosophy is a particularly challenging topic for the early adolescent. It is also an area that may bring about anxiety for some parents. This book is not for every child or for every school district. Although written with sensitivity, the topic can cause concern for some people. NCSS, however, through its annual listing of notable trade books for young people, strongly recommended the book; it does much to make philosophy accessible to middle school scholars. The major philosophers are profiled, and the biographic sketches are expanded by sidebars and illustrations that make the philosopher appear less remote (e.g., "Socrates' wife was annoyed that he would not teach for money." "He went barefoot, even in winter"). The last half of the book consists of a chronological discussion of the various schools of philosophy, which examines the beliefs of the philosophers mentioned earlier.

1. Compare the information in this work—be sure to include the glossary in your evaluation—with standard reference books such as the *World Book Encyclopedia*. Which do you think makes philosophy more accessible? Why? Be specific.
2. The author of this work encourages his readers to reflect on the large questions of life. After reading the book, how would you answer these questions that have long occupied the minds of philosophers: Why are we here? What does it mean to be human? What is the point of life?

HOW RUDE! THE TEENAGERS' GUIDE TO GOOD MANNERS, PROPER BEHAVIOR, AND OF GROSSING PEOPLE OUT

Alex Packer. Illustrated by Jeff Tolbert. (Minneapolis, Minn.: Free Spirit Publishing, 1997) 472 pages. ISBN 1-57542-024-4. Performance expectations: a, b, d.

Etiquette is all about establishing and maintaining relationships. As such, books of etiquette are always prized by social historians; these books provide insight into the norms of groups and institutions. This book is no exception. Much of this lengthy tome is commendable. Each chapter provides guidelines in behavior; possible or probable questions by adolescents follow. It is contemporary in perspective and content. For example, there is a chapter on etiquette concerning "Going Online Without Getting Out of Line" and a section titled "Pollution Prevention." The book, however, is not without controversy. For example, in responding to the question "Who's supposed to bring the condom, the boy or the girl?", the author notes, "An excellent question, because no teenager today who chooses to be sexually active should have intercourse or oral sex without protection." After two commendable sections on stopping sexual harassment and "Besting Bigots" comes a surprising response to the question "What's so bad about ethnic jokes? They're funny." The author responds, "A Jewish joke that makes fun of rabbis, yarmulkes or gefilte fish is probably pretty safe to tell in the proper context. A 'Jewish' joke about the Holocaust is likely to offend listeners no matter what the context may be." Packer explains that context means "where, when, and to whom are you telling the joke." Packer's response may not be well received by those who believe politically correct behavior is correct behavior.

1. Summarize Packer's advice on responding to bigoted jokes and comments. Survey members of your class who may have heard such jokes or comments, and discover which response works best for them.
2. Select one of the pages the author has indicated may be reproduced. These pages range in topics from family etiquette and etiquette for divorced parents to "toiletiquette" and telephone etiquette. Copy the page, attach the page to a poster, and fill the border with appropriate captions.
3. E-mail the author with your comments about his advice, or suggest other topics that should be covered in a future work, at help4kidsfreespirit.com.

CAJUN HOME

Raymond Bial. (Boston, Mass.: Houghton Mifflin, 1998) 48 pages. ISBN 0-395-86095-4. Performance expectations: a, b, d, e, f.

Bial's photography beautifully highlights the trek of the Cajun people to find a home. Rebelling against what they perceived as royal and ecclesiastical tyrannies of France, they settled in Acadia, which is now New Brunswick, Nova Scotia, and Prince Edward Island. There they thrived for more than one hundred years, until, reluctant to submit to either the British or the French in the French and Indian War, they moved once again. They were finally allowed to remain in the bayous of Louisiana. An adaptable people, the Cajuns live by the rule of "love of life" or "joie de vivre," and their livelihood is often due to their craftsmanship and interdependence. Their past has led them to relish their tightly knit communities.

1. Create a timeline that highlights the "major moves" of the Cajun people. On the top of the line, write the date. Just below it, write a short description of why the move was necessary.
2. How does being "Cajun" influence one's life? Write an overview of what "A Day in the Life of Cajun Family" would be like.
3. Throughout their history, the Cajun people rebelled against outside authority. Identify three kinds of control that violated the Cajuns' desire to be free.
4. Few of the photographs in this book include pictures of people. Do the pictures that were included help you get a sense of the Cajun people? Why or why

not? Create a two-column chart to record your thinking on these questions, and then share your results with a small group or your whole class. Invite discussion.

THE STRENGTH OF THESE ARMS: LIFE IN THE SLAVE QUARTERS

Raymond Bial. (Boston, Mass.: Houghton Mifflin Co., 1997) 48 pages. ISBN 0-395-77394-6. Performance expectations: a, b, c.

Bial challenges the notion of kind owners and happy slaves. In a non-emotional style enhanced by historic photographs of life on the plantation, he demonstrates that slavery was a brutal institution. Despite those conditions, the enslaved African Americans maintained their dignity.

1. Some educators believe that children learn more effectively by viewing a photograph, rather than an illustration, of an event. Many of the photographs in this work are in color because they were taken in a museum. Discuss where you stand on the premise that photographs are a more meaningful way of studying history than are works of art created through the interpretive eye of an artist.

2. The photographs in this book include the exterior of a plantation and a formal dining room set with expensive china and crystal, as well as other elegant rooms. Upon an initial viewing, some would probably call them beautiful. Beautiful is that which delights the senses or the mind. View all of the pictures carefully. What is truly beautiful? Write an essay on what you think is superficially beautiful and what is absolutely beautiful.

I WAS BORN A SLAVE: THE STORY OF HARRIET JACOBS

Jennifer Fleischner. Illustrated by Melanie K. Riem. (Brookfield, Conn.: Milbrook Press, 2000) 96 pages. ISBN 0-7613-0166-6. Performance expectations: a, b, c, d, e.

This is a unique work not only because of the arresting woodcuts that will attract the interest of even the most distractible young adolescent but also because of the origin of the text. The author has taken Harriet Jacobs's original "slave narrative" and woven original dialog and information from Jacobs's autobiography into the book.

1. Your life experiences probably are not as dramatic as are those of Harriet Jacobs, but begin your efforts to define yourself by writing your story. Be sure to address these two questions: What has happened to you? What have you made happen?

2. In the persona of Harriet, write a series of poems, expressing your fears, beliefs, and other feelings.

SEPARATE BUT NOT EQUAL: THE DREAM AND THE STRUGGLE

James Haskins. (New York: Scholastic Press, 1998) 192 pages. ISBN 0-590-45910-4. Performance expectations: a, b, c, d, e, f, g.

This Haskins work is as readable and enjoyable as ever; he has once again taken a complicated topic and made it understandable. Known for his nonfiction writing, Haskins is a master of explanation, knowing when to provide needed background information and when more would overwhelm the topic at hand. Haskins never shies away from the truth. He tells readers what needs to be stated, never sensationalizing for effect. His texts are enjoyable reading—even when the news is not good—because he makes knowledge accessible, and "knowledge is power." In fourteen chapters, he traces the history of the "struggle." After an important preface, which focuses on Little Rock, Arkansas, Haskins begins his commentary about black education in colonial America and concludes with "Public Education in the Late Twentieth Century."

1. Haskins states, "This book is about the struggle of African Americans for equal rights to education, perhaps the most important right an American can enjoy" (p. 6), and "Knowledge is power" (p. 7). Agree or disagree with either or both of these statements, explaining why you believe as you do.

2. Read *The Story of Ruby Bridges* (Robert Coles, illustrated by George Ford; Scholastic, 1995, 32 pages, ISBN 0-590-57281-4). Using a Venn diagram, compare Ruby's first day of school with that of Elizabeth Eckford's.

3. Read Ann Rinaldi's *Hang a Thousand Trees with Ribbons* (Harcourt Brace, 1996, 337 pages, ISBN 0-15-200877-2), a biography of Phillis Wheatley. Then find a collection of her poems or just one of her poems in another poetry book. Practice reading it aloud, and then share the poem and some related event in Phillis's life with your class.

4. For a more detailed look at the past one hundred years of interracial relationships in this country, read the Delaney sisters' book *Having Our Say: The Delaney Sisters' First 100 Years* (Dell, 1996, 299 pages, ISBN 0-440-22042-4). Find at least three anecdotes to share (that Haskins does not include in his book) that illustrate the difficulties faced by black people in the United States in the past century.

5. Make a poster highlighting the most important information of the five key cases that Haskins includes in this book.

6. Complete the "chronology" as included in the end of the text by noting important dates and events before 1861.

THE LOST GARDEN

Laurence Yep. (New York: William Morrow & Co., 1996) 118 pages. ISBN 0-688-13701-6. Performance expectations: a, b, d, f, g.

For anyone familiar with Laurence Yep's work, this autobiography is particularly fascinating; the reader learns "the inside story" of many of Yep's texts. Yep explains how writing helped him figure out the "puzzle" of himself as he tried to discern where he fit in: he felt like an American because he could not speak Chinese or converse with his grandmother, but felt not American when attending the "white" school or living in his integrated neighborhood. He understood while growing up that there were "invisible barriers that separated the wealthy whites from the Chinese who cleaned their apartments or waited on their tables. The Chinese could see and even touch the good life: but they could not join in" (p. 63). Regarding the stereotype that Chinese people wanted to live in Chinatown, "The fact was that before the fair housing laws they often had no choice" (p. 62). Such is the world Yep knew growing up—reading and writing were his means of understanding and decoding his sense of self.

1. As you read this memoir, keep a list of the "inside stories" that Yep provides for various books. After you have finished recording this information, review your list and choose one to read. Then do a book talk for the class.
2. What events in Yep's life helped him sort out who he was as a person with Chinese heritage but as a citizen in the United States? After you list as many events as you can find, see if you can find a pattern in these "memorable moments."
3. Yep talks of being the victim of racism. With your class, define racism and discuss whether racism exists in your school.

DEAR OKLAHOMA CITY, GET WELL SOON: AMERICA'S CHILDREN REACH OUT TO THE PEOPLE OF OKLAHOMA

Jim Ross and Paul Myers (Editors). (New York: Walker Publishing Co., 1996) 48 pages, ISBN 0-8027-8436-4. Performance expectations: b, d, e, g.

This unusual work is a collection of writings, drawings, and responses by children to the bombing of the Alfred P. Murrah Federal Building in Oklahoma City, Oklahoma. The pieces that have been included are both poignant and inspiring. They suggest not only that children care but also that they have the ability to hope for the better.

1. The children in this book were reaching out to help ease pain and to dry tears. Discuss what you, or your class, might do for someone who is experiencing a tragedy.
2. Choose one action and do it.

VOICES FROM THE STREETS: YOUNG FORMER GANG MEMBERS TELL THEIR STORIES

Beth Atkin. (Boston, Mass.: Little, Brown and Co., 1996) 131 pages. ISBN 0-316-05634-0. Performance expectations: a, b, c, d, e, f, g.

This author of the acclaimed *Voices from the Fields* (Little, Brown and Co., 1993, 96 pages, ISBN 0-316-05633-2) profiles nine young people who have escaped from "the life." The stories are profiles of courage and of dysfunctional families. In most of the stories, it is clear that part of the appeal of the gang is the appeal that should come from being a member of a family. This work might not prevent a determined youth from becoming a member of a gang, but it may deter others because it provides an image of gang membership as a bond of desperation—not glamour.

1. In the section "Intervention Programs," the author provides the addresses of most of the individuals described in the book. As a class or individually, write letters of encouragement to the people in the book.
2. Contact the chief administrator of the largest school district in your area and find out if there are any equivalent programs that might provide a guest speaker to your class. If so, write a letter of invitation to that person. After his or her presentation, write a thank you letter.

Novels, Stories and Folk Tales

THE WITCH OF BLACKBIRD POND

Elizabeth Speare. (New York: Laurel Leaf, 1978) 223 pages. ISBN 0-440-99577-9. Performance expectations: a, b, c, d, e, f, g.

Newbery winner in 1959, Speare's novel highlights what occurs when belief systems clash. When Kit arrives in Puritan Connecticut Colony from Barbados, she finds herself suddenly in a frighteningly different environment. Unaccustomed to her aunt and uncle's strict Puritan traditions, Kit is in frequent conflict with them, especially when she befriends the Quaker woman, known as the "witch of Blackbird Pond," at the edge of the village. Accused of being a witch herself, in part, amazingly enough because she teaches a young child to read, Kit stands trial. Some background knowledge of this time period may be needed if students read the book independently; if read aloud, however, commentary may work well.

1. How does the community's Puritan code infringe on Kit's sense of self? Make two lists. In the first, write down the expected behaviors within the community. In the second, record what Kit would prefer to be the standard. Write a final paper arguing either for Kit's right to be herself or for the conformity that must be required for the greater good of the community.

2. In the persona of Kit, write a letter to Grandfather, explaining how much you miss him and how different life is for you now.

3. What evidence, through research, can you find that people truly feared "witches" in 1687? Write a report and share what you learned with your classmates.

4. Although the story itself is fictitious, some of the "players," such as the governor, Sir Edmond Andros, and Captain Samuel Talcott, were actual persons. What can you find out about these men? Which of the other "players" were true personages of this time? Research them, too.

ALL IS WELL

Kristin Embry Litchman. Illustrated by Warren Chang. (New York: Yearling, 1999) 128 pages. ISBN 0-440-41488-1. Performance expectations: a, b, c, d, e, f, g.

This short but powerful book focuses on people of the Mormon faith in Salt Lake City in 1885. Although it is a book that supports Mormon tenets—and clarifies what and why people of this faith believe—it is also a book about acceptance. Ma says, "Emmy, don't think unkindly of Gentiles. Most people—Saints or Gentiles—want to do what is right. Most want to follow God's laws. Problems come when people have different ideas about what God wants them to do." Ma understands both positions because for much of her live she was a Gentile. She understands why Gentiles want to persecute her husband for polygamy; she understands why the Saints expect her husband to have more than one wife. Despite the center stage that religion has in this book, its purpose is not to convert, but to inform and help readers understand why conflict exists and how it might be resolved. Beyond the marriage issue, the values supported by characters of both faiths are ones with which few of us would quarrel; this is an important book for middle graders to read or hear read aloud.

1. Research the history of the Mormon religion in this country. Create a timeline of significant events in Mormon history.

2. After researching the history of the Mormons, create a map showing Mormon communities throughout the United States.

3. The essence of this book is friendship. Have you ever had to be a "faithful friend" as Emmy had to be for Miranda? Write a personal narrative explaining what you had to do and why you chose to do it.

4. Miranda's father works for the newspaper. From the point of view of a U.S. government offical, write a description of one of the events of the novel. As an editor would do, be sure to tell the "who, what, when, where, why, and how" of the story. If you told the same story from a Mormon's point of view, how might you portray the same event?

DREAMS IN THE GOLDEN COUNTRY: THE DIARY OF ZIPPORAH FELDMAN, A JEWISH IMMIGRANT GIRL, NEW YORK CITY, 1903

Kathryn Lasky. (New York: Scholastic, 1998) 190 pages. ISBN 0-590-02973-8. Performance expectations: a, b, d, g.

With her sisters and mother, twelve-year-old Zipporah comes from Russia to the new world, exuberantly ready to begin again in the "Golden Country." After being apart for two years, her parents find it difficult to be together again. Zipporah's father has become more "Americanized" than his wife would like, and she seems steadfastly rooted in the ways of the "Old Country," particularly in matters of faith. This familial conflict provides a forum for Zipporah to determine what she truly values as she sees the strengths in both of her parents' positions. Her new understandings are nurtured by her own sense of self as an actress. Zipporah Feldman became one of Yiddish theater's most beloved stars, earning an Academy award nomination for *A Treacherous Woman*. A real life hero, she and her husband Yitzy (whom she meets soon after her arrival in New York) worked passionately to get Jewish children out of Germany during World War II.

1. Imagine that you were Zipporah as she came through Ellis Island. What if a nurse had written an "E" on the back of your coat? Knowing what the consequences were of not passing the examination, would you have done as Zipporah did? Why or why not?

2. The pressures of religion both enhance and restrict Zipporah's life, as her sister Miriam knows as well. Accordingly, Miriam is considered "dead" by her own mother when she gets married out of the faith to an Irishman named Sean. Zipporah is devastated by her sister's departure. She never successfully contacts her sister—despite various attempts to do so. What do you think Miriam would have liked to tell her sister? What do you think Zipporah wanted to tell Miriam? In the persona of one of the sisters, write a letter to the other one explaining your feelings during this confusing time.

3. "Institutions" usually promote conformity. Zipporah's father plays in an orchestra, which promotes a kind of conformity. Or does it? Is this good or bad? Tovah "gets" her union. Is a union an "institution"? Again, is this good or bad? Can an institution meet both individual needs and the common good? Write an essay exploring this issue of the social responsibility of institutions.

4. Make hamantaschen using the recipe in the back of the book. Serve the cookies to your classmates, recounting the tale of Queen Esther as you do—the person the cookies were created to commemorate.

5. Kathryn Lasky wrote another "immigrant" diary as well, *A Journey to the New World: The Diary of Remember Patience Whipple* (Scholastic, 1996, 173 pages, ISBN 0-590-50214-X). Compare and contrast the journeys of the two girls.

VOYAGE ON THE GREAT TITANIC
Ellen Emerson White. (New York: Scholastic, 1998) 197 pages. ISBN 0-590-96273-6. Performance expectations: a, b.
This book was published just as the popular movie *Titanic* opened. Because the book was a particularly timely work, one might expect it to be poorly crafted, but this is not the case. As with other authors in the Dear America series, White tells the yarn well. Robert, an impoverished Irish orphan, is hired to be a companion to a rich American woman who is returning to America on the *Titanic*. White highlights the issues of social class, as one would expect, and introduces a romantic interest not unlike that in the movie (Robert also dies a hero). Readers will gain the understanding that while the *Titanic* sunk quickly, issues of social class distinctions have not died, but linger painfully.

1. Using the novel along with the historical notes and photographs, write a description of what life was like then, from two points of view—from those of the upper decks and from those in steerage.

2. Using the word *Titanic*, do a title search of books in the public library. Prepare a list of published works and note the dates of publication. In your research, you probably will learn that there was an earlier film about the *Titanic* titled *A Night to Remember*, available at video stores.

ESPERANZA RISING
Pam Munoz Ryan. (New York: Scholastic, 2000) 262 pages. ISBN 0-439-12041-1. Performance expectations: a, b, c, d, e, f, g.
Drawing on the experiences of her maternal grandmother, Ryan has woven a Cinderella tale—in reverse. Her grandmother Esperanza, once the privileged child of a wealthy landowner in Mexico, is forced to immigrate to the United States when her father dies unexpectedly. Although Esperanza's father left their house and its contents to his wife Ramona, he left the land to his brother Luis, which meant that Luis had become Ramona's landlord. Luis's solution? To marry Ramona and send his niece Esperanza to boarding school. Wishing not to marry again and wanting to keep her daughter with her, Ramona chose to steal away in the night to the United States. Their "freedom" in 1924 in the United States required that Ramona and Esperanza work from dawn until dusk in the fields. The chapters in the book are each named for the crop that Esperanza harvested in a given year, which was her way of keeping track of time. The issue of individual need versus the common good is a theme throughout the novel. As the field workers debated among themselves the value of unionizing, Esperanza struggled with learning how to be a productive part of their close-knit community in her new life as a laborer.

1. Has the life of a migrant worker changed much since Esperanza was a child? Using newspapers, magazine articles, and the Internet, research the life of current migrant workers. What has remained the same? What is different? Make a poster to share with your class.

2. Read *The Circuit: Stories from the Life of a Migrant Child* (Houghton Mifflin, 1999, 144 pages, ISBN 0-395-97902-1) by Francisco Jimenez. Find examples of how "groups and institutions" influenced Francisco's life. After compiling the list, discuss your findings with your classmates.

THE WELL

Mildred Taylor. (New York: Dial, 1995) 92 pages. ISBN 0-803-71802-0. Performance expectations: a, b, c, d, e, f, g.

Like Taylor's other short novels, *The Well* packs a powerful punch. During a drought, the Logan family—ever generous—willingly shares the water from its well with all of its neighbors, even with a white, prejudiced family. Although the adults are capable of walking this precarious societal line of the era, hot-headed Hammer, the eldest Logan son, finds it difficult to handle Charley Simms's taunting simply because he and his family are black.

1. List the actions of the characters in this novel that would no longer be legal in our society.
2. In the persona of David, write a letter to your father explaining what really happened when he tried to help Charley get the wheel back on his wagon.
3. Read any of the other books about the Logan family:
   Roll of Thunder, Hear My Cry (Puffin, 1997, 276 pages, ISBN 0-140-38451-0); *The Road to Memphis* (Puffin, 1992, 290 pages, ISBN 0-140-360-77-8); *Let the Circle Be Unbroken* (Puffin, 1991, 394 pages, ISBN 0-140-34892-1);
   Song of the Trees (Laureleaf, 1996, 52 pages, ISBN 0-440-22699-6); *Mississippi Bridge* (illustrated by Max Ginsburg; Bantam Books, 1992, 62 pages, ISBN 0-553-15992); or
   The Friendship (illustrated by Max Ginsburg; Puffin, 1998, 56 pages, ISBN 0-140-38964-4). Compare the actions of Logan family members in any of these situations with their actions in this book.

MY LOUISIANA SKY

Kimberly Holt. (New York: Yearling, 2000) 208 pages. ISBN 0-4404-1570-5. Performance expectations: a, b, d, f, g.

In this tender but not sentimental story, twelve-year-old Tiger Parker negotiates her role as daughter to a mother whose mental age is about six and a father whose mental capabilities are limited as well. Tiger's mental capabilities, however, are not limited, a phenomenon that townspeople in the small town of Saitter, Louisiana, in the 1950s frequently comment on. Tiger's grandmother, Jewel Ramsey, is a source of security in Tiger's life until Jewel dies of a heart attack while picking butter beans. Shaken, Tiger looks to her mother's sister, Dorie Kay, for comfort, and debates whether to go and live with her in Baton Rouge. Dorie Kay's "colored maid," Magnolia, comes to Saitter to help Tiger's Momma through the immediate sorrow of her

mother's death. She helps Tiger, too, to see the possibility of her family becoming whole once more. Issues of age, race, and gender are part of this story, as is the issue of social expectations of the 1950s.

1. In the 1950s before civil rights really took hold, what was life like for a person of color in the South? How did it differ for a person of color in the North? Write a paragraph comparing and contrasting life in each.
2. The arrival of the television set is a major event in Tiger's life. Trace the development of the television set, both in size and power, by making a timeline. Additionally, create a chart that shows the growing number of television sets per household in the last fifty years.
3. Dorie Kay "escapes" to Baton Rouge. Ultimately, Tiger has to make the same decision: to stay in Saitter or to be with Aunt Dorie Kay. Write a letter to Tiger encouraging her to decide one way or the other.
4. After the hurricane, the church's piano fund is given to a church in Cameron that suffered damage. Sister Margaret says, "It's the Christian thing to do." What other explanation could be given to support this generous act?
5. What causes hurricanes to form? Draw a diagram showing how this natural phenomenon occurs, and include an explanation telling why some parts of the world are more susceptible to hurricanes than are others.

GO AND COME BACK

Joan Abelove. (New York: DK Publishing, 1998) 176 pages. ISBN 0-7894-2476-2. Performance expectations: b, c, d, f, g.

The author is an anthropologist, and this is her first book. She wisely chose to write about an experience she knows well, the work of an anthropologist in a "primitive" society. Yet she uses an original twist. The story is written from the point of view of one of the people being studied. This young girl finds the anthropologists to be quite primitive and funny. She notes their strange values and behavior. In the end, the tribe appears to have had a greater impact on the anthropologists than vice versa. A note of caution: although nothing graphic is described, the promiscuity of women in this Peruvian tribe is described in a sympathetic manner.

1. Write the story, or important incidents in it, from the American "lady's" point of view.
2. From clues given in the book, try to find out where this fictional village could be located. Draw a map,

marking "X" on the spot you choose and write a brief explanation justifying your choice.

3. Consider some rituals that Americans engage in. Assume that you were an anthropologist writing about our practices and describe them, highlighting what might appear to be the ironic or odd twist. For example, how might Halloween seem to others? Valentine's Day parties? Try to view these and other cultural practices you think of from another person's perspective.

RAVEN IN A DOVE HOUSE
Andrea Davis Pinkney. (New York: Jump at the Sun Publishers, 1999) 224 pages. ISBN 0-786-81349-0. Performance expectations: a, b, d.

This book looks at the paradox of being within a culture and also outside of it. It is incredibly well written. Pinkney's way with words is most memorable, and her dialog rings so true to the ear that readers believe the characters are actually saying the words in their presence. Twelve-year-old Nell arrives at her Aunt Ursa's house one day soon after school is out—just like always—to discover that her cousin Foley and his best friend Slade have seemingly grown up quite a bit since the previous vacation. They ask her to hide a "Raven," a .25 pistol, in her old doll house, which is known as "Dove House." Tragedy strikes, and despite promises to keep various secrets surrounding the pistol to herself, Nell eventually confides in those adults who are most important to her, her father and aunt. The summer brings new understandings about what it means to belong to a family and a culture—without losing one's individuality.

1. Nell's father attended Morehouse University. Consult the Internet and find out what you can about Morehouse University.

2. Nell has a difficult time deciding when to tell the "whole" truth. Telling only part of the truth, is, she believes, a "lie of omission." Do you think she should have told the "whole" truth earlier? Would it have prevented the tragedy? Find someone who disagrees with you, and then the two of you should present both sides to the class, ending with a class debate.

3. Read Gary Paulsen's *The Rifle* (Laurel Leaf, 1997, 105 pages, ISBN 0-440-21920-5-4). Then write a letter to Foley and Slade explaining why you think they should or should not have a Raven.

4. Andrea Pinkney has written a variety of books. Find out what other books she has written, read at least two, and then present a short book report to your classmates.

FLYING SOLO
Ralph Fletcher. (New York: Clarion, 1998) 138 pages. ISBN 0-395-87323-1. Performance expectations: a, b, d, f, g.

Flying Solo is the story of one sixth grade class on the day the substitute teacher does not report to work—and the class does not report her absence. The students do report to the office with the attendance list, and they do complete their assignments (almost cheerfully), hoping to make it through the day without adult assistance. Although class members are not in unanimous agreement that such a plan is wise, the majority rules, and much is gained. Two factors make this book especially appropriate for this strand. First, one of the students, Rachel White, has not spoken a word aloud—either at school or at home—since a classmate died earlier in the year—an interesting way to look at individual choice in a social setting. Second, because the students do so much of the writing in this book, which is set up rather like a log, with dates and times specified, individual responses to collective actions can be discussed and analyzed. Thus, individual voices can be "heard" against the backdrop of the entire story.

1. What would you do if the substitute teacher did not report to your class one day? Would you report her absence to the office? Why or why not? After you write this response, think about how your classmates might influence you. Make a list of these factors. Discuss both your response and your list with your class, either in a whole group or small-group session.

2. Ralph Fletcher also writes poetry. With three friends, each writing from the perspective of one of the major characters—Karen Ballard, Sean O'Day, Bastian Fauvell, or Rachel White—create a poem that explains your perspective at the close of the "Ritual of the Rock."

3. Read other novels by Ralph Fletcher such as *Spider Boy* (Yearling, 1998, 183 pages, ISBN 0-4404-1483-0) and *Fig Pudding* (Yearling, 1996, 136 pages, ISBN 0-04404-1203-X). Present an oral book report to your classmates.

THE VIEW FROM SATURDAY
Elaine Konigsburg. (New York: Aladdin, 1999) 163 pages. ISBN 0-689-82964-7. Performance expectations: a, b, d.

Winner of the Newbery Medal in 1997, *The View from Saturday* chronicles the success of the sixth grade Academic Bowl team. Konigsburg does so in a most interesting fashion, weaving the stories of the four team members throughout the book as she simultaneously weaves in the final Academic Bowl match. This novel, which is exuberant and substantial, is also funny, and is sure to delight a middle school audience.

1. At one point in the book, Mrs. Olinski admits that she does not know why she chose the four students she did for the Academic Bowl team. Why do you think she chose the four she did? Use the novel to support your answers. Hint: Why do team members think of themselves as "The Souls"?
2. In "Nadia Tells of Turtle Love," Konigsburg presents information about the importance of watching out for loggerhead turtle nests that are not in safe positions for hatching. What else can you find out about loggerhead turtles and their safety as a species? What other endangered animals live in Florida?
3. Konigsburg's *T-Backs, T-shirts, Coat, and Suit* (Hyperion, 1995, ISBN 0-786-81027-0) also addresses issues of conformity for the "public good." Read the book and decide with which group you would stand.

SEEDFOLKS

Paul Fleischman. Illustrated by Judy Pedersen. (New York: Harper Collins, 1999) 69 pages. ISBN 0-064-47207-8. Performance expectations: a, c, g.

Using a technique not unlike that used in *Bull Run* (see #2 immediately below), Fleischman brilliantly tells the story of the conversion of a littered vacant lot to a community garden, which helps individuals of various ethnic groups discover their common humanity. The characters represent the variety of persons one might find in a typical low-income neighborhood. Fleischman chronicles the development of the garden by devoting each chapter to one person who lives in the neighborhood. Told in the first person, this book provides readers with insights into that person's hopes and fears, and at the same time, shares information about the success of the garden project.

1. Consider the development of a school garden. Explore with classmates and the principal the challenges of starting a community school garden.
2. Read Fleischman's *Bull Run* (illustrated by David Frampton; Harper Trophy, 1995, 104 pages, ISBN 0-064-40588-5). Compare and contrast *Seedfolks* to *Bull Run*. Create a two-column chart listing how the books are similar, in one column, and how they are different, in the other.
3. Decide which four characters would be the best guests on a talk show such as *Oprah*. With four friends, stage a mock television talk show and have the rest of your classmates act as the audience.

WHIRLIGIG

Paul Fleischman. (New York: Laurel Leaf, 1999) 144 pages. ISBN 0-4402-2835-2. Performance expectations: a, b, c, d, e, g.

Not often is such a powerful, eloquently composed novel created for middle school students and young adults. Brent is another "adolescent lost in his growing up," and he decides to commit suicide by drinking and driving. Instead, he escapes with minor injuries but kills a popular, intelligent, compassionate young woman, Lea. Her parents do not sue, but the mother asks for "four whirligigs, of a girl that looks like Lea. Put her name on them. Then set them up in Washington, California, Florida, and Maine—the corners of the United States." Her mother's wish is to "Let people all over the country receive joy from her even though she's gone. You make the smiles that she would have made." Brent does just that, traveling by bus across the country, fully coming to realize that "We never know all the consequences of our acts," both bad, which he knew about, and good—which he comes to know. This is a virtuoso performance by a Newbery-winning writer.

1. Design and construct your own "whirligig," integrating it with its surroundings just as Brent does.
2. What is the local percentage of arrests for driving under the influence of alcohol in your town or city per year? How does this rate compare with the national rate? Create a chart showing the data; then write a short analysis of the information presented.
3. Make a poster encouraging your peers not to drink and drive.
4. Read Cynthia Voight's *Izzy, Willy Nilly* (Aladdin, 1986, 280 pages, ISBN 0-689-80446-6). Write a letter to Izzy.

Poetry

THE PALM OF MY HEART: POETRY OF AFRICAN AMERICAN CHILDREN

Davida Adedjourma. Illustrated by Gregorie Christie. (New York: Lee & Low Books, 1997) 32 pages. ISBN 1-880-00076-8. Performance expectations: a, b, d.

Winner of the Coretta Scott King Illustrator Honor Award in 1997, this book is distinctive because the poems, written by children, are all responses to what it means to be a "black" individual in our society. Editor Davida Adedjourma has selected the twenty poems from students' work in writing workshops that she has conducted. She hopes that this anthology "will challenge other African American youth to explore creativity as a means of self-definition. Because they who control the image, control the idea. And they who control the idea, control the mind."

1. Which of the poems speaks to you most boldly? Read it aloud and explain why.

2. As a group, what does this volume of poetry say to you? Write a review.

3. How are you and your classmates alike? Find a concept with which you can all relate and write a poem about it. Add illustrations. Be sure to include an "About the Poets" section as this book does. Title your work so that it is clear you understand the concepts in this strand.

Notes

1. This section is directly quoted from National Council for the Social Studies, *Expectations of Excellence: Curriculum Standards for Social Studies* (Washington, D.C.: Author, 1994), 91.

CHAPTER EIGHT

ⓥ POWER, AUTHORITY, AND GOVERNANCE

Performance Expectations

Social studies programs should include experiences that provide for the study of *how people create and change structures of power, authority, and governance*, so that the learner can:

a. examine persistent issues involving the rights, roles, and status of the individual in relation to the general welfare;

b. describe the purpose of government and how its powers are acquired, used, and justified;

c. analyze and explain ideas and governmental mechanisms to meet needs and wants of citizens, regulate territory, manage conflict, and establish order and security;

d. describe the ways nations and organizations respond to forces of unity and diversity affecting order and security;

e. identify and describe the basic features of the political system in the United States, and identify representative leaders from various levels and branches of government;

f. explain conditions, actions, and motivations that contribute to conflict and cooperation within and among nations;

g. describe and analyze the role of technology in communications, transportation, information-processing, weapons development, or other areas as it contributes to or helps resolve conflicts;

h. explain and apply concepts such as power, role, status, justice, and influence to the examination of persistent issues and social problems;

i. give examples and explain how governments attempt to achieve their stated ideals at home and abroad.[1]

Picture Books

TOUSSAINT L'OUVERTURE: THE FIGHT FOR HAITI'S FREEDOM

Walter Dean Myers. Paintings by Jacob Lawrence. (New York: Simon & Schuster, 1996) 40 pages. ISBN 0-689-80126. Performance expectations: a, b, c, d, f, h, i.

In this picture book meant for middle grade students and beyond, Lawrence's paintings and Myers's words describe the liberation of Haiti. Myers recounts this island's bitter history, beginning with Columbus's occupation in 1492 and ending with Toussaint L'Ouverture's role in its final peace. L'Ouverture's life as a slave and his generosity toward his slave owners provide inviting points of discussion: How can one be treated so cruelly and still be capable of such kindness? Because this book focuses on revolution, issues of how to obtain power and who should govern could be interesting points to contemplate.

1. Read *Taste of Salt* (Harper, 1994, 180 pages, ISBN 0-064-47136-5) by Frances Temple. This novel presents the current day struggle of the Haitian people to govern themselves. It is told from two points of view: that of a young man who has been injured in the political battles and that of a young woman who cares for him at the hospital. As you read the novel, take notes, writing down passages that reveal how each feels about governance in their lives.

2. Research the life of one of the persons Jacob Lawrence mentions in his foreword: Frederick Douglass, Marcus Garvey, Harriet Tubman, Nat Turner, or Denmark Vesey. Focus on the "deeds" that made him or her a "hero" in young Jacob's eyes. Compile your short biography with others from your classmates to create a book to share with the class.

3. Write a biography of either Walter Dean Myers or Jacob Lawrence, focusing on events in their lives or other works they have created that show their commitment to helping all people be free.

4. Create a timeline for Haiti beginning with Christopher Columbus's "discovery."

5. Write an elegy, a poem that honors the dead, celebrating Toussaint, his character, and his accomplishments.

THE YELLOW STAR: THE LEGEND OF KING CHRISTIAN X OF DENMARK

Carmen Agra Deedy. Illustrated by Henri Sorensen. (Atlanta, Ga.: Peachtree, 2000) 34 pages. ISBN 1-56145-208-4. Performance expectations: a, b, c, d, f, h, i.

"Without the yellow star to point them out, the Jews looked like any other Danes." Exactly. And as legend has it, when King Christian X wore a yellow star, so did all Danes, confounding the Nazi plan. Such is an example of "power, authority, and governance" for the good of humanity. This is a heartwarming and inspirational legend about a king and his people, all of whom acted with one heart.

1. In her author's note, Carmen Deedy provides some interesting facts about the Danish people. What additional information can you find, of both legend and documented fact?

2. The last two paragraphs of this note read: "What if it had happened? What if every Dane, from shoemaker to priest, had worn the yellow star of David? And what if we could follow that example today against violations of human rights? What if the good and strong people of the world stood shoulder to shoulder, crowding the streets and filling the squares, saying, 'You cannot do this injustice to our sisters and brothers, or you must do it to us as well,'" and then Deedy asks, "What if?" Indeed. What if? Lead a discussion with your class. What would the world be like? How would your school change? Your classroom? Your place of worship? Your neighborhood? Your home?

SMOKY NIGHT

Eve Bunting. Illustrated by David Diaz. (San Diego, Calif.: Harcourt Brace, 1999) 36 pages. ISBN 0-15-20188-40. Performance expectations: a, b, c, d, e, f.

Young Daniel watches as looters destroy the stores in his neighborhood. This picture book is about rioting—unregulated power in the streets. His mother defines it: "It can happen when people get angry. They want to smash and destroy. They don't care anymore what's right and what's wrong." Shortly after he goes to sleep that night, Daniel is awakened because his building catches fire and Daniel, his mother, and all of the residents are forced to evacuate. At the shelter, Daniel worries about his cat Jasmine, wondering whether she has survived. A firefighter delivers her to Daniel, as well

as the orange cat that belongs to their neighbor Mrs. Kim. Daniel's mama, who previously did not shop at Mrs. Kim's store, preferring to buy goods "from our own people," invites Mrs. Kim to come over when things settle down. Mrs. Kim accepts. The illustrations of this 1995 Caldecott are as bold as the theme of the text: Knowing one another enables liking one another, which builds productive and caring communities.

1. This picture book is dedicated to "The peacekeepers." Who do you think Bunting had in mind with this dedication? Write an essay explaining how each of us has the potential to be a "peacekeeper."

2. What cities have experienced riots in recent history? Building on Mama's explanation, why does rioting occur? More important, what can be done to curb this behavior generally? Specifically, what might be done in your school to make it a safer place, that is, to reduce violent conflict?

Non-Fiction

THE SMITHSONIAN BOOK OF THE FIRST LADIES: THEIR LIVES, TIMES AND ISSUES

Doris Faber and Edith Mayo. (New York: Henry Holt and Co., 1996) 352 pages. ISBN 0-8050-1751-8.

FIRST LADIES: WOMEN WHO CALLED THE WHITE HOUSE HOME

Beatrice Gormley. (New York: Scholastic, 1997) 96 pages. ISBN 0-590-255185. Performance expectations: a, b, c, f, h, i.

These are two similar books that can be compared and contrasted. Both books contain two- to three-page biographies of the first ladies. The Smithsonian edition, however, also adds sections of similar length to introduce historic eras such as the New Nation, 1830-1865, and 1865-1920. Eleven brief essays are also included, which relate to the movements or perplexing issues that occurred during certain presidential terms, such as "What Was Woman's Suffrage?" and "How Have First Ladies Contributed to Campaigning?"

1. The book published by the Smithsonian costs more than four times that of the one by Scholastic. After reading both, prepare an advertisement for each one.

2. Select a president's wife (good choices might be Jackie Kennedy, Eleanor Roosevelt, Dolly Madison, or Edith Wilson) and compare and contrast the chapters about the two women in the two books.

3. A popular activity among historians is to classify the presidents as "Great," "Near Great," and so forth. Abraham Lincoln, George Washington, and Franklin D. Roosevelt invariably are classified as

"Great." Restricting yourself to the information in either of these books, do the same for the first ladies.

THE VOICE OF THE PEOPLE: AMERICAN DEMOCRACY IN ACTION

Betsy Maestro. Illustrated by Guillermo Maestro. (New York: Mulberry Books, 1998) 48 pages. ISBN 0-688-16157-X. Performance expectations: b, c, e, h, i.

This colorful, oversized book begins by restating the familiar, but its format may make that information more accessible to students. It concludes with a discussion of elections and information that may be particularly appealing to children.

1. Create a rap song using the brief descriptions of some of the seven articles of the Constitution and/or the amendments.
2. Review the additional information on the last three pages and then prepare two lists. Title one column "Information people should know," such as how the president is elected, and title a second column "It was interesting to learn," including information such as how many presidents died in office. Compare and contrast the two lists. Did some items appear on both lists?

TERM LIMITS FOR CONGRESS

Barbara Silberdick Feinberg. (New York: 21st Century Books, 1996) 64 pages. ISBN 0-8050-4099-4. Performance expectations: a, b, c, e, h, i.

The great debate about term limits is accessible in this relatively short work that begins with the earliest debates, which, in America, predate the Constitution. A review of the activities of Congress is followed by a discussion of various attempts at term limits. The author concludes with a particularly valuable chapter that briefly outlines the arguments of both sides and includes rebuttals to those arguments. This section is a good source for discussion in the classroom.

1. Using the information in the last chapter, create two teams to debate the issue. Ask a student who particularly enjoys history to introduce the debate by providing the historical background.
2. Organize a values clarification activity that could be used in conjunction with the debate. After reading the chapter or learning about it through the debate or a handout, ask your classmates to move to one of five areas of the room according to their position on the issue: "Strongly Agree," "Somewhat Agree," "Undecided," "Somewhat Disagree," or "Strongly

Disagree." Once your classmates are in their areas, allow them a few minutes to identify their reasons for being there. Then engage the class in a debate.

AFFIRMATIVE ACTION

A. E. Sadler. (San Diego, Calif.: Greenhaven Press, 1995) 94 pages. ISBN 1-56510-386-6. Performance expectations: a, b, c, d, f, h.

Although this book might be more appropriate for high school students, Greenhaven Press has a reputation for making information on difficult topics accessible for novices. After providing a two-page introduction, the author offers a series of essays by academics, as well as one by Jesse L. Jackson. Although students might be awed by the footnotes, the essays of three to four pages are tightly written, and students reading at the junior high level should be able to understand them.

1. Find seven friends and ask them to assume the role of the authors of the different chapters. Ask eight others to assume the roles of members of a congressional committee reviewing existing affirmative action programs. Ask the "authors" to make their cases for the committee. What conclusions does the committee come to? As a group, write a final position paper noting your support for continuing affirmative action guidelines or not.
2. For one of the chapters, list the types of evidence (e.g., anecdotal, documental, numerical) and the rhetorical strategies the authors used. Do you find this information and form of argument persuasive? Why or why not? Write a final commentary.

THE DISABILITY RIGHTS MOVEMENT

Deborah Kent. (New York: Children's Press, 1996) 32 pages. ISBN 0-516-20223-5. Performance expectations: a, c, g, h.

This brief work, part of the Cornerstones of Freedom series, includes many contemporary photographs and uses the experiences of two activists to describe and explain recent legislation.

1. Follow the local press for two weeks to see if there is any news about the rights of people with disabilities where you live.
2. How would a ten-year-old deaf student receive an education in your school district?

IRREPRESSIBLE SPIRIT: CONVERSATIONS WITH HUMAN RIGHTS ACTIVISTS

Susan Kuklin. (New York: Putnam, 1996) 240 pages. ISBN 0-399-23045-9. Performance expectations: a, d, f, h, i.

This is not a book for the timid or squeamish. It contains a number of first-person recollections of individuals who have experienced oppression in places such as China, Cuba, Bosnia, and Cambodia. Some stories are told by victims, others by young idealists associated with the Human Rights Watch. Child prostitution, rape, and the death penalty are some of the topics explored in these first-person narratives.

1. Explore the quotation by Vaclav Havel: "Each one of us can come to realize that he or she, no matter how insignificant or helpless he may feel, is in a position to change the world. . . . If he does not even try, it is quite certain he will achieve nothing." Write an essay discussing why some do try and why others do not. Can you think of times when you could make a difference in someone's life?

2. One of the stories deals with a minister's opposition to the death penalty, which he considers a violation of human rights. Debate this issue. Does the topic of the death penalty belong in a book about human rights activists?

THE CHILDREN OF TOPAZ: THE STORY OF A JAPANESE-AMERICAN INTERNMENT CAMP BASED ON A CLASSROOM DIARY

Michael Tunnell and George Chilcoat. (New York: Holiday House, 1996) 74 pages. ISBN 0-8234-1239-3. Performance expectations: a, b, c, d, f, h, i.

This nonfiction text is primarily a diary that a third grade class kept while interned in the camp in Topaz, Utah. The authors provide a comprehensive, although not overwhelming, introduction to the diary, providing the necessary context for middle grade students to understand this "story of a Japanese-American internment camp." The book includes photographs of the diary pages and evacuation trains, and shows children arriving at the camp, sitting in the classroom, eating in dining halls, and attending scout meetings.

1. Read Sheila Hamanaka's *The Journey: Japanese Americans, Racism and Renewal* (Orchard, 1995, 40 pages, ISBN 0-531-07060-3). Do her paintings help to retell this history?

2. Was life inside the camp more democratic than was life outside the camp? Explain your answer. Write an editorial for the "camp newspaper."

A FENCE AWAY FROM FREEDOM

Ellen Levine. (New York: G. P. Putnam's Sons, 1995) 260 pages. ISBN 0-399-22638-9. Performance expectations: a, b, c, d, f, h, i.

This nonfiction text provides an extensive picture of one of the least acknowledged times in American history, the incarceration of at least 120,000 Americans whose "crime" was to be of Japanese ancestry. Levine begins the book with the years before Pearl Harbor, followed by the bombing of Pearl Harbor and the evacuation orders. Most of the book details the effects of this event on those forced to move to the camps and the special populations of the camps—the homeless children, Japanese Peruvians, and Nisei who fought on the Western Front as U.S. soldiers. Understanding this era in history necessitates discussion of "ideals, principles, and practices of citizenship in a democratic republic" so that students understand why the U.S. government officially apologized to Japanese Americans in 1988.

1. Yoshiko Uchida wrote two novels for middle grade students that are based on her own experiences in Topaz, one of the prison camps. Read *Journey to Topaz* (illustrated by Donald Carrick; Creative Arts, 1985, 149 pages, ISBN 0-916870-85-5) or the sequel, *Journey Home* (illustrated by Charles Robinson; Aladdin, 1992, 131 pages, ISBN 0-689-71641-9), to more fully understand what it was like being a child in the camps.

2. In tribute to those Japanese Americans who willingly fought as U.S. soldiers because they believed in their country—despite their country's treatment of them—plan a Day of Remembrance. Write speeches or poems, design posters or banners, and find appropriate music and food to make it a special day of remembering.

3. Review the Bill of Rights. How were the Japanese Americans' legal rights abridged? Write a "legal brief" describing these discrepancies.

A SPECIAL FATE

Alison Leslie Gold. (New York: Scholastic, 2000) 177 pages. ISBN 0-439-25968-1. Performance expectations: a, b, c, d, f, h, i.

Chiune Sugihara has become known as a "Hero of the Holocaust" because of his courageous acts during World War II. Although breaking rules was not his nature, this Japanese diplomat serving in Lithuania did so by writing visas for Jews who needed to escape from the Nazis. Nearly six thousand Jews are indebted to Sugihara. The stories of two of them, who were children when Sugihara wrote visas for their families, are woven into this biography of Sugihara.

1. Schindler was also credited with saving the lives of thousands of Jews. Research his actions and compare them with those of Sugihara.

2. Sugihara was awarded the Righteous Among the Nations medal by Yad Vashem, Israel's Holocaust

Memorial and Museum. What are the qualifications for this award? Who else has won it? Why exactly would Sugihara have won it? Write a newspaper article about Sugihara's receipt of it as if it had just happened. Weave background information about the medal itself into the article.

3. Sugihara disobeyed his government when he wrote the visas. Were Sugihara's actions right or wrong? As citizens of any country, should we *always* follow the country's laws? Or are there exceptions?

BAYARD RUSTIN: BEHIND THE SCENES OF THE CIVIL RIGHTS MOVEMENT

James Haskins. (New York: Hyperion Books for Children, 1997) 121 pages. ISBN 0-7868-0168-9. Performance expectations: a, b, c, d, f, h, i.

A 1998 Coretta Scott King Honor winner, this book, in its cover jacket, describes Rustin this way: "He was not a famous orator like Martin Luther King Jr., or a flamboyant personality, like Adam Clayton Powell Jr., or even the head of any major civil rights organization. But for many years, Rustin was a key player in every major civil rights initiative in the United States." He certainly was. His crowning achievement was the 1963 March on Washington when a quarter of a million American citizens came together as a sign that it was time for the most encompassing civil rights legislation this country had ever witnessed to be passed. This biography is fascinating as it provides a behind-the-scenes look at an incredibly important time in history.

1. Rustin worked as a civil rights advocate around the world. Create a map that notes the people, their causes, and the countries he worked in.

2. With several of your classmates, write a "collective" biography of Bayard Rustin. After each has chosen a chapter or two, read them, and then write a brief summary of the significant events in Rustin's life, as if you were preparing a script to highlight his life's work for a documentary. Making sure the "parts" flow together, present your report to the class.

3. As you read, keep a list of the occasions on which Haskins discusses Rustin's ideas about how economic issues are the root of the problem with racial equality. Then write an essay of your own supporting Rustin's position or providing a counterargument.

4. Or, as you read, keep a list of all of the people who were involved in the civil rights movement. Choose one of them and do a little more research about the person's contribution. Then present your findings to your classmates in the form of a poster, highlighting that person's contributions.

5. Read Walter Dean Myers's account of Malcolm X's life, *Malcolm X: By Any Means Necessary* (Scholastic, 1998, 224 pages, ISBN 0-590-29912-3). Write a brief essay stating what you find most compelling about his story.

OH, FREEDOM! KIDS TALK ABOUT THE CIVIL RIGHTS MOVEMENT WITH THE PEOPLE WHO MADE IT HAPPEN

Casey King and Linda Barrett Osborne. (New York: Knopf, 1997) 144 pages. ISBN 0-679-89005-X. Performance expectations: a, f.

Three sections (life under segregation, moves to end segregation, and the struggle to end poverty and discrimination) are introduced with a narrative providing middle grade students with necessary but not overwhelming information about the era. The photographs are sometimes more telling than is the narrative. Following each introduction is a series of interviews written by middle grade students who interviewed people about their experiences during that era. The interviews are appealing and should provoke questions by children.

1. Interviews were done by and of whites, as well as blacks. Interview someone who is older than sixty years of age and ask him or her some of the questions that you found most interesting. Compile your findings into a book.

2. Pretend that your child is interviewing you twenty years from now. Write down some questions that your child might ask you about life today.

Novels, Stories and Folk Tales

KAI: A MISSION FOR HER VILLAGE, AFRICA 1440

Dawn Thomas. (New York: Aladdin, 1996) 64 pages. ISBN 0-689-80986-7. Performance expectations: a, c, f, h, i.

This short chapter book effectively addresses the question of gender roles and power. In Kai's culture, only men could be craftsmen, casting the sculptures that her people were famous for, and only men could have friends for life, "ore ko-ri-ko-sun," because women were expected to leave their villages upon marrying. Still, it is Kai and her sister who are sent on the mission to save the village, an intriguing place to start a discussion about power.

1. Read one of the other Girlhood Journey books: *Juliet: A Dream Takes Flight, England 1339* (Anna Kirwan, illustrated by Lynne Marshall; Aladdin, 1996, 72 pages, ISBN 0-689-81137-3); *Marie: A Summer in the Country, France 1775* (Ellen Krieger, illustrated by Lyn

Durham; Aladdin, 1997, 72 pages, ISBN 0-689-81562-X); or *Shannon: A Chinatown Adventure, San Francisco, 1880* (Kathleen Kudlinski, illustrated by Bill Farnsworth; Aladdin, 1996, 71 pages, ISBN 0-689-80984-0). Then compare their discoveries with the ones that Kai makes.

2. Do further research about the Yoruba people in what is now Western Nigeria. If you lived there now, what would your life be like?

3. Keep a list of all of the new and foreign words in the book; then alphabetize them and create a glossary.

BREAKING FREE

Louann Gaeddert. (New York: Avon, 1996) 144 pages. ISBN 0-380-72520-7. Performance expectations: a, f, h.

Set in 1800, this novel looks at power and governance from a teenage Richard's perspective. After his mother and Aunt Ruth die, it is decided that Richard must go and live with Uncle Lyman, his mother's brother. While Richard's Uncle Ambrose, husband of Aunt Ruth, would have willingly remained Richard's guardian and Richard would have preferred such an arrangement, blood ties—not compatibility—and an extra pair of hands on the farm prove to be the deciding factors. The overriding question of this novel is "Who has the ultimate control?" Richard ultimately realizes that he does, and that others cannot stop any of us from living out our own beliefs and dreams.

1. Write a letter to Uncle Ambrose as if you were Richard; tell him how you really feel about living with Uncle Lyman.

2. Research the varying laws about slavery, as Gaeddert mentions on page 103.

3. A Quaker saved Dina. Why? Read other stories of Quakers saving slaves such as *Amos Fortune: Free Man* (Yates, 1989, illustrated by Nora Unwin, Puffin, 181 pages, ISBN 0-14-034158-7) and then write your own versions as a collection of short biographies.

ONCE ON THIS ISLAND

Gloria Whelan. (New York: Harper Trophy, 1996) 186 pages. ISBN 0-06-440619-9. Performance expectations: a, b, c, d, f, g, i.

This book deals with the War of 1812 and the British occupation of Mackinac Island. Twelve-year-old Mary and her older siblings, Angelique and Jacques, strive to maintain their farm when Papa leaves the island to join American troops in Detroit, Michigan. Jacques follows in his father's footsteps and finds himself in battle face-to-face with his boyhood friend Gavin (who, because of his Native American ancestry, finds himself on the side of the British). Both run from the other, realizing that war is hardly a game and that "duty" can create false allegiances. Still, Papa writes in a letter to his children, "I . . . only pray that I have done the right thing to fight for my country against those who have long threatened our liberty" (pp. 68-69). Middle grade students may eagerly argue for and against who should govern—and how.

1. Create a map showing where each of the Indian tribes mentioned in the novel lived (Sauk, Winnebagoes, Ottawas, Chipewas, Menomonees, and Potawotami).

2. Choose one of the tribes and write a report describing its way of life in the early 1800s. Then compare its way of life with the tribe's current way of life.

3. Maintain a glossary of French words and their meanings as you read the book.

4. Design a travel brochure inviting people to visit present-day Mackinaw Island. What historical places might they visit? What stories might they hear?

WASHINGTON CITY IS BURNING

Harriette Gillem Robinet. Illustrated by Gabriela Dellosso. (New York: Atheneum, 1996) 149 pages. ISBN 0-689-80773-2. Performance expectations: a, b, c, d, f, h, i.

In August of 1814, the month the British came to Washington, D.C., and burned much of the city, a slave named Virginia came to the White House to be of service to the president. Virginia believed that Miss Dolley, President Madison's wife, had asked her to come, but she quickly realizes that she has been chosen by Tobias, a coachman to the president. She also finds out that Tobias expects her to join in an illegal activity: helping her own people, those of African ancestry, escape from slavery. In a momentous decision, she decides to remain a slave "by choice." She decides that she owns herself—and that is the ultimate power. "I had made a choice for the next two years: to aid those who wanted to escape. If I had gone to freedom, there would have been one free slave girl. If I stayed like Tobias and Aunt Sally, there might be hundreds of slaves that I could help" (p. 141). Questions of political power, authority, and governance are all at play in the novel.

1. Draw a map of Washington, D.C., in 1814; draw a map showing the city as it is now. Then create a Venn diagram comparing features of the city then and now.

2. The War of 1812 is not as well known as are some other wars. What were the central issues of conflict? Prepare a short report on what this war was all about.

3. Was Virginia courageous or foolhardy to give up her chance for freedom? Find someone who disagrees with you and prepare a debate for the class, citing as many historical reasons as each of you can to support your positions.

4. Read another of Robinet's work, *Children of the Fire* (illustrated by Tristan Ellwell; Aladdin, 2001, 135 pages, ISBN 0-689-83968-5). Set in Chicago during the Great Fire, this story of two young girls tells how prejudice is learned—and can be unlearned—through experience. Read the book, and then prepare an oral book report for your classmates on the lessons the characters in this novel learned.

NIGHTJOHN

Gary Paulsen. (New York: Laurel Leaf, 1995) 92 pages. ISBN 0-440-21936-1. Performance expectations: a, b, c, d, h.

The vivid imagery in this book is unforgettable. This historical fiction work is about a black man who understands that the hope for his people is to know the power of literacy. The setting for this book occurs in the days before the Emancipation Proclamation, when it was illegal for slaves to learn to read and write. Nightjohn defied this rule, sneaking onto plantations to invite slaves to his "pit schools," where under cover of night, clusters of people would come together to learn. Paulsen does not sanitize the dangers. In one scene, a woman who is accused of teaching twelve-year-old Sarny the alphabet is stripped, made to pull a buggy, and whipped, to make a point to the slaves who are forced to watch. In another, Nightjohn himself loses the middle toe on each foot to a chisel and a hammer as punishment for teaching. He heals and returns to teach. His dreams are greater than are the master's punishments.

1. Why was it illegal for slaves to learn to read and write? Why would a government make such a law?

2. The brutality of the masters is clearly present in this book, making it a "hard" read for some. How does the vividness of Paulsen's language affect you? How does this affect your understanding of the concepts of this strand, "Power, Authority, and Governance"?

3. Although Nightjohn is a fictional character, his actions are based on the experiences of real slaves. Write a ballad to commemorate their valor.

4. Read the sequel to the novel, *Sarny: A Life Remembered* (illustrated by Jerry Pinkney; Laurel Leaf, 1999, 192 pages, ISBN 0-440-21973-6). Report to your class "the rest of the story."

5. Another novel that addresses the power of literacy is *Miles' Song* (Alice McGill; Houghton Mifflin, 2000, 224 pages, ISBN 0-395-97938-2). Read this book and then compare Miles's song with *Nightjohn* by creating a Venn diagram.

THUNDER ON THE TENNESSEE

Clifton Wisler. (New York: Scholastic, 1997) 153 pages. ISBN 0-590-13178-8. Performance expectations: a, b, c, d, f, g, h, i.

The "thunder on the Tennessee" was the relentless cacophony from the battles fought during the Civil War, not only from the canons and muskets but also from the cries of agony and despair from the soldiers—on both sides. The nature of military command is powerfully revealed in conversations among fifteen-year-old Willie, his father, and the other officers. The final "power" of death is sometimes rather graphically revealed, which works well to dispel the myths of the glamour and glory of war. The personal and political issues of governance are the core of this historical novel. As Willie's father says, "What's really at stake is the deciding . . . When somebody decides for you or sends an army down to make up your mind, you've got to fight it" (p. 13).

1. Read another book that portrays battle(s) during the Civil War such as Stephen Crane's *The Red Badge of Courage* (Random House, 1998, 308 pages, ISBN 0-679-60296-8). Write a short paper describing how the two books portray war similarly.

2. Read Avi's *The Fighting Ground* (Lippincott, 1987, 157 pages, ISBN 0-064-40185-5). Although this book is about the Revolutionary War, consider the similarities between this one and the Civil War. Then, using Avi's book as a model, write a similar version, describing the battle at Shiloh over a twenty-four-hour period.

3. Read Paul Fleischman's *Bull Run* (illustrated by David Frampton; Harper Trophy, 1995, 104 pages, ISBN 0-064-40588-5), which shows how the battle of Bull Run was esxperienced by different people. Then, using that book as a model, write a similar version for *Thunder on the Tennessee* showing how a battle was viewed from different perspectives. Finally, recruit some friends to perform this Readers Theater for your class, other classes, or a school assembly.

A DIFFERENT KIND OF COURAGE

Ellen Howard. (New York: Atheneum, 1996) 170 pages. ISBN 0-689-80774-0. Performance expectations: a, b, f, h, i.

Set in France in 1940 as the German army nearly reaches Paris, this story is about Bertrand, his little sister, and Maman, who are forced to flee. Maman gets them safely to the south of France to a convent where she then works to get them out of the country. The core of this novel deals directly with the concept of power and who has it. Bertrand feels powerless because he is forced to leave his Paris home, required to stay at the convent, and finally sent to America—without his Maman. He takes a small pair of scissors before leaving the convent so that he feels "powerful and safe," but when he actually lashes out and hurts a fellow evacuee, he realizes that he does not "want to hurt anyone anymore" even if he is "still afraid" (p. 164). He realizes that even adults are afraid and that they can still act bravely, that "one could be good, yet still do bad things sometimes. But one could choose" (p. 165). Indeed. The choosing is the powerful message about power, authority, and governance in this novel, an important understanding for middle grade students who are increasingly given the power to make decisions in their own lives.

1. Find out about the evacuation efforts in England during World War II. Create a bulletin board showcasing the most interesting findings of your research.
2. In the persona of one of the children in Bertrand's group, create and illustrate a poem about the experience. Be sure to include details from the text or clearly link the emotions portrayed in the book to the significant events in the text.

NUMBER THE STARS

Lois Lowry. (New York: Laurel Leaf, 1998) 137 pages. ISBN 0-440-22753-4. Performance expectations: a, b, c, d, f, g, h, i.

In this relatively short novel, Lowry provides insight into one of the defining moments of World War II, when the Danish people, in a matter of just weeks, rescue some seven thousand Jews living within their borders to the safety of neutral Sweden. Instead of the horror of war, this novel records the actions of the righteous, those who knew that Hitler and his plan were wrong. The story is told through ten-year-old Annemarie's eyes as she is personally forced to deal with the German occupation when the order comes to "collect" all the Jews. Her best friend, Ellen, is Jewish. Ellen and her parents escape to freedom—through the courage of Annemarie, her parents, and others in the resistance.

1. A high-ranking German official, G. F. Duckwitz, is credited with passing the information to the Jewish leaders about their imminent danger. How do you think he had the courage to do this? Why do you think he did it? What further information can you find about his heroic act? Report your findings to the class.
2. The Danish people sunk their own navy in 1943 so that Hitler could not use it for his purposes. Where do you think this kind of commitment to righteousness came from? Did other nations make similar commitments to stopping Hitler? What examples can you find of other nations using their power (in ways other than through the military) to thwart Hitler's plans? With a small group, research the general topic, divide up it up into specific topics, and create a bulletin board of the results of your study.
3. Storytellers often look for stories such as this one to promote a feeling of universal humanity and connectedness. Summarize this one, highlighting the goodness of the people involved. Practice telling it before the class.

BROKEN BRIDGE

Lynne Reid Banks. (New York: Avon, 1996) 314 pages. ISBN 0-380-72384-0. Performance expectations: a, b, c, d, f, g, h.

In this sequel to *One More River*, a powerful story takes place twenty-five years later. As the book begins, Nili is returning to her native Israel after a vacation with her Uncle Noah and his son Glen in London. Because Nili's grandmother is often confused by international time zones, Nili's parents are two hours late picking up the teenagers at the airport. Deciding not to just sit around and wait, the pair leaves the airport to visit an aunt who lives in nearby Gilo. En route, however, Glen is stabbed and killed by an Arab—and Nili is unaccountably spared. The rest of the novel explores the aftermath of this frightening event on their families' lives—Grandpa, who helped create the state of Israel, his son Noah who fled from the principles supporting the kibbutz, and Donna, the Gentile mother of Glen who remained in the kibbutz after her divorce from Noah. This is a family touched by the hatred and mistrust of the Palestinian-Israeli conflicts.

1. Read *One More River* (Banks; Harper, 1993, 256 pages, ISBN 0-380-71563-5). Then provide a biography of Noah to explain further why he left the kibbutz to live and work in Canada.
2. Research and write a history of the country of Israel.

3. Find out what it would be like to live on a kibbutz. Write a diary entry explaining your daily routine as well as that of your parents. Then explain the philosophy behind such a life.

4. Grandpa says, "You can't have a nice, kindly, humane occupation of one people by another. Never, not in history, not in this world" (p. 238). Do you agree? Write an editorial revealing your position.

DRIVE-BY

Lynne Ewing. (New York: HarperCollins, 1998) 96 pages. ISBN 0-06-440649-0. Performance expectations: a, b, c, f, h.

> The gunshots exploded.
> White angry fire flashed from the backseat of the car. . . .
> Jimmy fell.
> I knew he was teasing, and it made me angry.
> I couldn't believe he'd tease me that way.
> I only thought that for a heartbeat. (p. 4)

This novel is not for the squeamish. The reality of gang life in Los Angeles hits hard. However, it is not written from the point of view of a gang member, but of Tito, the twelve-year-old brother of a gang member. Tito finds it hard to comprehend that his brother was, indeed, a gang member, even after his brother's death. Clearly, the issues of power, authority, and governance come into play in this book because the "rules" are written by the gangs. Students will be drawn to this story, and teachers will want their students to learn from Tito's wisdom.

1. Using the Internet and newspaper and magazine articles, research what gang life is all about. Then compare it to the events in this story. Write a review of the book.

2. Write a letter of invitation asking a police officer to visit your classroom to talk about gangs in your area. Before the officer arrives, lead your class in a discussion of the kinds of questions you want to ask. Record these questions. Finally, write a thank you note after the officer's visit.

3. Pretending you are Tito, write a letter to Jimmy. Include the range of emotions that you feel about Jimmy's "secret" life and untimely death.

4. For another view of the effects of gang life, read Sharon Draper's *Romiette and Julio* (Simon and Schuster, 1999, 236 pages, ISBN 0-689-82180-8).

CAMOUFLAGE

Gloria Miklowitz. (San Diego, Calif.: Harcourt Brace, 1998) 166 pages. ISBN 0-15-201467. Performance expectations: a, b, c, d, h, i.

Fourteen-year-old Kyle thought visiting his dad in Michigan would be the answer to avoiding a seriously boring summer. After all, Kyle's dad promised to teach him how to shoot a gun at the gun club he started. Kyle wins his mom's permission, and the visit begins even better than Kyle expects—his dad gives him the chance to try a cigarette and to drive home from the airport. Some of Kyle's questions, however, remain unanswered until it is nearly too late; Kyle discovers his father's involvement with a right-wing militia group. Although the book ends realistically, it does not end happily, which is the strength of the book. "Power, authority, and governance" is a theme that ripples throughout the book, from families, to communities, to states, and to the nation as a whole. It is a powerful text for confronting these issues.

1. Reread the Bill of Rights. Which amendments most clearly address the conflict Kyle is feeling? How?

2. Does the government have the right to make rules for "our own good"? To begin thinking about this issue, list some of these specific rules—such as seat belt laws. Weave these examples into your essay.

3. Kyle's dad says, "I'll teach you how to handle firearms. Then, son, you'll really be a man." Do you agree? Is this a measure of a man? If not, what is? Write a paper describing what makes one a "man" or "woman."

THE KID WHO RAN FOR PRESIDENT

Dan Gutman. (New York: Scholastic, 1996) 157 pages. ISBN 0-590-93988-2. Performance expectations: b, e.

This funny book actually provides a great deal of information about the election process. Twelve-year-old Judson Moon runs for president—and wins! In doing so, the reader is taken on as an "insider" in the entire process, from Judson's getting on the ballot for the presidency in Wisconsin to amending the Constitution so that a person of any age may run for president. Middle school students will thoroughly enjoy this novel and learn much about the democratic process as well.

1. Suppose you were going to campaign for Student Council. Keep a list of all of the information you gather about running for a presidential or other office that could help you run a more successful campaign.

2. Choose one of the issues mentioned in the book, such as affirmative action, gun control, nuclear

power, the death penalty, or the environment. Find out what current policy is and then write a position paper taking a stand supporting the existing policy or changing it.

3. Find a copy of Nixon's "Checkers" speech. Write a paper comparing and contrasting it with Judson's speech.

4. Read the sequel, *The Kid Who Became President* (Scholastic, 1999, 176 pages, ISBN 0-509-02376-4). Make a list of "facts" that Gutman wove into the novel about the duties and responsibilities of the president.

HELP! I'M TRAPPED IN THE PRESIDENT'S BODY

Todd Strasser. (New York: Apple, 1997) 144 pages. ISBN 0-590-92166-5. Performance expectations: c, d, e.

This fun, lighthearted book could easily accompany *The Kid Who Ran for President*. Its punch comes in the last third of the novel when Jake, who has switched bodies with the president while he was visiting Jake's school, takes a stand and says what he really thinks—as opposed to what he believes people want or expect to hear—in the final debate before election day. While "president," Jake also creates a "Commission on Teenage Attitudes" so that the "president" can stay in touch with the voters of tomorrow—an idea that middle school students may applaud.

1. What if you were on the "Commission on Teenage Attitudes"? Find three other classmates who want to serve on this council. Meet together, brainstorm ideas that you believe "the administration" should know about, and then write a letter sharing your concerns with the president.

2. Is there any scientific evidence that it is possible to transfer learning from one animal to another? Are there any reports of a system like DITS (Dirksen Intelligence Transfer System)? Search diligently and report your findings to the class.

Notes

1. This section is directly quoted from National Council for the Social Studies, *Expectations of Excellence: Curriculum Standards for Social Studies* (Washington, D.C.: Author, 1994), 94.

CHAPTER NINE

⑦ PRODUCTION, DISTRIBUTION, AND CONSUMPTION

Performance Expectations

Social studies programs should include experiences that provide for the study of *how people organize for the production, distribution, and consumption of goods and services,* so that the learner can:

a. give and explain examples of ways that economic systems structure choices about how goods and services are to be produced and distributed;

b. describe the role that supply and demand, prices, incentives, and profits play in determining what is produced and distributed in a competitive market system;

c. explain the difference between private and public goods and services;

d. describe a range of examples of the various institutions that make up economic systems such as households, business firms, banks, government agencies, labor unions, and corporations;

e. describe the role of specialization and exchange in the economic process;

f. explain and illustrate how values and beliefs influence different economic decisions;

g. differentiate among various forms of exchange and money;

h. compare basic economic systems according to who determines what is produced, distributed, and consumed;

i. use economic concepts to help explain historical and current developments and issues in local, national, or global contexts;

j. use economic reasoning to compare different proposals for dealing with a contemporary social issue such as unemployment, acid rain, or high quality education.[1]

Picture Books

MARKET!

Ted Lewin. (New York: Lothrop, Lee & Shepard Books, 1996) 32 pages. ISBN 0-688-12161-6. Performance expectations: a, b, d, e, f, g, i.

In resplendent illustrations, Lewin shares the world of commerce with readers. In markets from Peru and Nepal to Ireland, Uganda, the United States, and Morocco,

Market! depicts the basics of economics from production to distribution and anticipated consumption of wares. This book shows particularly well the universality of economics, that all societies come to "market."

1. Choose a country other than one mentioned in this book and find out what a typical "market" might look like, focusing on the products that would be available.

2. Choose one of the countries mentioned in the book and research the different kinds of money that would be exchanged at the market. Draw a picture of the various coins and paper money, and after consulting a newspaper or the Internet, provide current U.S. equivalent values.

3. Choose one of the places mentioned in the book and show how the products brought to market are either specific to that location and people or are also products of other countries or peoples. You could do this by first listing the product on the left side of a poster board and then providing options or a rationale why this product is unique to this location.

4. Create a map of the places mentioned in the book, labeling each in its appropriate location.

VISION OF BEAUTY: THE STORY OF SARAH BREEDLOVE WALKER

Kathryn Lasky. Illustrated by Nneka Bennett. (Cambridge, Mass.: Candlewick Press, 2000) 48 pages. ISBN 0-763-60253-1. Performance expectations: a, b, c, e, f, j.

The life of the woman better known as Madame C. J. Walker is wonderfully portrayed, beginning with her childhood and continuing through her accomplishments. She is especially noted for her focused nurturing of other black women to help them succeed and for her extensive philanthropy, especially in Indianapolis, Indiana.

1. What specific information guided Walker's decisions as a business woman? What choices did she make about goods and services? How did she use the concepts of supply and demand, pricing, incentives, and profits to guide her decision making? After learning what she did, write her "marketing plan."

2. Explain and illustrate how Walker's values and beliefs influenced her economic decisions. Share your conclusions with your class by creating a poster that gives visual evidence of the cause and effect of your conclusions.

3. What do you believe is Madame C. J. Walker's greatest legacy? Is it that she was America's first black female millionaire? Or do you think it's something else? Explain your answer using as much detail as possible from the text and epilogue.

THE PIANO

William Miller. Illustrated by Susan Keeter. (New York: Lee & Low Books, 2000) 32 pages. ISBN 1-880000-98-9. Performance expectations: a, b, c, f, g.

Young Tia loves music so much that she is willing to trade her work as a maid for piano lessons. Although Miss Hartwell does not take Tia up on her offer, the idea of exchange of services is reinforced when Johnny finds a new job chopping firewood and lighting the fire that was to pay a nickel more. While Johnny wishes for Tia "a better job, too," Tia has no interest in another position. "All she cared about was the piano, making the music Miss Hartwell taught her to play." She tells Miss Hartwell she can take care of the house, that she doesn't need Johnny. "I can do his chores and mine. Then we can play the piano." Although Miss Hartwell fears that Tia will hurt herself, she finally acquiesces to Tia's request for that day. A special bond is forged forever. Set in the early 1900s in the deep South, this friendship is all the more notable because Miss Hartwell is white and Tia is black.

1. Miss Hartwell chooses to share her knowledge about the piano with Tia without compensation. Why? Does this mean Miss Hartwell does not place a value on her time and energy? Justify her decision by discussing how this decision shows her values. Be sure to consider the time and place of this story.

2. Why does Johnny change jobs? Using his decision as an example, explain how the concepts of supply and demand, prices, incentives, and profits apply in the market system of the early 1900s. Do these concepts hold fast in contemporary society?

PAPERBOY

Mary Kay Kroeger and Louise Borden. Illustrated by Ted Lewin. (New York: Clarion, 1996) 32 pages. ISBN 0-395-64482-8. Performance expectations: a, b, f, i.

Written by two Cincinnati authors, *Paperboy* is set there in 1927. Lewin's warmly shaded drawings accentuate this story of a young boy's desire to help his family through lean years by selling newspapers on street corners. A key event centers on the Dempsey-Tunney boxing match, the fight that decides the Heavyweight Champion of the World; Willie signs up to sell the "Fight Extra." Unfortunately, Dempsey, the "workingman's hero," does not win, but Willie does—through his perseverance.

1. "Willie Brinkman always stood a little taller when he brought money home." Is money the issue? Or what it represents? Write an essay on how a person's ability to perform worthwhile duties or earn money influences how that person feels about himself or herself.

2. Willie intuitively knows an important lesson about being an employee. His boss reinforces this lesson in a significant way by giving Willie more than double his usual number of papers and by changing his corner after he shows up to sell the papers that "no one wanted to hear." What is the lesson that Willie knows? Create a list of suggestions for anyone interested in getting a job, keeping that position, and advancing in it.

THE GARDENER

Sarah Stewart. Illustrated by David Small. (New York: Farrar, Straus Giroux, 1997) 32 pages. ISBN 0-374-32517-0. Performance expectations: a, c, d, i.

In this visually appealing picture book (a 1998 Caldecott Honor Book), Stewart presents a compelling story about a young girl, set in the Great Depression. The text of the book is a series of letters that Lydia Grace writes to her parents and grandmother while she is away. Contrary to the typical pattern during the Great Depression, Lydia's parents send Lydia from their home in the country to the city where her uncle is a baker. There they believe Lydia will be more assured of getting sufficient food. Lydia shares her knowledge of the Latin names for flowers with Emma, one of Uncle Jim's employees, and Emma shares her knowledge of bread making, showing Lydia the principle of barter and exchange. Lydia's "work" ethic in relation to her surprise for Uncle Jim will also prompt much discussion about "value" versus money.

1. Write a definition of the historical term *Great Depression*. Be sure to include the years that are typically called the "Depression era" and the reasons for these difficult times.

2. Read Jerry Stanley's *Children of the Dustbowl* (Crown, 1992, 85 pages, ISBN 0-517-58782-3). Choose one of

the photographs and write a narrative poem telling the "story" of the child pictured.

3. Using graph paper, plan and then draw a garden for your school. Consult planting guides to find out each plant's needs and growth expectations, as well as weather patterns for the timing of your planting. Finally, create a budget for your project. If possible, present your proposal to the principal for acceptance.

ONCE UPON A COMPANY: A TRUE STORY

Wendy Halperin. (New York: Orchard, 1998) 40 pages. ISBN 0-531-30089-7. Performance expectations: a, b, c, e, f.

One day in November when her three children were bored with nothing to do, Halperin challenged them to start a business selling wreathes. Their grandfather got in on the activity and suggested they begin a college fund, and so the company got its name, The College Fund Wreath Company. In the second year, they added a summer business as well, The Peanut Butter & Jelly Company. The book documents the history of the business through its sixth year and includes an enormously helpful glossary of terms. The art is richly detailed, as are the entrepreneurial aspects of this story of a business.

1. What other products could this company offer? In the persona of a business adviser, make a list of suggestions this company could consider. Be sure to take into account the number of employees, physical limitations of production space, time, supply and demand, potential market, and, of course, profit.

2. With a small group, design your own company and plan for its implementation.

Non-Fiction

MONEY

Caroline Grimshaw. (Chicago: World Book, 1998) 32 pages. ISBN 0-7166-1309-3. Performance expectations: e, g.

By using a vividly colorful and busy format, this book's designers successfully demonstrate that learning about money is not boring. The book's format consists of fifty-two questions about money. Typical questions include the following: "Can we tell how people lived by looking at their money?" "Can power create wealth?" and "Why are some countries rich and some poor?"

1. List the twelve questions you think are the most interesting and present them to your classmates, asking them to name the three that are the most intriguing to them. Tally your results, and then give

an oral report on the questions that your classmates thought were the most intriguing.

2. This book contains a lot of data. List the fifteen most interesting pieces of information in this book. Then list the fifteen pieces of information you would have excluded if you had written the book. Explain your choices.

3. Prepare two timelines on an economic topic of your choice. The second one should include only events from this century.

NEALE S. GODFREY'S ULTIMATE KIDS' MONEY BOOK

Neale S. Godfrey. Illustrated by Randy Verougstraete. (New York: Simon & Schuster, 1998) 128 pages. ISBN 0-689-81717-7. Performance expectations: a, b, e, g.

Godfrey is able to make complex economic concepts simple, recognizing the limited attention span of adolescents. She combines her skills with those of an equally competent illustrator. The book's cartoon figures, color photographs, and appealing formatting create a highly recommended work. This is a "browse through" book. Banking, credit cards, starting a business, money, and stocks and bonds are some of the many topics in this appealing work.

1. Continue the book's list of "What's in a job?" using the want ads in the local newspaper.

2. Choose a famous person whose salary is very high, and prepare a weekly budget for him or her (such as that provided in the chapter on saving and spending).

3. At the end of each chapter are three to four activities. Select an activity from one of the chapters and use your response to give a book report.

THE KIDS' BUSINESS BOOK

Arlene Erlbach. (Minneapolis, Minn.: Lerner, 1998) 64 pages. ISBN 0-8225-98213. Performance expectations: a, b, f.

Written in a colorful format that may appeal to middle school students, this book profiles successful young business owners. The book describes familiar businesses such as dog walking and baby-sitting, and also includes descriptions for unfamiliar businesses such as those that manufacture T-shirts, bead jewelry, and gingerbread houses. The last part of the book contains a lot of how-to-do-it information in a limited space. Offering an authentic way of discussing the free enterprise system, this book describes basic economic principles in a way that children will understand.

1. Select one or more of the businesses described in the book and do a market survey. Investigate the

supply and demand for the various services and the range of prices in your area. Create several charts to present your findings.

2. Make a list of "talents" you could "market." Choose one. Create a business plan to launch your business.

THE LEMONADE STAND: A GUIDE TO ENCOURAGING THE ENTREPRENEUR IN YOUR CHILD

Emmanuel Modu. (Newark, N.J.: Gateway, 1996) ISBN 1-887-64603-5. Performance expectations: a, b, f.

This is technically not a book for children, but they may read it if they are interested in starting a business. Or perhaps they will become curious when they see that the book is written for parents. One lengthy chapter, as in Erlbach's book noted above, describes in great detail successful teenage business owners. Another chapter focuses on business ethics. The chapter on business concepts includes an introduction to terms such as *supply and demand* and *opportunity cost.*

1. Either independently or as a class project, complete the survey written for entrepreneurs that is found in Chapter 17. Compare the results from the class with that from young people who wish to be or are entrepreneurs (as seen in the book).

2. Review business ideas such as helping elderly persons, buying goods at auctions, cleaning houses, tutoring, washing windows, and others. Create a survey for your classmates to discover what they would like to be paid in order to do activities such as these. Chart your results and make some inferences about what your classmates value.

SUGARING

Jessie Haas. Illustrated by Joseph A. Smith. (New York: William Morrow, 1996) 24 pages. ISBN 0-688-14200-1. Performance expectations: a, b, f.

This brief, simple, illustrated work uses a story format to explain how maple syrup is produced.

1. Buy some Vermont Maple Syrup. Compare its cost with that of synthetic syrup. Conduct a blind taste comparison. Survey a group and ask if the difference in cost is worth it.

2. Given the premium cost of maple syrup, prepare an advertisement for it. In your advertisement, justify to potential consumers the additional cost.

3. The making of Vermont Maple Syrup is labor intensive. Read the story, study the pictures, and then identify how production methods could be modernized. How would you cut costs? Write a letter of recommendation to the president of Vermont Maple Syrup, Limited.

HOW ARE SNEAKERS MADE?

Henry Horenstein. (New York: Simon & Schuster, 1993) ISBN 0-671-77747-5. Performance objective: e.

This aptly titled book uses color photographs taken inside the Converse sneaker factory, and terse prose to help children learn about the process of production. After reading this book, an insightful student will probably get a sense of the tediousness of factory work.

1. The best way to understand an assembly line or specific task production is to experience it. Ask your class to decide on a product to be manufactured. Decorated cookies are a favorite, but bead animals would work, too. Divide the work into tasks, and assign the labor cost of each task.

2. Design a format for a book—like this one—which would explain how something is done in your family. You could consider a "service" such as getting the family up and out of the house in the morning or mowing the lawn. You could consider a "product" if your family makes pizza or dessert "from scratch." Decide what you would need to photograph for your book and how large it should be. Decide what prose would be necessary to explain what is happening.

FROM HEAD TO TOE: HOW A DOLL IS MADE

Susan Kuklin. (New York: Hyperion, 1994) 32 pages. ISBN 1-56282-666-2. Performance objective: e.

This book tells the story of how dolls are manufactured, including the work of designers and the role of market forces.

1. Compare and contrast the manufacturing of dolls with the manufacturing of sneakers (see *How Are Sneakers Made?*, immediately above). Where would you rather work? Identify the photograph that most influenced your decision.

2. In reviewing the work that is done in the manufacturing of dolls versus the work that is done in the manufacturing of sneakers, decide which job would be the most appealing to you. Assume that everyone would earn the same income and would have the same job security. What is it about the job you think you would prefer that would make it more appealing than the other job?

NEVER WERE MEN SO BRAVE: THE IRISH BRIGADE DURING THE CIVIL WAR

Susan Provost Beller. (New York: Margaret McElderry, 1998) 96 pages. ISBN 0-689-81406-2. Performance expectations: a, b, f, i.

The economic impetus for the Irish immigration to America comes through clearly in the opening chapters of this book. The Irish, literally starving to death because of the English Penal Laws and the Potato Famine of the 1840s, needed a way to survive, and so they came to America. Beller speculates that perhaps because the Irish knew all too intimately the cruel yokes of dominance by others—in the name of economics—they could so readily fight for the freedom of the slaves. Just as the British tried to keep the Irish people servile through economic sanctions, so, too, did southerners want to keep their slaves.

1. After reading this text, see what other comparisons you can find between the plight of the slaves and that of the Irish. Create a Venn diagram by drawing two intersecting circles. Write the similarities in the middle area, distinctive characteristics of the Irish in the left, and distinctive characteristics of the slaves in the right.
2. Create a timeline of the life of Thomas Francis Meagher.
3. Create a timeline summarizing the history of the Irish Brigade.
4. Consult the Internet and a library. What information can you find about the Irish Brigade, especially its involvement at the Battle of Gettysburg? Prepare the script for a "broadcast" about the Brigade's deeds.

STOLEN DREAMS: PORTRAITS OF WORKING CHILDREN

David Parker, Lee Engfer, and Robert Conrow. (Minneapolis, Minn.: Lerner, 1997) 112 pages. ISBN 0-8225-2960-2. Performance expectations: a, d, e, f, i, j.

The author, a physician and photographer, tells the story of young people who work as carpet weavers in Pakistan, factory workers in Nepal, and migrant workers in the United States, as well as children who become soldiers or prostitutes. The author acknowledges the harsh reality that, in many cases, children work so that their family can eat. He reminds us that not only do these children lose the opportunity for an education, but their health and safety suffer as well. Most important, they lose their childhood.

1. The author includes a section titled "Ask some questions." His intent is to cause reflection. His list is an effective resource for a class discussion or journal entries about child labor.

2. The book describes the murder of a twelve-year-old Pakistani boy who had organized a protest against bonded child labor. The American students described in the book responded by writing letters to the editor of their local newspaper. After reading this book, write a letter to the editor of your newspaper noting your thoughts about bonded child labor.
3. Children can make a difference. The author lists organizations fighting child labor. Write to those organizations to learn how children in America might help in this struggle.

KIDS AT WORK: LEWIS HINE AND THE CRUSADE AGAINST CHILD LABOR

Russell Freedman. Photographs by Lewis Hine. (New York: Clarion, 1998) 112 pages. ISBN 0-395-79726-8. Performance expectations: a, d, f, i, j.

In this dramatic and compelling text, Hine uses photographs and Freedman uses prose to paint a vivid portrait of how children were exploited in U.S. factories and mines up until the late 1930s. It was not until 1938 when President Roosevelt signed the Fair Labor Standards Act that a minimum wage and maximum hour standards for all workers in interstate commerce were set and limitations were placed on child labor.

1. Which photograph strikes you as the most powerful? In the persona of the child in the picture, tell "your" story, the kind of life you would have lived as a cotton mill spinner, cannery or glass factory worker, or any of the other positions children had.
2. Create a timeline of legislation concerning child labor laws.
3. Create a graph comparing "salaries" of various positions that children might have had.
4. Make a chart listing of all the jobs that children might have had according to their age. What job might even a three-year-old have had? What kind of jobs did older children have?
5. Write a brief biography of Lewis Hine.

GREAT AFRICAN AMERICANS IN BUSINESS

Pat Rediger. (New York: Crabtree, 1996) 64 pages. ISBN 0-8605-817-2. Performance expectations: a, b.

Brief biographies of contemporary and past successful African American business owners are provided in this colorful format that profiles their business successes. (Note: The piece on Madame C. J. Walker mislabels her first house as her very impressive Hudson River estate. This is inaccurate.) This work should be inspiring to all youth, but may appeal to young African Americans in particular.

1. Compare the profile on Madam C. J. Walker given in this book with the biography in *Madam C. J. Walker, Building a Business Empire* (Penny Colman; Millbrook, 1994, 48 pages, ISBN 1-562-94338-3). Does the Colman book give you more information about how goods and services are distributed and the role of supply and demand? Create an "Economics" vocabulary list with your own definitions of these words.

2. This work includes descriptions of some successful African Americans. Are there common characteristics that show up in the profiles, such as area of endeavor, market audience, education, age at the time of first success, or personality? Make a chart comparing and contrasting these characteristics, and then write a summary of your findings.

3. Assume you are to become a great business person. Use the format in this book to write your autobiography. Be sure to include "Personality Profile" and "Accomplishments."

Novels, Stories and Folk Tales

THE SLAVE DANCER

Paula Fox. (New York: Laurel Leaf Library, 1989) 127 pages. ISBN 0-440-96132-7. Performance expectations: c, e.

This Newbery Award winner deserves its reputation as a book that is not only an exciting read but also one that teaches us about a shameful time in our history. Thirteen-year-old Jessie, the son of an impoverished family, is kidnapped by seamen from a "slaver," a ship that brought slaves from Africa to America. The book recounts Jessie's adventures on board the ship that eventually sinks, killing all but Jessie and an African boy who becomes his friend. The book does not hesitate to show not only the brutality of the slave trade but also the consequences to those who were participants in this evil trade.

1. Draw two maps, one showing the voyage of *The Moonlight* and another showing Jessie's possible return route to New Orleans from the shipwreck.

2. Consider this adage: "Power corrupts; absolute power corrupts absolutely." Explore how this is true when reviewing the attitudes of the seafaring men, especially Purvis, an Irish American, who does not see the similarities between the Irish experience and that of the Africans.

3. The illustrator introduces each chapter with a drawing. Assume the publisher wanted two drawings for each chapter. Describe what you would recommend to the publisher for the second drawing.

SO FAR FROM HOME, THE DIARY OF MARY DRISCOLL, AN IRISH MILL GIRL

Barry Denenberg. (New York: Scholastic, 1997) 166 pages. ISBN 0-590-92667-5. Performance expectations: a, b, d, e, f, i.

This fictional diary, one of the Dear America series, chronicles the life of a young immigrant girl in the 1840s. Mary works far from her family in a textile mill in Lowell, Massachusetts. Few were happy in this early era of technology, but Denenberg tells well this tale of death, poverty, and prejudice.

1. How did technology change the lives of the Yankee and Irish girls? In the persona of a worker in the mill, write a letter advising a sister about work in Lowell.

2. Because of laws designed to protect workers, much of Mary's story could not happen today in America. Review the story, research current U.S. laws, and specify how the story is "dated."

3. Prepare an "Afterword" for this book. Write how the entrepreneurial culture was responsible for the "advances" in Lowell. Are the advances worth the consequences?

4. Read another of Denenberg's works: *Voices from Vietnam* (Scholastic, 1997, 272 pages, ISBN 0-590-43530-2) or *When Will This Cruel War Be Over? The Civil War Diary of Emma Simpson* (Scholastic, 1996, 156 pages, ISBN 0-590-22862-5). Then review the book for your class or a small group.

AN ACQUAINTANCE WITH DARKNESS

Ann Rinaldi. (San Diego, Calif.: Harcourt Brace, 1999) 356 pages. ISBN 0-15-202197-3. Performance expectations: a, b, c, d, e, f, i, j.

This novel offers a fascinating (and historical) way to look at "supply and demand," and is set at the time of Lincoln's assassination. Fourteen-year-old Emily is confronted with myriad changes in her own life. Her mother has just died, her best friend Annie Surratt's mother has been arrested for taking part in the assassination, and Emily, a minor, is forced to live with her mother's brother, Uncle Valentine, a man who her mother hated. Never understanding her mother's dislike for Valentine, who is a doctor, Emily decides to overlook his peculiar behavior when he saves her mother's grave from gravediggers. His sudden appearance one night from behind a gravestone, however, still puzzles her. The plot thickens, as they say, and Emily ultimately finds herself part of a grave-robbing network, headed by Uncle Valentine—all in the name of medicine.

1. Explain the principle of "supply and demand" in relation to the cadavers.
2. Conduct research into medical schools' need for cadavers in the mid 1800s. What is the current policy for finding cadavers for today's medical schools?
3. Find out more about Mary and Johnny Surratt's involvement in Lincoln's assassination. Do you think Mary Surratt should have been hanged? Make a case supporting or rejecting the court's decision.

JASON'S GOLD

Will Hobbs. (New York: Harper Trophy, 1999.) 221 pages. ISBN 0-380-72914-8. Performance objectives: a, b, f, g, i.

As soon as fifteen-year-old Jason hears the news of the riches of the Klondike fields in Alaska in 1897, he heads back home to Seattle, despite the fact that it had taken him a year to journey to New York City and he had arrived only five days earlier. Such was the allure of the adventure—and the gold. Jason was not alone. In the author's note at the end, Hobbs writes, "Of the approximately one hundred thousand people who set out for the Klondike, around forty thousand made it to Dawson City. Of those, only half are thought to have even looked for gold. Of those, only four thousand are thought to have found gold. Of the four thousand, only several hundred struck it rich." In this carefully documented novel, there is much to be learned about how both "goods and services" were a part of the Gold Rush, which was particularly influenced by supply and demand, especially in light of anticipated profits. This novel is not only incredibly "rich" in economic concepts but is also a real page-turner.

1. Create a timeline of events in the novel. Label each event with an appropriate economic concept.
2. Were all "players" in this story equally committed to the gold? Make a list as you read the novel and place the name of each on a "Commitment to Gold Continuum." Ask a classmate to do the same, and then compare your perceptions.
3. Young Jason meets Jack London. Find out more about London's involvement with the Gold Rush, read at least one of London's books, and share the highlights of both with the class in the form of an oral report.
4. Read the sequel, *Down the Yukon* (Harper Collins, 2001, 139 pages, ISBN 0-688-17472-8). Write a news article telling Jamie's and Jason's story.

THE ORPHAN OF ELLIS ISLAND

Elvira Woodruff. (New York: Scholastic, 1997) 176 pages. ISBN 0-590-48245-9. Performance expectations: f, i, j.

In this time-travel novel, Dominic Cantori, a young boy who does not want his fourth grade classmates to know that he is an orphan, finds himself transported to Italy in 1908 through a "conversation" with an old man at the Ellis Island museum. The economic conditions of early twentieth century Italy clearly become the impetus for "young" Francesco Cantori's immigration to America.

1. Research immigration patterns to Ellis Island for the past one hundred years. What were some of the primary motivations for such immigrants? Write a poem titled "An Appeal from Your World Neighbors" explaining why you would want to come to America.
2. Again, review immigration records for the past century. How have immigration patterns changed? Draw several maps showing where the immigrants have come from during these years. Then write a brief commentary explaining why these patterns have changed.
3. In this novel, Dominic, Antonio, and Francesco dream about what they want to be when they grow up. What do you dream of becoming? Is your potential income a factor? Why?

NOWHERE TO CALL HOME

Cynthia DeFelice. (New York: Farrar Straus Giroux, 1999) 200 pages. ISBN 0-37435552-5. Performance expectations: a, b, d, g, i, j.

Set during the Great Depression, this novel focuses on Frances Elizabeth Barrow's apprenticeship into the "real" world. Born into wealth, she suddenly becomes penniless at twelve when her father commits suicide. Frances rebels against being sent to live with an aunt whom she has never met. Instead, Frances decides to become a "'bo," someone who will "hop a freight," but not a "bum," someone who "gives an honest 'bo a bad name. A bum begs and steals and drinks wine and whiskey till he can't see straight. He's shiftless, you see." Although most of those riding the rails were men, many women, too, were homeless. With great attention to detail, as in her other novels, DeFelice shares the lives of those who experience the Great Depression. This book offers much depth and even greater heart. In her travels, twelve-year-old "Frankie" learns significant lessons about the power of money, individuals, and groups.

1. Not only is Frances suddenly homeless following her father's death, but the house servants are as well. Research the number of homeless people during the

years of the Great Depression. Create a graph of your results. Analyze your numbers further. Did some areas of the country have more homeless people than did others? How can you account for this?

2. What caused the "Great Depression"? Write a one-page report and present it to your class.

3. Frankie and Stewpot dig potatoes one day. They are not paid in money but in lunch and potatoes. What is this arrangement called, and why was it a particularly good deal for them? This economic practice occurred nearly sixty years ago. Is it still used today? When? Where?

4. Create a glossary of words and their meanings unique to one who is living life as a "bo."

5. Read other books of historical fiction by Cynthia DeFelice, such as *The Apprenticeship of Lucas Whitaker* (Camelot, 1998, 151 pages, ISBN 0-3807-2920-2) or *Weasel* (Camelot, 1991, 112 pages, ISBN 0-3807-1358-6). In some fashion, share your impressions of the book after you finish reading it.

Notes

1. This section is directly quoted from National Council for the Social Studies, *Expectations of Excellence: Curriculum Standards for Social Studies* (Washington, D.C.: Author, 1994), 96.

CHAPTER TEN

⑧ SCIENCE, TECHNOLOGY, AND SOCIETY

Performance Expectations

Social studies programs should include experiences that provide for the study of *relationships among science, technology, and society*, so that the learner can:

a. examine and describe the influence of culture on scientific and technological choices and advancement, such as in transportation, medicine, and warfare;

b. show through specific examples how science and technology have changed people's perceptions of the social and natural world, such as in their relationship to the land, animal life, family life, and economic needs, wants, and security;

c. describe examples in which values, beliefs, and attitudes have been influenced by new scientific and technological knowledge, such as the invention of the printing press, conceptions of the universe, applications of atomic energy, and genetic discoveries;

d. explain the need for laws and policies to govern scientific and technological applications, such as in the safety and well-being of workers and consumers and the regulation of utilities, radio, and television;

e. seek reasonable and ethical solutions to problems that arise when scientific advancements and social norms or values come into conflict.[1]

Picture Books

STARRY MESSENGER

Peter Sis. (New York: Farrar Straus & Giroux, 1996) 36 pages. ISBN 0-374-37191-1 . Performance expectations: a, b, c, e.

The history behind Galileo's realization that the Earth was not the center of the universe and his inability to "prove" it to society's leaders—at that time, the officials of the Church—resulted in Galileo's spending the last nine years of his life under "house arrest." He gave his contemporaries a new way to envision the world, a vision some could not accept.

1. Sis uses several timelines to help the reader "visualize" the information. Create one timeline showing significant events in Galileo's life.

2. After Galileo heard about a telescope, he created one for himself. What else did he invent?

3. Imagine you were Galileo's lawyer. How would you have argued his case in the Pope's court? Prepare your opening statement.

4. Imagine you were a fellow citizen watching the trial. Do you think the sentence Galileo received was appropriate or fair? Why or why not?

OLD HOME DAY

Donald Hall. Illustrated by Emily Arnold McCully. (San Diego, Calif.: Browndeer Press, 1996) 48 pages. ISBN 0-15-2768963. Performance expectations: a, b, c.

Using the fictional town of Blackwater, New Hampshire, Hall tells the story of its growth from prehistory to the bicentennial celebration of its founding. Students will discover how technology causes communities to change. Hall, in his "Author's Note," invites readers to think ahead: "In the future, maybe the computer, the fax, the modem—and goodness knows what else—will allow more people to return to the countryside, where they can conduct business from the wilderness as if they commuted regularly to a city office."

1. Trace the history of your own community. Investigate the advancements in transportation that influenced the development of your community separately from advancements in medicine, utilities, communication, or general technology. Make a timeline showing how each influenced your town's growth.

2. Are science and technology always good? Write an essay stating and supporting your position using changes in your own community as examples.

CHATTANOOGA SLUDGE: CLEANING TOXIC SLUDGE FROM CHATTANOOGA CREEK

Molly Bang. (San Diego, Calif.: Gulliver, 1996) 42 pages. ISBN 0-15-216345-X. Performance expectations: d, e.

In this unique book, the author illustrates her work with pictures that combine photographs, drawings, and cartoon figures whose balloon dialog provides both humor and information to supplement the story. A scientist is trying to find an economical means of removing the poisons from Chattanooga Creek. At the end of the book, the scientist is still working on a solution.

1. Read *811 Mistakes that Worked* by Charlotte Foltz Jones (illustrated by John O'Brien; Doubleday, 1994, 78 pages, ISBN 0-385-32043-4). Select one invention and write and illustrate the story using Molly Bang's format.

2. Lorraine Egan, in her book *Inventors and Inventions* (Scholastic, 1997, 80 pages, ISBN 0-590-10388-1), suggests this activity: Create a survey instrument to determine how many of your classmates think like an inventor. Ask them which of the following characteristics describe(s) them, using a Lickert scale. This means that for each characteristic, your classmates are to decide whether they "Strongly agree," "Somewhat agree," are "Undecided," "Somewhat disagree," or "Strongly disagree" that the characteristic describes him or her. Graph and chart your responses. The characteristics include the following: (1) Share your ideas with others. (2) Concentrate. (3) Try something new—able to turn a problem upside down. (4) Keep an open mind. (5) Take chances; learn from your mistakes; overcome failures. (6) Take time to dream; ask the question "What is it . . . ?" (7) Keep pushing. Don't give up. (8) Relax and tinker. (9) Be positive. (10) Overcome failures. (11) Learn from your mistakes.

THE BOBBIN GIRL

Emily Arnold McCully. (New York: Dial, 1996) 40 pages. ISBN 0-8037-1827-6. Performance expectation: e.

Mill owners and Yankee farm girls hired to tend the machines came into conflict when mill owners began to forgo their commitments to making the workplace desirable for young girls. The heroes in this book challenged oppressive working conditions through a strike. Although a strike can be a means of solving the problem of abuse of labor resulting from the side effects of technological advances, in this case, the strike failed.

1. Explore the ethics of striking. What makes a strike justifiable? People in certain careers cannot go on strike; who are these people? What can people such as air traffic controllers or physicians do if there is a conflict with an employer? Write a short report of your findings.

2. This book is written from the perspective of a worker. The owners are portrayed in a most unflattering way. Assume the role of a manager and tell his side of the story.

ARTHUR'S COMPUTER DISASTER

Marc Tolon Brown. Illustrated by author. (Boston, Mass.: Little Brown and Co., 1999) 32 pages. ISBN 0-316-10534-1. Performance expectations: b, e.

This book, another of Marc Brown's delightful stories, is probably appropriate for only the earlier middle grades. It provides an interesting stimulus for discussions of contemporary life and technology. Arthur is told not to use Mom's computer for games but does so and "breaks" it.

1. Leading a discussion with a small group, ask, (a) How is life different in Arthur's household because of the computer? Would you agree that your younger brother or sister believes having a good video game is worth not being "tucked in"? (b) Review the steps Arthur took to fix the computer. Why didn't Arthur make the obvious phone call? Would other parents respond the same way that his did? and (c) What are the possible consequences of using a computer designated for the family's business? Was the punishment harsh enough?

2. How have computers changed the world we live in? Brainstorm a list of ways you come into direct contact with computers and their power. Then brainstorm a list of ways computers affect your life indirectly—like regulating the electric company. Finally, write a paragraph or two explaining whether you would be willing to give up this aspect of technology in your life. Be sure to include your reasons for your position.

THE TOWER TO THE SUN

Colin Thompson. (New York: Alfred A. Knopf, 1997) 32 pages. ISBN 0-679-883347. Performance expectations: a, d.

The story is simple. One hundred years have passed. The story implies that because society has abused the environment, there is little fuel and one cannot see the sky or sun due to the haze of the atmosphere. Above the land are clouds and a yellow mist. The richest man in the world wants his grandchild to see the sun. A tower is built so that all may enjoy the sun, "the warmth of life." Fascinating illustrations that may appeal to students and teachers alike show the jumble of architecture and artifacts across cultures that are used in the construction of the tower. This book should be carefully studied and, hopefully, its message fully heard.

1. Make a list of the consequences of using fossil fuels.

2. The cover illustration, as well as the detail of the tower, shows examples of cultures long ago and far away. Attempt to identify those structures, including their time

and place, and then make inferences about the choices that society made because of its technology in those eras.

3. What laws or governmental polices are you aware of that are in place to protect the safety of workers or consumers? Interview neighbors and friends. Think, for example, of the entertainment, transportation, and food industries.

4. Can you think of any additional laws that should be added to protect society from technology? If there is interest, have a debate. Statements for debate might include the following: (a) People should not be allowed to use wood-burning fireplaces. (b) If families have two cars, the second one should be an electric one or mini car. And (c) To encourage people to use public transportation, all rides should be free. People would pay for the extra costs through an increase in the gasoline tax.

Non-Fiction

BIODIVERSITY
Dorothy Hinshaw Patent. Photographs by William Munoz. (New York: Clarion, 1996) 96 pages. ISBN 0-395-68704-7. Performance expectations: a, b, c, d, e.

The connection between science and humanity is clearly made in this readable nonfiction text. Humanity's relationship with the environment is emphasized, particularly our need to preserve biodiversity. After all, we have "only one earth." Munoz's photographs are perfect complements to Patent's text.

1. Choose any plant native to your area. Study it firsthand. Write down everything you notice. Try to figure out how it reproduces. If there were a fire, could it survive to a next generation? If there were a flood? A freezing rain? Finally, check out a reference book and see how the plant you chose is connected to other plant families in other habitats.

2. Create a map of the major types of habitats in the United States. Be sure to include a legend.

WEAPONS AND WARFARE: FROM THE STONE AGE TO THE SPACE AGE
Milton Meltzer. Illustrated by Sergio Martinez. (New York: HarperCollins, 1996) 86 pages. ISBN 0-06-024875-0. Performance expectations: a, b, c, d, e.

Meltzer writes about weapons and warfare in a way that is thought provoking. The subtitle, "From the Stone Age to the Space Age," tells much about the folly of man. As technology progresses, we are becoming increasingly capable of destroying one another, not only with nuclear weapons but also with guns. He states, "In the United States: A handgun is manufactured every 20 seconds. A person is shot every two minutes. A person dies from a gunshot wound every 14 minutes. Every two hours a child dies from gunshot wounds" (p. 74). In fifty-nine brief sections, each about a page in length, and with plentiful drawings, Meltzer considers both the technology of warfare and the humanity of it: "Do people kill because it comes naturally? Does it make sense?" Readers are left with substantial information with which to draw their own conclusions.

1. What do you think? Do people kill because it comes "naturally"? Write a draft of a letter to the editor of a local paper or to a magazine, stating your opinion. Use evidence from the book to support your position.

2. Read *Scorpions* (Harper, 1990, 216 pages, ISBN 0-064-47066-0) by Walter Dean Myers. In this Newbery-award winning book, a gun plays a central role. What message do you think Myers was trying to convey by including it? Give an oral book report to your class.

3. Or read *The Outsiders* (Puffin, 1997, 180 pages, ISBN 0-140-38572-X) by Susan Hinton. The weapon here is a knife. Does this reflect a more sane world? With those who read *Scorpions*, have a debate about which "gang's" behavior makes more "sense"? Or do you have a better solution?

WHEN PLAGUE STRIKES
James Cross Giblin. Woodcuts by David Frampton. (New York: Harper Trophy, 1997) 240 pages. ISBN 0-06-446195-5. Performance expectations: a, b, c, d, e.

Giblin does amazingly well in showing the similarities between what he calls the three "plagues": the Black Death, smallpox, and AIDS. In a text whose central theme may be considered gruesome, Giblin highlights the interaction between science and society. The history behind these ailments is actually fascinating, although a little scary. Giblin's prose reminds readers, "The enemy is alive and well," the title of the last section. He closes the book stating, " Finding ways to treat and cure [any new disease] soon becomes the concern of everyone on the planet." Note: Some people might say the content of the book is unsuitable for students as young as ten, the age designated on the book's cover.

1. Choose two friends. Each should select one of the three ailments to study. Then make three timelines, highlighting the events of each disease. Finally, hang

the timelines on a bulletin board, study their similarities, and present to the class the commonalities of how each disease affected society.

2. For what age levels so you belive this book is most suitable? Take a stance and then support is in a fully developed paragraph.

WHY DO WE USE THAT?
Jane Wilcox. (New York: Franklin Watts, 1996) 32 pages. ISBN 0-531-14395-3. Performance expectations: a, b.

This cleverly written book reflects the preference of many early adolescents for colorful, entertaining means of acquiring information. Fifteen topics are explored. The titles suggest the writing style: "A Clean Start" (bathrooms) or "Getting Comfy" (chairs, air-conditioning). The book may provide a stimulus for thinking about technology, especially for those who consider themselves "scientifically challenged."

1. Which of the inventions described has the most interesting "story" behind it? With five classmates who chose other inventions, write up your own version of the story and read it to the class in a Readers Theater format.

2. What invention was omitted from the book? What can you find out about it? Write about what you find in as similar a fashion as that of the book's descriptions as possible.

GIRLS THINK OF EVERYTHING: STORIES OF INGENIOUS INVENTIONS BY WOMEN
Catherine Thimmesh. Illustrated by Melissa Sweet. (Boston, Mass.: Houghton Mifflin, 2000) 57 pages. ISBN 0-395-93744-2. Performance expectations: a, b.

This fascinating book describes how women, across time, have responded to daily challenges and invented "solutions" to immediate needs. From the invention of "Toll House Cookies" to "Windshield Wipers" to "Scotchguard," women saw the necessity of an alternative and rose to the occasion.

1. Which of these inventions do you think is the most creative? Why? Explain to your class the impetus behind the invention and why you believe it was so "inspired."

2. Study the "endpapers" of the book that create a timeline of other women and their inventions, from 3000 B.C. to 1995 A.D. Choose one of the women and find out the impetus behind her invention; then write a brief report like Thimmesh has in this text.

53 1/2 THINGS THAT CHANGED THE WORLD AND SOME THAT DIDN'T
Steve Parker. Illustrated by David West. (Westbrook, Conn.: Millbrook, 1995) 64 pages. ISBN 1-56294-894-6. Performance expectations: a, b.

Originally published in England, this information-packed paperback provides both historical information and technical information about our most significant inventions. The illustrations are colorful and cartoon-like in their appeal. (Fusion power is the 1/2 invention.) The style is light and should be appealing to middle school students. A word of caution: In the introductory notes the following sentence appears, which may require an explanation: "Why did people invent spirits, gods and prophets? Maybe they wanted to explain mysterious happenings."

1. Make a list of ten inventions for which you believe people are most grateful. Then survey your classmates and see if they agree. Next, ask them to survey two adults (twenty-one years of age or older) they know. Compile the results. Do the different generations agree on which inventions are the most important in their lives?

2. Imagine inventing something you think would be particularly useful to you in the future. In writing, speculate why, when, where, and how it will be invented.

3. Make a timeline predicting the dates of future inventions.

4. Using the text, create a timeline showing twenty inventions and when they were created. Consider making a parallel timeline showing twenty key political events.

FAILED TECHNOLOGY: TRUE STORIES OF TECHNOLOGICAL DISASTERS, VOL. 1
Fran Locher Frieman and Neil Schlager. (New York: Gale Research, Inc., 1997) 392 pages. ISBN 0-8103-9794-3. Performance expectations: d, e.

Volume 1 of this series focuses on forty-four disasters of all kinds, involving ships, automobiles, bridges, dams, and nuclear plants, as well as environmental and medical disasters. A listing of related magazines and books completes the description of each disaster. This is a rich resource for student research papers.

1. Which disaster surprised you most in terms of its impact on society? Why?

2. Are all of the disasters included in this book part of the "common knowledge base" of American citizens? Or does it seem that some are less well known than others? Why would anyone try to keep these incidents hidden? Why should citizens know about

all of them? What recommendations could you make for protecting citizens from disasters in the future?

TECHNO LAB: HOW SCIENCE IS CHANGING ENTERTAINMENT

Carol Anderson and Robert Sheely. (New York: Silver Moon, 2000) 58 pages. ISBN 1-881889-63-7. Performance expectations: a, c.

Although the language is sometimes childlike, the authors identify five topics—movies, sound recordings, television, video games, and virtual reality games—and then provide information about the historical origins and scientific principles. Each chapter is introduced by a fictionalized event that uses familiar names or places.

1. With four friends, summarize the book. Each student should select one of the topics, write a summary, and create a poster to highlight and extend the written report. Be sure to include the report on the poster.

2. Interview your grandparents or another person over fifty years old. Ask them what activities were "entertainment" for them when they were your age. Ask yourself the same question. Compare their answers with yours. What conclusions can you draw about how technology has changed? Share your findings with the class.

THE UNITED STATES IN THE 19TH CENTURY

David Rubel. (New York: Scholastic, 1997) 192 pages. ISBN 0-590-72564-5. Performance expectations: a, b, c, d, e.

With a format sure to engage middle school students, this book describes life in the nineteenth century through four strands, including Science and Technology. Students can read the book straight through focusing only on this strand, or they can read the information in this strand while sampling information from the other three categories: Politics, Life in the Nineteenth Century, and Arts and Entertainment. Because the information is also placed in sections by time periods within this century, beginning with Federalism (1800-1814) and ending with the Gay Nineties (1890-1899), students may find it easy to focus on a particular year or group of years. Whether used as a reference or free choice book, students may find the reading enjoyable and satisfying because entries are thorough but not overwhelming.

1. Choose one of the many inventions described in the text and find out more. Invite your classmates to do the same and then create your own invention timeline for the class.

2. Read one of the books described in the "Arts and Entertainment" section. What references to science and technology can you find? Do they appear to be accurate? Do an oral book report for your class, sharing not only a short summary of the book and your impressions of it but also the information you can find about how technology (or the lack of technology) affected the lives of the characters.

DAILY LIFE IN A VICTORIAN HOUSE

Laura Wilson. (New York: Puffin, 1998) 48 pages. ISBN 0-140-56368-7. Performance expectations: a, b.

Featuring a discussion of this period of sophisticated technology, this book, which focuses on the things of the Victorian era, may help today's students understand technology by looking at "technology" from another era. The photographs of rooms and of objects, as well as the description of the Victorian life-style, help make the time period come alive. Although the book might be criticized for focusing on the upper middle class, there is recognition in the text of the life of the common folk.

1. Other than emptying chamber pots, which of the chores of the servants would you find most unpleasant? Which would you find the most agreeable?

2. Pretend that Mary, a sixteen-year-old housemaid in this Victorian house, is a friend of yours. Write a dialog trying to explain how your life is different from her life because of the technology available to you.

THEY NEVER KNEW: THE VICTIMS OF NUCLEAR TESTING

Glenn Cheney. (New York: Franklin Watts, 1996) 128 pages. ISBN 0-531-11273-X. Performance expectations: a, b, c, d, e.

The impact of technology on society is clear in this fascinating text about the history of nuclear weapons testing: "One hundred and forty-nine atomic bombs have exploded over America. No one knows how many people these bombs have killed" due to cancer caused by radioactive fallout. This book spares no detail, telling as accurately as possible the global effects of the nuclear arms race.

1. After reading this book, choose one of the incidents and write a short story from a young person's point of view explaining how the bomb affected his or her life. If you want, pretend you are the person whose life was affected by the bombing.

2. Read *Hiroshima* (Apple, 1996, 64 pages, ISBN 0-590-20833-0) by Laurence Yep or *Hiroshima* (Vintage, 1989, 152 pages, ISBN 0-679-72103-7) by John Hersey.

Compare what you learn from either of these books with the information in *They Never Knew*. Prepare an opinion piece to share with your classmates.

INCREDIBLE PEOPLE: FIVE STORIES OF EXTRAORDINARY LIVES

Frederick Drimmer. (New York: Atheneum, 1997) 192 pages. ISBN 0-689-31921-5. Performance expectations: a, b, c.

Drimmer does, indeed, tell stories of "incredible people": the gentle giant, Jack Earle; the last "wild" Indian in North America, Ishi; Siamese twins Violet and Daisy Hilton; a pygmy, Ota Benga; and a "wild" boy, Victor. Carefully and poignantly, Drimmer reveals their stories against the backdrop of the eras in which they lived, when medical theory and practice were not what they are now. Generally, society's interests were hardly altruistic, although each of these special people eventually had guardians who strove to act in their best interests. Middle grade students may at first be interested only in these stories because the people are so "different," but this book will lead them to see the human needs that are common among these five people—and the reader.

1. Choose one of these people and research that person's history further. What else can you find to enhance the portrait of your chosen person? After writing a short report adding the additional details, consider how medical science or technology could have enhanced the person's life. If medical science or technology could not have improved the person's life, or could not have fully improved it, decide how society could have done so.

2. Read one of Drimmer's other books, such as *Very Special People: The Struggles, Loves and Triumphs of Human Oddities* (ISBN 0-806-51253-9) or *Born Different: Amazing Stories of Very Special People* (ISBN 0-553-15897-X).

Novels, Stories and Folk Tales

LYDDIE

Katherine Paterson. (New York: Puffin, 1995) 182 pages. ISBN 0-140-37389-6. Performance expectations: a, b, c, d, e.

Set in the 1840s, this book describes how Lyddie leaves the farm she loves in order to work in the mills of Lowell, Massachusetts. Determined to pay off the family farm's debts, she endures the outrageous hours and factory conditions. Lyddie finds the courage to stand with Diana, a leader for social change, in confronting the mill's owners.

1. Diana tries to get all of the workers to belong to the Female Labor Reform Association. What can you find out about it? What did it eventually accomplish?

2. In some ways, the mills did enhance life for those who lived in this era. How? What were the negative effects on individuals, the physical environment, and the community in general? Make two lists, one of the benefits and another of the disadvantages.

3. Near the end of the novel, after deciding to head to Ohio where there is a college "that will take a woman just like a man," Lyddie says, "It'll be years before I come back to these mountains again. I won't come back weak and beaten down and because I have nowhere else to go. No, I will not be a slave, even to myself." How does Lyddie's experience in the factory nurture this decision? Write a short biography of Lyddie's life, focusing on actions that would help her reach this decision.

4. To what Ohio college was Lyddie referring? Write a brief history of this college and its open enrollment policy.

THE APPRENTICESHIP OF LUCAS WHITAKER

Cynthia DeFelice. (New York: Farrar Straus Giroux, 1998) 151 pages. ISBN 0-380-72920-2. Performance expectations: a, b, c, e.

Like DeFelice's other works, this historical novel is compelling and thought provoking. Based on a gruesome practice of the mid-1800s by people desperate to "cure" their loved ones of consumption—which is now known as tuberculosis—this novel clearly shows the conflict between science and superstition. Twelve-year-old Lucas, having just lost his entire family to consumption, wanders away from his Connecticut farm because of grief and guilt. At that point, he believes that if he had only listened to his neighbor explain the "cure," his mother might still be alive. Thankfully, he becomes the apprentice of Doc Beecher, who helps him understand the scientific method and the hope and heartbreak of being a doctor in any age—when human need outstrips medical knowledge.

1. Read *Weasel* (Camelot, 1991, 119 pages, ISBN 0-380-71358-6), also by DeFelice. This book is set in Ohio. Decide how "science, technology, and society" have changed since the events in this story occurred. Share your analysis with the class.

2. Research other medical practices that have changed over time, such as using leeches or "bleeding" patients. Describe each procedure as it was done then, including why it was thought to be helpful, and then

explain why it was stopped, detailing its replacement practice.

3. Research the development of the microscope. Include a drawing for each major stage in its development, labeling how it has changed from the previous version.

THE BOMB

Theodore Taylor. (New York: Avon, 1997) 176 pages. ISBN 0-380-72723-4. Performance expectation: a, d, e.

Although World War II had ended, the U.S. government continued to experiment with nuclear weapons. This is the story of the people who lived on the Bikini Atoll, where a test bomb was dropped. Although fictional, this book accurately describes what happened to the people who were uprooted.

1. Imagine that your homeland is to be destroyed for the sake of science. Create a plan to capture the attention of the media so they will promote either not dropping the bomb or destroying some other place instead.

2. Research other books by Theodore Taylor. Choose one that has a technological subject, read it, and report on how technology changes the lives of the people in the book.

THERE'S AN OWL IN THE SHOWER

Jean Craighead George. Illustrated by Christine Herman Merrill. (New York: Harper Trophy, 1997) 134 pages. ISBN 0-06-440682-2. Performance expectations: b, d.

Although improbable, this story provides rich arguments for the preservation of endangered species. The son of a logger, whose job is eliminated because a court mandates that spotted owl nesting sites be protected, finds a lost owlet and raises it to maturity. In the process, he becomes an "owl lover."

1. Role play an argument between Borden's father and another boy's father who is not convinced of the importance of protecting endangered species.

2. Draw a poster supporting the protection of either the spotted owl or the loggers' jobs, as was done in the book.

3. Identify an environmental need in your area and learn what is (or is not) being done about it.

ADEM'S CROSS

Alice Mead. (New York: Laurel Leaf, 1998) 132 pages. ISBN 0-440-22735-6. Performance expectations: a, b.

Fourteen-year-old Adem is tired of the oppression resulting from the four-and-a-half years of Serbian occupation of his land, Kosovo. He is an Albanian Muslim and is personally committed to nonviolent resistance. Adem witnesses beatings, murder, and other forms of terror. His cross was a literal one, ironically an Orthodox one, carved into his chest by Serbian soldiers not much older than he was. This book, however, is about all of those who exist in this war-torn land because all bear the cross of their ancient hatred. This graphic novel is realistic and important; it is contemporary "news" from the television made personal.

1. Create a scrapbook of news stories you find in newspapers and magazines about the conflicts in this part of the world. Read them as you find them, keeping track of significant events by posting them on a "Did you know . . . ?" chart.

2. Write a "protest poem" in the persona of Adem, giving voice to his fears, frustrations, and hopes.

VIRTUALLY PERFECT

Dan Gutman. (New York: Hyperion, 1999) 123 pages. ISBN 0-7868-1316-4 . Performance expectations: a, b, c, d, e.

When Yip's father brings home software that creates vactors—virtual actors—Yip tries it out and creates Victor! Charming and wonderful at first, Victor soon reveals his potential for good and evil. In this completely readable and thoroughly enjoyable text, Gutman provides the impetus for significant discussions: Given that such a software program could exist in the years to come, should it be marketed? If so, who should have access to it? How should it be programmed? Or should such software be developed at all? This text would make a particularly good read aloud, and whole class discussions would lend themselves easily to students addressing these issues further in more specific ways.

1. Consider how such an invention—creation of virtual actors, or people—could affect our world. Could using such vactors benefit medicine? World politics? Scientific progress? Choose one area and write a description of the potential of virtual actors (vactors) in the year 2025.

2. Consider the impact of using vactors in your home. How might having a new "sibling," with qualities like Victor's, change your life? Argue, either in written or verbal form, for or against adding such a new "family member."

3. Victor makes some errors in judgment. If these were to be rectified, what principles or philosophies would Victor have to acquire? Make a list of the "ethical" beliefs that Victor should have as a part of his data base in order to create a more harmonious world.

AMONG THE HIDDEN

Margaret Haddix. (New York: Aladdin, 2000) 153 pages. ISBN 0-689-82475. Performance expectations: a, b, c, d, e.

Luke is a shadow child, the third child in a family. Third children are "forbidden"—such is the premise of *Among the Hidden*, a novel of some future American society. Such is already the reality in some countries, like China, where the number of offspring is limited. The Population Police enforce this rule, but Luke, always hidden, has made it to age twelve. His family members accept the government's mandate. Should they?

1. Is this law requiring population restriction one that protects the safety and well-being of the rest of the population? Is the government justified or has it intruded on the rights of private citizens? Is technology to blame because it is so useful in ferreting out lawbreakers? Is this an ethical solution? Write a position paper stating your perspective, citing as much evidence from the book as possible.

2. How has this rule changed family life? What risks did Luke's parents face for having disobeyed the law? What risks did Luke's brothers face? Was it fair for the parents to put their children in this position? In the persona of one of Luke's brothers, write a letter to your parents explaining why or why not they should have broken the law.

3. Read the sequel, *Among the Impostors* (Simon & Schuster, 2001, 172 pages, ISBN 0-689-83904-9). Five additional sequels are planned. Hypothesize whose story Haddix will tell next. Outline a potential plot outline for the future novels.

4. Read another of Haddix's works of science fiction, *Turnabout* (Simon & Schuster, 2000, 223 pages, ISBN 0-689-82187-5), which explores the concept of "un-aging," or *Running Out of Time* (Aladdin, 1997, 184 pages, ISBN 0-0689-81236-1), which chronicles parallel time periods—a contemporary "entertainment park" in Indiana that is a fully functioning village of inhabitants who live in a world of more than a century and a half ago and do not know they are actually an exhibit. How does either or both of these texts look at the relationships among "science, technology, and society"?

VIRTUAL WAR

Gloria Skuraznski. Illustrated by Francesca Caseres. (New York: Simon & Schuster, 1999) 160 pages. ISBN 0-689-82425-4. Performance expectations: a, b, c.

This futuristic novel centers on the question of our age: Will there be a war to end all wars? In this novel, war nearly did destroy Earth. Wars after this near-destruction can be fought virtually—with hardly any fatalities. A team of players, in this case, fourteen-year-old Corgan and his teammates Sharla and Brig, fight the war to decide whether the Pacific, Eurasia, or Western Hemisphere Federations will claim ownership of the Isles of Hiva, the only noncontaminated land left in the world. In Corgan's world, all is controlled, from his physical world to the intellectual world to the spiritual one. Why are he and his teammates trained to fight this war? "It was a reminder of what happened when wars used to be fought the old way. It was meant to show why humans can no longer solve disputes by killing one another. . . . So that thousands of others will be spared. With the world so sparsely populated now, peace is the only way to achieve survival" (pp. 135-136). This captivating novel relays well a possible fate of humans who fail to recognize the power of technology—for both good and evil.

1. Near the end of the novel, Corgan has to decide for himself who to believe, his mentor Mendor or Sharla and Brig. What factor do you think was the most influential in causing Corgan to go on with the war? In the persona of Corgan, write a letter to the Supreme Council explaining your current perception of reality.

2. Corgan's life is different from ours. Compare his lifestyle with yours using a Venn diagram. In the center of two intersecting circles, write how your lives are alike. On the right side, list how your life is like Corgan's. On the left side, list how Corgan's life is different from yours.

3. Sharla is fascinated with DNA and how genes divide. What can you find out about it? Write a short report to explain how DNA works. Be sure to include some drawings to support your text.

THE GIVER

Lois Lowry. (New York: Bantam, 1999) 180 pages. ISBN 0-553-57133-8. Performance expectations: a, b, c, d, e.

This captivating book considers life in the future, when technology has evolved to such a point that even people are genetically engineered for sameness; cultural diversity is no more. There is no war. Medicine now makes life nearly pain-free . . . and even emotion-free.

1. The Giver is the only one who knows the history of the people. Is this dangerous? Santayana said that those who refused to learn from history were doomed to relive it. Is this appropriate for the world Jonas inhabits? Why or why not? Explain your answer in a position paper.

2. What if you were Jonas? Would you want to become the Giver? Why or why not?

3. Is the world Jonas lives in a better world than is the one in which we currently reside? Why or why not? Make your argument in a persuasive essay.

THE LAST BOOK IN THE UNIVERSE

Rodman Philbrick. (New York: Scholastic, 2000) 223 pages. ISBN 0-439-08758. Performance expectations: a, b, c, d, e.

"If you're reading this, it must be a thousand years from now. Because nobody around here reads anymore. Why bother, when you can just probe it? Put all the images and excitement right inside your brain and let it rip. There are all kinds of mindprobes—trendies, shooters, sexbos, whatever you want to experience." So begins this incredible futuristic novel about a world that is controlled by different "latches," where poverty reigns except for those who have been genetically altered to be perfect—proovs. This book may stimulate significant conversation about the state of our world now and its direction for the future.

1. As you read the book, create a "New World" glossary of words and their contemporary (as we know them) counterparts. For example, "mindprobe" could be defined as an "electrode needle that gives or stimulates mental images, depending on its placement and type. There are at least three types of mindprobes: trendies—about living in Eden; shooters—violent action; and sexbos—sequences focusing on sex."

2. Most of us would not choose to live in this futuristic version of our world. Where do you think things went wrong? Can you pinpoint a particular insight from the novel that seemed to be the point of no return for this created world? Are there lessons to be learned from this story? What are they? Create a list of "Rules" that you believe would protect us from evolving into such a society.

Notes

1. This section is directly quoted from National Council for the Social Studies, *Expectations of Excellence: Curriculum Standards for Social Studies* (Washington, D.C.: Author, 1994), 99.

Chapter Eleven

ⓘ GLOBAL CONNECTIONS

Performance Expectations

Social studies programs should include experiences that provide for the study of *global connections and interdependence*, so that the learner can:

a. describe instances in which language, art, music, belief systems, and other cultural elements can facilitate global understanding or cause misunderstanding;

b. analyze examples of conflict, cooperation, and interdependence among groups, societies, and nations;

c. describe and analyze the effects of changing technologies on the global community;

d. explore the causes, consequences, and possible solutions to persistent, contemporary, and emerging global issues, such as health, security, resource allocation, economic development, and environmental quality;

e. describe and explain the relationships and tensions between national sovereignty and global interests in such matters as territory, natural resources, trade, use of technology, and welfare of people;

f. demonstrate understanding of concerns, standards, issues, and conflicts related to universal human rights;

g. identify and describe the roles of international and multinational organizations.[1]

Picture Books

GRANDFATHER'S JOURNEY

Allen Say. (Boston, Mass.: Houghton Mifflin, 1993) 32 pages. ISBN 0-395-57035-2. Performance expectation: a.

In glorious illustrations that are so realistic they appear to be photographs, this 1994 Caldecott-winning picture book recounts a Japanese American man's love for two countries. Author and illustrator Allen Say tells the story of his grandfather's life, as he left Japan as a young man and came to America. After exploring much of the country, he settled in San Francisco, where he married, and then had a daughter. Once the daughter was grown, Say's grandfather longed for the land of his childhood, so he and his family returned to Japan where the daughter married and had a son. Although Say's grandfather did not have the chance to return to California because of World War II, Say did. He, too, came to America as a young man, feeling an important link with his grandfather that he had not known before. Say writes that, like for his grandfather, "The funny thing is, the moment I am in one country, I am homesick for the other."

1. What does Say's grandfather like about America? Do you appreciate these qualities about your homeland, too, or are there other ones you appreciate more?

2. Have you ever felt this tug at your heart, wanting to be one place (it does not have to be another country) until you are there and then wanting to be back home? Write a poem providing the details of this experience.

3. Suppose you were to move to another country next month. Choose a country and imagine what might be different about it. What could you (reasonably) take with you to make it seem more like "home"?

CHERRY PIES AND LULLABIES
Lynn Reiser. (New York: Greenwillow, 1998) 40 pages. ISBN 0-688-13391-6.
TORTILLAS AND LULLABIES
Lynn Reiser. (New York: Greenwillow, 1998) 40 pages. ISBN 0-688-14628-7. Performance expectations: a, f, g.

Cherry Pies and Lullabies is about four generations of mothers who sing lullabies, bake a favorite food, make a quilt, and create a crown of flowers. *Tortillas and Lullabies (Tortillas y Cancionitas)* follows the same idea, but it features Costa Rican women. The paintings were done by a group of women who were taught to paint by an American Peace Corps volunteer. Although picture books are usually intended for primary grade children, they can be a rich resource for middle grade students, who can study pictures and make comparisons between cultures, coming to an understanding of the most universal of human groups—the family.

1. The book *Tortillas and Lullabies (Tortillas y Cancionitas)* is about an American Peace Corps volunteer who helped a group of women in Central America establish a cottage industry. If you were willing to spend two years of your adult life in a less

developed country, where would you serve? What skills or services would you bring to that country? Write a "letter of application" explaining where you would like to go and what talents you could bring.

2. Using the Internet, visit www.peacecorps.gov or www.law.vill.edu/fed-agency/fedwebloc.html to find out about the Peace Corps. Share your information with your classmates.

3. Plan your own picture book on the United States comparing it with a country you may have studied or visited. What activities would you choose to compare the two countries and show both commonalities and differences? Fishing? Playing catch? Check out the format of Reiser's books for ideas.

Non-Fiction

WHAT DO WE KNOW ABOUT ISLAM?
Shahrukh Husain. Illustrated by Celia Hart. (New York: Peter Bedrick, 1996) 40 pages. ISBN 0-87226-388-6.

WHAT DO WE KNOW ABOUT CHRISTIANITY?
Carol Watson. Illustrated by Celia Hart. (New York: Peter Bedrick, 1997) 48 pages. ISBN 0-87226-390-8. Performance expectation: a.

Colorful photographs are a particularly appealing aspect of this series. The format groups encyclopedic entries around basic questions that young people might have such as, How do Muslims worship? How did Islam begin? What is Haj? Why is Mecca important? The work on Christianity has been included in this list of recommended books to help Christian children gain greater perspective on how their own religion is described to others. Many Christian students may be familiar with works about minorities and non-Christian religions, but it might be helpful to these students to read a work in which their own religion is profiled as if it were less well known.

1. Choose another book in the series about a religion that is well known to you and read it. What topics do you think should receive additional treatment or could be added to the series? What do you perceive are the strengths or weaknesses of this work?

2. Choose one of the books about a faith less well known to you. Write questions for an interview that would help you understand this faith more fully. Then compare and contrast this set of beliefs with your own.

3. After reading about a religion less well known to you, do a "K W L," making a list of information underneath each key letter. K—What did you Know about that religion before you read the book? W—What did you Want to learn? L—What did you Learn about the religion? What questions were not answered in this book?

4. Contrast two works in this series and attempt to identify commonalities of the religions.

STORY OF THE UNITED NATIONS
Conrad Stein. (San Diego, Calif.: Greenhaven Press, 1994) 32 pages. ISBN 1-516-06677-3. Performance expectations: b, e, f.

Although not lengthy, this book provides much information about how the United Nations (UN) came to be and what its role in the world is currently. The photographs are excellent, and complement the text well.

1. Create a one-page "fact" sheet about the UN. In other words, present an overview of what the United Nations is and what it does.

2. Near the end of the book, several UN agencies are described briefly. In groups of three, find out more about these three agencies. Then, as a group, create a tri-fold board sharing what you learned.

ISOLATION VS. INTERVENTION: IS AMERICA THE WORLD'S POLICE FORCE? (ISSUES OF OUR TIME SERIES)
Karen Bornemann Spies. (New York: Twenty-first Century Books, 1995) 64 pages. ISBN 0-8050-3880-9. Performance expectations: a, b, e, f.

This informational book would be an ideal companion to *Story of the United Nations*. This book opens by posing these questions: "How involved should the United States be in the affairs of other countries? When, if ever, should this country declare war? Bring 'democracy' to other countries? Donate food and medical supplies to nations fighting civil wars? Have colonies overseas? Send troops to other nations—or sell those nations weapons?" The book concludes with a chapter titled "Where Do We Go from Here? Because the conclusion is open ended, students at the middle grade level may enjoy deciding which route they believe is in the world's best interest.

1. Create a timeline showing when the United States was choosing to be isolationist or when the United States was choosing to be interventionist.

2. The glossary in this text is brief. Add brief descriptions of specific decisions or events, such as the Marshall Plan, the Cold War, and the Bay of Pigs. Include as many as you think would be helpful. Hint: Use the index to provide some guidance regarding which event or decision to include.

GAMES PEOPLE PLAY: MEXICO (SERIES)

Conrad Stein. (Chicago, Ill.: Children's Press, 1995) 64 pages. ISBN 0-516-04439-7.

GAMES PEOPLE PLAY: INDIA (SERIES)

Dale Howard. (Chicago, Ill.: Children's Press, 1996) 64 pages. ISBN 0-516-04437-0. Performance expectations: a, b, d, f, g.

This series, which also includes books on England, Japan, and the United States, addresses one of the primary ways people connect around the world—through sports. In fact, the text on Mexico begins with a chapter called "The Passion for Sports." Other chapters that address "global connections" particularly well are "Olympic Glory" and "Mexican-American Athletes." Similarly, the book on India includes a chapter on "International Sports." The cooperative nature of sports is emphasized well because it is clear that "games" can unite the world.

1. If you were going to choose one sport that you believe best unites the world, which one would it be? Be sure to explain why in your persuasive essay.
2. Each of these books includes background information about a country. Write a one-page overview of a country. Then analyze which sports are most popular in that country. Considering the geography of the country as well, explain why the popularity of its sports "fits" that country.
3. The Olympics are the best example of a global sports connection. Find out when the original Olympics began, and summarize their history. See if you can identify which sport draws competitors from the most countries; document your findings.

THE INTERNET KIDS AND FAMILY PAGES

Jean Armour Polly. (Berkeley, Calif.: Osborne/McGraw Hill, 1999) 784 pages. ISBN 0-072-11849-0. Performance expectations: c, d, e, f.

This book includes more than one hundred pages of descriptions of web sites related to different countries, as well as map web sites. This book is not only clearly written to appeal to children and busy parents but also is candid about risks involved in sending messages over the Internet. As the Usenet Newsgroups for Kids section states, "Part of Usenet is just for kids. However, it is important to remember the following: Even in areas set aside for kids, adults can send messages. You might even find adults pretending to be kids." Still, under careful control, the Internet can provide a wonderful opportunity for learning. A few of the recommended sites (and activities) are listed here:

1. Endangered and Extinct Species: Learn about plans to recover species on the brink of extinction. Address: www.fws.gov.

2. Energy: Renewable Energy Education Module. Learn about five types of renewable energy—a suitable site for a beginner. Address: solstice.crest.org.

THE INTERNET FOR YOUR KIDS

Denen Frazier, Barbara Kurshan, and Sarah Armstrong. (Almedia, Calif.: Sybex, 1998) 353 pages. ISBN 0-7821-2167-5. Performance expectations: c, d, e, f.

Although this work does not include as many web sites as does *The Internet Kids and Family Pages*, it, too, has an appealing format and contains an appendix that has a listing of many good sites, such as Voices of Youth, at www.un.org/youth. The book also contains hints for readers on using the various web sites. Of particular interest to those wishing for help in nurturing students' learning about global interactions is Chapter 2, "Making Global Connections," and Chapter 4, "Changing the World with a Few Friends."

1. After reading Chapter 4, evaluate the steps and sites recommended by the authors for making changes. Write a review to share with your class.
2. Discover strategies that other kids in other communities are using. Take a look at www.teaching.com.

THE WORLD WIDE WEB

Christopher Lampton. (New York: Franklin Watts, 1997) 64 pages. ISBN 0-531-15842-X. Performance expectations: c, d, e, f.

This brief work is an excellent introduction for a student—or teacher—to the web. Included in a chapter describing a few web sites is one on the White House (www.whitehouse.gov). Although this book isn't as comprehensive as are longer works of web sources, this is a good resource for getting started on the Internet.

1. This book is particularly good for someone who is just learning about the Internet. Using as many of the words in the glossary as possible, explain simply how the Internet works, making sure to include why it is called the WORLD Wide Web.
2. Using this text as a starting place, explain how the Internet began and what its original purpose was. Was it initially a global endeavor? (You will need to consult other resources as well.)

ON-LINE KIDS: A YOUNG SURFER'S GUIDE TO CYBERSPACE

Preston Gralla. (New York: John Wiley and Sons, Inc., 1996) 281 pages. ISBN 0-471-13545-3. Performance expectations: c, d, e, f.

This reference book is written in a conversational style that should appeal to middle school students. Some of the web sites suggest activities, such as writing to the president of the United States. The Virtual Schoolhouse, at sunsite.unc.edu/cisco/schoolhouse.html, provides information about school subjects, as well as a Yahoo List of Elementary or Middle schools (www.yahoo.com/Education/K_12/Elementary_Schools/ or www.yahoo.com/Education/K_12/Middle_Schools). The author evaluated sites on the basis of usefulness and "coolness."

1. Using Chapter 19 as a guide, create a home page with your social studies class "to broadcast to the world" your accomplishments.

2. Choose one of the web sites with "global" possibilities and rate it yourself; then compare your rating with the author's on both usefulness and "coolness."

Novels, Stories and Folk Tales

NZINGHA: WARRIOR QUEEN OF MATAMBA, ANGOLA, AFRICA, 1595

Patricia McKissack. (New York: Scholastic, 2000) 136 pages. ISBN 0-439-11210-9. Performance expectations: a, b, d, e, f.

This is Patricia McKissack's debut in the Royal Diary Series. Nzingha is indeed a "warrior queen." In this book inspired by a brief note on a poster presenting "Great Kings of Africa" by the Anheuser Busch Brewery company, McKissack presents the story of a woman of high moral principles—a woman for all time. Like her father before her, Nzingha strove to keep the Portuguese from conquering the land of the Mbundu, her people. Although most of the book focuses on her early teenage years, the epilogue provides a most satisfying conclusion. The supplementary information and pictures that conclude the text also add depth to the subject.

1. Early in the diary (August 1595), Nzingha tells the "story" of her mother through the creation of a shell bracelet. Retell Nzingha's life story in a similar way, perhaps even drawing a picture of the shells you place on her bracelet.

2. Nzingha was vehemently against the slave trade. In the persona of Nzingha, draw a map of the Portuguese slave trade routes and write an editorial that includes the information Nzingha discovered about slavery when she went to Luanda. Present the map and the editorial to your classmates as if they were clansmen you needed to convince of the reality of the Portuguese threat.

3. Find out more about the Gullah people of the Sea Islands off the coasts of South Carolina and Georgia; then make a presentation to your class highlighting the information you find on a tri-fold board.

4. Research life in present-day Angola. Then, by accenting Angola's key features, create a brochure for the state commerce board inviting people to live there.

SOS TITANIC

Eve Bunting. (San Diego, Calif.: Harcourt Brace & Company, 1996) 246 pages. ISBN 0-15-201305-9. Performance expectations: a, b, d, e, f.

Fifteen-year-old Barry is traveling to America from Ireland on the *Titanic* to join his parents after a long separation. With visions of American life occupying his thoughts on the journey, Barry realizes the shortcomings of the Irish class system. This realization becomes pivotal when he determines that peers from his hometown, traveling in steerage, will be the last to be "welcomed" into the lifeboats as the *Titanic* sinks. "Who's in control?" and "Why?" are central questions of this novel, and middle school students may eagerly explore them.

1. Do some additional research on the *Titanic*. Create a poster listing all of its features, both "unsinkable" and "fashionable," to convince people that taking a cruise on board the *Titanic* would be the "thing to do."

2. In the persona of either of Barry's parents, write a letter to Barry telling him why he or she wants him to join them in America.

TIES THAT BIND, TIES THAT BREAK

Lensey Namioka. (New York: Laurel-Leaf, 2000) 154 pages. ISBN 0-440-41599-3. Performance expectations: a, b, f.

This fascinating novel, set in the 1920s, chronicles the story of Third Sister Ailin, who refused to follow the Chinese custom of having her feet bound. Ailin's refusal leads to her being considered an unsuitable Chinese wife. Her engagement with Hanwei is broken, and Ailin loses status within her own family. Consequently, she becomes a nanny for the children of a missionary family in China, and when they return to the United States, she accompanies them. There she stays, marrying a young Chinese man who believes that a wife is a partner, not a possession.

1. Research the custom of binding feet. Share your information with the class. What do your classmates think of this practice? Do women in America wear healthy shoes?

2. Did Ailin have a "universal human right" not to have her feet bound? In the persona of her lawyer, plead her case in either an oral or written form.

BLOOMABILITY

Sharon Creech. (New York: Harper Collins, 1998) 273 pages. ISBN 0-06-026994-4. Performance expectations: a, b.

An "opportunity" came to thirteen-year-old Domenica Santolina Doone, or Dinnie, as she was whisked from Albuquerque, New Mexico, to live with her aunt and uncle in Lugano, Switzerland. There, Uncle Max would be headmaster, Aunt Sandy would teach, and Dinnie would be enrolled in the middle school of the American School, which accepted students from all over the world. Dinnie, a veteran of new schools through her father's many "opportunities," quickly realizes that kids will be kids and readily appreciates the diversity, although all of her classmates do not. The curriculum is not all that different from the curriculum in other schools that she has attended, she decides, although perhaps it is more varied, given the vast array of experiences of students who enter the school. But it is Global Awareness Month that really helps Dinnie make significant "global connections," comprehending more fully the realities of man-made and natural disasters, such as ozone depletion, poverty, and AIDS. She also learns about "knowledge of art and beauty and music and laughter"—and the gift of being able to make informed choices as an adult.

1. Which of Dinnie's new classmates would be the one that you hope would choose you as a friend? How would you choose? How would this choice facilitate global understanding?

2. The night that Lila has dinner with Dinnie and her aunt and uncle, Lila makes stereotypical remarks about various kinds of people. Why would Lila do this? Why do others do this? Does this practice promote global misunderstandings? How can such misconceptions be changed into greater understandings? In a small group, create a classroom policy statement that honors global communities.

3. Read other Sharon Creech novels, such as her Newbery Award winner *Walk Two Moons* (Harper Trophy, 1996, 280 pages, ISBN 0-0644-0517-6). Other possibilities are *Absolutely Normal Chaos* (HarperCollins, 1997, 230 pages, ISBN 0-0644-0632-6), *Pleasing the Ghost* (Harper Trophy, 1997, 96 pages, 0-0644-0686-5), or *Chasing Redbird* (HarperCollins, 1998, 261 pages, ISBN 0-0644-0696-2).

JAGUAR

Roland Smith. (New York: Hyperion, 1999) 249 pages. ISBN 0-7868-1312-1. Performance expectations: a, b, c, d, e, f.

After Jacob's mother dies, Jacob's dad finds ways to leave Jacob and Poughkeepsie to ease his feelings of loss. When he heads to Brazil to create a jaguar preserve, his original plan is that Jacob will stay in high school, visiting his father only during spring break. When a massive explosion destroys Jacob's father's boat and one of his father's partners is killed, the only person who can help fulfill the mission is Jacob. This amazing adventure highlights the consequences of greed, on both the spirit and the environment, and the potential of citizens of various countries to work together for the good of the Earth.

1. What do you know about the Amazon River? With three classmates, read about the region; then write a report, each person choosing one of the following topics: vegetation, animals, native peoples, or the effect of technology on the land.

2. Are there currently any jaguar preserves in Brazil, in any other South American country, or in a country outside of South America? How "endangered" are jaguars?

3. What international organizations support global human or animal rights projects? Using the Internet, make a list and post it on the bulletin board.

HABIBI

Naomi Shihab Nye. (New York: Aladdin, 1999) 272 pages. ISBN 0-689-82523-4. Performance expectations: a, b, d, e, f, g.

Habibi, meaning "darling" in Arabic, centers on the life of fourteen-year-old Liyana. Liyana's doctor father has lived in the United States for half of his life, and decides he is ready to return to the land of his birth—Palestine. So, along with Liyana's brother Rafik and mother, they leave St. Louis, Missouri, to live in Jerusalem. There, Liyana learns to love her father's mother, Sitti, and all of his family members as she grows to understand them and this world that is now hers as well. This is a valuable and compelling story because few stories of this part of the world are told from an Arab perspective. When Liyana's Jewish friend Omer visits Sitti's village, he tells them he wishes "they didn't have all these troubles in their shared country." Sitti responds, "We have been waiting for you for a very long time." This book's heart is the pursuit of peace. Its author believes that hope for the future rests with the young. This inspiring story reminds the reader that even in a land known for conflict, new visions can be born.

1. To provide more context for this novel, write a history of Israel's past fifty years.
2. As teenagers, what could Liyana and Omer actually do to promote peace in their country? What plan could they create and actually carry out?
3. As teenagers in the United States, what can you and your classmates do to help students like Liyana and Omer live in peace? What can you and your classmates do to promote peace worldwide?

HOMELESS BIRD

Gloria Whelan. (New York: HarperCollins, 2000). 240 pages. ISBN 0-060-28454-4. Performance objectives: a, b, d, f.

Winner of the National Book Award in 2000, *Homeless Bird* is an exceptional book of a culture underrepresented in young adult literature. Set in contemporary India, this book provides readers with insights into a culture that is probably much different from their own. Following her family's wishes, thirteen-year-old-Koly marries Hari; her family does not know until after the wedding that he is quite ill with tuberculosis. His family arranges the wedding so that they can use Koly's dowry to pay for his doctor and a trip to the holy Ganges River in hopes of a miracle. He soon dies, nevertheless, and according to custom, Koly now belongs to his family, who sees her only as a reminder of their dead son. Eventually, her mother-in-law abandons her in Vrindavan, a city of widows, and Koly begins a new life, one where she begins to control her destiny, not having to be subservient to others.

1. Make a list of the marriage customs that Koly and her family followed. Choose another culture. Make a chart noting how its marriage customs are similar or different.
2. In Whelan's author's note at the end of the text, she states that Rabindranath Tagore (1861-1941) was one of India's greatest poets. Find some of his poetry, perhaps reading Selected Poems (William Radice, Editor, South Asia books, 1995, 208 pages, ISBN 0-140-18366-3). Choose your favorite one, perhaps "Bride," and share it with the class.
3. Whelan also notes that Tagore won the Nobel Prize in 1913. Do a bit of research and find out why he was so honored. Create a poster highlighting his artistic accomplishments.
4. Koly speaks Hindi, one of the many languages of India. Create a pie chart, showing the other major languages spoken there and the percentage of speakers of each.

5. Koly is of the Hindu faith. What are the tenets of this religion? Write a one-to two-page paper describing this perspective.
6. The economic plight of the people, especially widows, is vividly portrayed. Mrs. Devi's son had one plan for helping the widows. What other ideas do you have for helping this group of people?

TALES OF THE SHIMMERING SKY: TEN GLOBAL FOLKTALES WITH ACTIVITIES

Susan Milord. Illustrated by JoAnn Kitchel. (Charlotte, Vt.: Williamson, 1996) 128 pages. ISBN 1-885593-01-5. Performance expectations: a, b.

Although we have not typically included books such as this in this bibliography (because the book already includes activities), it may be helpful to use with younger middle school students. The tales themselves span the globe—as the sky links us all—and facilitate the first performance objective particularly well, as do most of the short informational sections that accompany each tale. Although some of the activities are just plain fun, there are several that link well to science and art.

1. Create a map showing where each of these tales originated.
2. Choose one of the stories and memorize it. Choose one of the activities and make preparations to tell the story, and lead either your class or a younger class in completing the activity.

THE GOLDEN HOARD: MYTHS AND LEGENDS OF THE WORLD

Geraldine McCaughrean. Illustrated by Bee Willey. (New York: Simon and Schuster, 1997) 130 pages. ISBN: 0-689-81322-8. Performance expectations: a, b.

Willey has illustrated with vibrancy this collection of twenty-two traditional tales from around the world. The diversity of cultures whose stories are presented is particularly broad. McCaughrean provides some notes about the origin of these stories at the end of the book.

1. Create a map showing where each of these tales originated.
2. The purpose of many traditional tales is either to explain why and how something was created (called a *pourquoi* tale), such as "How Music Was Fetched Out of Heaven," or to maintain the social order, as in "The Golden Wish." Read three tales and write a paragraph about what the purpose of each seems to be.

Poetry

A SUITCASE OF SEAWEED

Janet Wong. (New York: Simon & Schuster, 1996) 42 pages. ISBN 0-689-80788-0. Performance expectations: a, b, c, d, e.

Divided into three sections, this unique collection of poems honors Wong's Korean mother, her Chinese father, and her American identity. Wong relates the actions and belief systems of each culture. In the Korean section, she describes the burial of kimchi and the tradition of removing shoes; in the Chinese section, she relates the gift of "poor girl's pearls, cooked fish eyes," and the sacredness of the tea ceremony; and in the American section, in a poem dealing with "Manners," she discusses the difficulty of deciding between Chinese and Korean eating customs.

1. Consider your own heritage. Write a poem that shares one of the dilemmas you face when in "mainstream" society, or one that describes Wong's dilemma.

2. Read Wong's other cultural collection of poems, *Good Luck Gold and Other Poems* (Margaret McElderry, 1994, 42 pages, ISBN 0-689-50617-1). Compare it with this book. Which do you like more? Why?

3. Which poems in all three sections reveal thoughts or beliefs you share with Wong? Make a list. Then choose one poem, memorize it, share it with the class, and explain why this poem makes so much sense to you.

Notes

1.   This section is directly quoted from National Council for the Social Studies, *Expectations of Excellence: Curriculum Standards for Social Studies* (Washington, D.C.: Author, 1994), 102.

CHAPTER TWELVE

⊗ CIVIC IDEALS AND PRACTICES

Performance Expectations

Social studies programs should include experiences that provide for the study of the *ideals, principles, and practices of citizenship in a democratic republic*, so that the learner can:

a. examine the origins and continuing influence of key ideals of the democratic republican form of government, such as individual human dignity, liberty, justice, equality, and the rule of law;

b. identify and interpret sources and examples of the rights and responsibilities of citizens;

c. locate, access, analyze, organize, and apply information about selected public issues—recognizing and explaining multiple points of view;

d. practice forms of civic discussion and participation consistent with the ideals of citizens in a democratic republic;

e. explain and analyze various forms of citizen action that influence public policy decisions;

f. identify and explain the roles of formal and informal political actors in influencing and shaping public policy and decision-making;

g. analyze the influence of diverse forms of public opinion on the development of public policy and decision-making;

h. analyze the effectiveness of selected public policies and citizen behaviors in realizing the stated ideals of a democratic republican form of government;

i. explain the relationship between policy statements and action plans used to address issues of public concern;

j. examine strategies designed to strengthen the "common good," which consider a range of options for citizen action.[1]

Picture Books

SO YOU WANT TO BE PRESIDENT?

Judith St. George. Illustrated by David Small. (New York: Philomel Books, 2000) 53 pages. ISBN 0-399-23407-1. Performance expectations: a, b, f.

The 2001 Caldecott Winner, *So You Want to Be President?*, is written with a great deal of humor. St. George reports that your path to the White House might be eased if your name were James (six presidents shared this name), you were born in a log cabin (eight presidents were), and you have brothers and sisters (every one of them did). Still, the concluding part looks carefully at those who have served—and those who have not—no women, no people of color, and no one who has not been either a Protestant or a Roman Catholic. This section also elucidates why people choose to be president and includes the oath of office each president has taken. This picture book provides serious food for thought about the concept of leading a democratic nation.

1. So, would you like to be president? Why or why not? State your position clearly, giving at least three reasons why or why not.

2. Ask your classmates whether or not they have thought about becoming president. Could the "white male" pattern change with your generation?

3. After reading this book, including pages 49-52, which president do you admire most? Why? Create a paragraph stating your choice and including at least three reasons for that choice.

MINTY

Alan Schroeder. Illustrated by Jerry Pinkney. (New York: Dial, 1996) 40 pages. ISBN 0-803-71888-8. Performance expectations: a, b, f, h, j.

The appeal of this biography of the early life of Harriet Tubman comes from its focus on the frustration that eight-year-old Harriet feels. Her father helps her to understand that she is not yet old enough to run away, let alone fulfill what will be her destiny—assuming the responsibility of leading about three hundred slaves to freedom. The power of this picture book is in Tubman's conviction to take action and do something against slavery.

1. "If your head is in the lion's mouth, it's best to pat him a little. Your head's in his mouth, Minty, but you sure ain't doin' any pattin'. You're just fixin' to get your head bit off." On a scale from 1 to 5, decide where you stand on that piece of advice. If you strongly agree, you are a 5; agree, 4; not sure or can't decide, 3; disagree, 2; and strongly disagree, 1. Pair off those who say "4" or "5" with those who say "1" or "2," and discuss whether the sentence is good or bad advice for those who are minorities or have little power.

2. Read a fuller account of Harriet Tubman's life, such as *Go Free or Die: A Story About Harriet Tubman* by Jeri Ferris (Carolrhoda Books, 1989, 64 pages, ISBN 0-876-14504-7) and compare it with this book.

3. Read *Sojourner Truth: Ain't I A Woman* by Patricia and Fredrick McKissack (Scholastic, 1994, 186 pages, ISBN 0-590-44691-6) and examine the similarities between the two women.

I HAVE A DREAM

Martin Luther King, Jr. Illustrated by fifteen Coretta Scott King Award and Honor Book Artists. (New York: Scholastic Press, 1997) 40 pages. ISBN 0-590-20516-1. Performance expectations: a, b, c, d, e, f.

On August 28, 1963, Dr. Martin Luther King, Jr., gave a speech that has become an American treasure. This richly illustrated version of his historic message is a most welcome and long overdue tribute to this man and his vision. King fervently wished that "people of all colors and religions could learn how to live together and treat each other like brothers and sisters," says his wife, Coretta Scott King, in a moving foreword.

1. King's speech was delivered during the March on Washington. Research the significance of this event and write a news report in the persona of a reporter attending the event on August 29, 1963.

2. On page 30, famous and not-so-famous African Americans are named in the background of the painting by Carole Byard. Choose one with whom you are unfamiliar and write a short report on a 4" x 6" or 5" x 8" index card. Choose several friends to do the same thing, and create a bulletin board highlighting the accomplishments of these important people.

THE DAY GOGO WENT TO VOTE: SOUTH AFRICA, 1994

Elinor Batezat Sisulu. Illustrated by Sharon Wilson. (Boston, Mass.: Little, Brown and Company, 1999) 32 pages. ISBN 0-316-70271-4. Performance expectations: a, b, c, d, e, f.

"Inspiring and moving," says Nelson Mandela of this powerful picture book that chronicles the first time black South Africans were permitted to vote in a governmental election. Thembi's great-grandmother, Gogo, who is so old she has not left the house in years, decides to vote and declares that six-year-old Thembi will accompany her. Overcoming the physical obstacles, Gogo does indeed vote and is honored as the oldest voter in her township. The significance and privilege of voting are not lost because of the simplicity of this story; indeed, the poignancy of the words and the warmth of the drawings support this basic premise and promise of democracy.

1. Find a biography of Nelson Mandela. Discover why he is so important to the history of South Africa. Then compare his life and his beliefs to those of Martin Luther King, Jr.

2. Determine what the products, both agricultural and manufactured, are from South Africa. Create a map showing where these products are made.

3. A "Glossary and Pronunciation Guide" precedes this text. It states that Xhosa and Zulu are two of the major dialects spoken in Soweto, where this story takes place. What else can you find out about these dialects and the culture of South Africa?

Non-Fiction

IF YOU HAD TO CHOOSE, WHAT WOULD YOU DO?

Sandra McLeod Humprey. Illustrated by Brian Strassburg. (Amherst, N.Y.: Prometheus, 1995) 115 pages. ISBN 1-57392-010-X. Performance expectations: b, d, j.

This is a collection of twenty-five social dilemmas, each of which can be read out loud to a class in less than ten minutes; each story concludes with discussion questions. Although intended to be used by a parent, this book is clearly appropriate for classroom application. The introduction stresses process and alternative solutions to problems, but the stories are not truly moral dilemmas. Rather, there is usually one choice that would be clearly honorable but might mean the loss of peer acceptance and a second choice that would clearly be dishonorable but would allow the person making the decision to save face.

1. In a small group, choose a story and act it out for your classmates, creating one or more alternative endings. Following the presentation of its last

ending, the group should share its recommended ending.

2. For one of the stories, to fully understand the issue, assume the identity of each character and write what each is feeling.

3. Choose a story. Identify two resolutions for the issue, and list the advantages and disadvantages of each. Try to see which principles are at stake, such as being liked versus being loyal to the family, or confronting a sister's drug problem versus having her be angry with you.

4. After reading, performing, or writing about a number of these episodes, write a letter to your teacher indicating why these topics should or should not be discussed in class further, being sure to address whether or not you feel such discussions are helpful in nurturing a sense of citizenship.

TAKE A STAND

Daniel Weizmann. Illustrated by Jack Keely. (Los Angeles, Calif.: Price, Stern & Sloan, 1996) 64 pages. ISBN 0-8431-7997-X. Performance expectations: a. b, d, e, f, g, h, j.

Using a creative format with a variety of illustrations, this work provides information about the U.S. government. Particularly helpful for classroom use are a sample preamble to a high school Constitution, and clear, simple, short explanations of the Bill of Rights. Much of the detail noted in the book could be used by a teacher to embellish his or her instruction. Although explanations are brief, the book does contain helpful information including addresses and web sites.

1. "Grass Roots Activities" included in the book are ways to get involved and make a difference. They include recycling, fundraising, and even picketing. As a class, choose one activity and discuss what kind of actions could be taken. The issue you choose may depend on the political situation in your community.

2. After choosing one of the listed issues as a class, or creating a different one, use the suggestions in the book to draft a persuasive letter to a decision maker who might be able to help further your cause. The addresses listed of key decision makers may be helpful.

3. If your class or school does not already have class or school elections, write a proposal to your teacher or principal suggesting that this means of student representation would help all students "live" civic ideals. If you are successful, run for office and use the tips on winning an election to help you do so.

TOUGH ISSUES, GOOD DECISIONS: STORIES AND WRITING PROMPTS

Lillian Putnam and Eileen Burke. (New York: Scholastic, 2001) 72 pages, 0-439-24117-0. Performance expectations: b, c, d, j.

Written for grades four to eight, and formerly published as *Stories to Talk About,* these stories deal with all-too-familiar classroom situations such as name-calling, stealing, drugs, practical jokes, and intolerance. The teacher's guide, which precedes the stories, provides a model for presenting each story: "Reflect on the story, identify the problem, propose alternative solutions, evaluate the consequences, and justify the choices." For each story, there are focused questions for discussions, as well as directions for a writing activity.

1. Write a personal or fictional narrative about how one of these issues affected your life. Read your finished story to the class.

2. In a small group, act out one of the stories using a courtroom as the setting.

REBELS AGAINST SLAVERY: AMERICAN SLAVE REVOLTS

Patricia McKissack and Fredrick McKissack. (New York: Scholastic, 1998) 176 pages. ISBN 0-590-45736-5. Performance expectations: a, b, f, h, j.

Masterful storytellers, the McKissacks tell the stories of slaves in and around America who resisted oppression. The familiar names include Harriet Tubman, Nat Turner, Cinque, and those who fought with John Brown, but they also include people who were part of the early resistance, such as the Maroons in Jamaica, and Toussaint L'Ouverture in Haiti. The stories, with few exceptions, are tragic and remind the reader of the consequences of oppression.

1. Each chapter focuses on a different person. Select one and assume that person's identity. Pretend you were able to write a letter to another hero in the book. In your letter, review your experiences and those of your correspondent. Be sure to explain why revolt seems necessary.

2. Be a talk show host. Design your own show and include as guests the heroes from the past featured in this book. (The title of the book should be the title of the show.) As the host, create a list of interview questions for each of your "guests" so that he or she will be comfortable being interviewed. Be sure that the audience understands the importance of your show's topic.

3. Divide a piece of paper vertically. As you read each chapter, write on one side of the paper, "Information I

learned." On the other side, write, "My feelings about that information."

BIG ANNIE OF CALUMET: A TRUE STORY OF THE INDUSTRIAL REVOLUTION

Jerry Stanley. (New York: Crown Publishers, 1996) 102 pages. ISBN 0-517-70097-2. Performance expectations: a, b, e, f, g, h, j.

This is the story of a woman who achieves great visibility in a turn-of-the-century miner's strike. It may appeal to students who identify with those who struggle against the powerful. The book provides insights into the realities of the labor struggles before the New Deal. The Afterword about the heroine's personal life is interesting.

1. What makes a citizen like Annie take action? She obviously influenced public policy, but she did so at great personal cost. Write down the factors that help someone acquire that kind of strength. Be as specific as possible.

2. Write a list of the decisions that Annie and the leaders made which influenced the larger community. Then decide which actions you think were the most effective. Do you think they would be as effective today? Why or why not? Write a one-page position paper.

3. This book was written by someone who is sincerely sympathetic to Annie. Write a book review from the perspective of the owners of the Calumet, which means that your review will be critical of the author and his perspective. After you have written the review, add an epilog that explains the perspective with which you are more comfortable.

4. With a small group of classmates who also read this book, discuss whether or not you would want Annie as your mother if your father were a miner in that community.

GANDHI: GREAT SOUL

John Severance. (Boston, Mass.: Houghton Mifflin, 1997) 144 pages. ISBN 0-395-77179-X. Performance expectations: a, b, c, d, e, f, g, h, i, j.

Gandhi, known for his nonviolent practices, addressed economics directly with his protests. His major protest against the British who were ruling India was an economic one—the 1930 Salt March to the sea. He urged all Indians to weave a coarse cloth called *khadi* for their clothing, thus avoiding the need to buy the more expensive cotton woven in England. He was convinced that Indian peasants needed to be more self-sufficient. Only then could India sever the British ties and attain *Purna Swaraj* or Complete Independence.

1. What was Gandhi's basic belief system? Write an "I believe" paper in the persona of Gandhi. Then share it with your classmates and ask them if they believe these things.

2. As you read the book, keep a list of Sanskrit words, writing down their English equivalents as well. Are these words a good description of Gandhi? Write a poem, using these words (and others) to describe Gandhi's life.

3. What places were important in Gandhi's life? Create a map, placing each location in the appropriate spot; then on an accompanying page, write a brief description of its significance in his life.

4. The last photograph in the book shows a collection of Gandhi's possessions at the time of his death. What do these possessions say about Gandhi? Write a tribute to this man and his accomplishments.

NO PRETTY PICTURES, A CHILD OF WAR

Anita Lobel. (New York: Greenwillow, 1998) 208 pages. ISBN 0-688-15935-4. Performance expectations: a, f, h.

Anita Lobel is a well-known author and illustrator of children's books. She is also a survivor of the Holocaust. This book is her story. It tells of her Christian maid, Niania, who hid Anita and her brother, and a Benedictine convent that provided shelter regardless of the consequences.

1. "Niania never really let us forget that we were not baptized, that we were Jewish children. She worshipped the Holy Mother, mistrusted Jews, yet she protected my brother and me with the flapping wings of a demented angel." There were other people like Niania, but too few. What do you think makes a person "a righteous one"?

2. Milton Meltzer, in his book *Rescue: The Story of How Gentiles Saved Jews in the Holocaust* (HarperCollins, 1991, ISBN 0-644-6117-3), profiles a number of "righteous ones," as does Steven Spielberg in his award-winning film *Shindler's List* (1993, ASIN 6303168507, Rated "R"). Read the book. What were some of the ingenious ways the Jews were saved from Hitler's plan?

3. For another view of the Holocaust, read *Torn Thread* (Anne Isaacs; Scholastic, 2000, 188 pages, ISBN 0-590-60364-7), the biography of Eva Buchbinder. What "civic ideals" and practices are noteworthy even within the most barbaric of places—a Nazi work camp? Make a list of people and their actions that exemplify the key to civility—honoring human dignity.

4. Look for other books by Anita Lobel in the library—especially ones she illustrated. See if you can note any references in her paintings that reflect her childhood experiences in Europe.

KINDERTRANSPORT

Olga Levy Drucker. (New York: Henry Holt, 1995) 146 pages. ISBN 0-805-04251-2. Performance expectations: a, b, c, f, g, h.

Kindertransport is Drucker's recounting of the six years she spent in England after having been sent there at the age of eleven by the *kindertransport*, literally, "child transport." In 1938, the Nazis gave the Jews no choice—either leave their homelands or die. After *Kristallnacht* on November 9, the Jewish Refugee Committee orchestrated the escape of ten thousand children, only one thousand of whom were eventually reunited with their parents. Olga was one of the lucky ones. This compelling story begins by describing what happened before Hitler came to power, which may prepare the reader more fully for understanding how the personal and civil rights of the Jews—and others Hitler felt were "undesirable"—were abridged.

1. Pretend you are Olga. Write a letter to your parents explaining how and why you feel your personal rights have been forgotten.
2. Find out more about *Kristallnacht*. Write a short report and share it with the class.
3. Research the *Kindertransport*, writing a brief biography of another of its participants.

LET IT SHINE! STORIES OF BLACK WOMEN FREEDOM FIGHTERS

Andrea Davis Pinkney. Illustrated by Stephen Alcorn. (San Diego, Calif.: Harcourt/Gulliver Books, 2000) 107 pages. ISBN 0-15-201005-X. Performance expectations: a, b, e, f, g ,h i.

In this amazing book, the sole 2001 Coretta Scott King Honor Book, Pinkney shares brief but brilliant biographies of ten extraordinary black women. Some of the portraits honor those who are already well known, including Harriet Tubman and Rosa Parks, but even these will reveal new information to most readers. Other portraits describe the lives of not-so-well-known women, such as Biddy Mason and Dorothy Irene Height. Indeed, these women are the embodiment of "civic ideals and practices." Each dedicates her life to the betterment of humankind.

1. With two classmates, choose one of the women. Specifically, how has she been a "light for America"? Write a tribute by recounting the woman's significant achievements.

2. Transform the prose tributes into poems; then read aloud your poetry as a Readers Theater.

Novels, Stories and Folk Tales

DATELINE: TROY

Paul Fleischman. Illustrated by Glenn Morrow and Gwen Frankfeldt. (Cambridge, Mass.: Candlewick Press, 1996) 80 pages. ISBN 1-56402-469-5. Performance expectations: a, b, e, f, h.

Juxtaposing newspaper clippings from the last century with the story of the Trojan War, Fleischman shows the timelessness of humanity's frailty. On the left side of each spread, Fleischman tells the story of Troy while on the right he places one or several newspaper articles that parallel the historical event with a more recent one. For example, Queen Hecuba's nightmare, as the story is retold, is interpreted to mean that "the child [the prince] will bring fire and ruin upon Troy." The accompanying newspaper clipping from the *Santa Cruz Sentinel*, dated May 4, 1988, bears this headline: "Reagans use astrology, aides confirm." The next page reveals that when the queen does indeed bear a son, he is sent away with a herdsman to be killed, in order to fulfill the priest's command: "When it's born, cut the infant's throat," in order to protect Troy. The following page leads with the headline "Newborn Found in Dumpster." In both stories, the babies are left to die—and are saved. Page after page, the humanity—or inhumanity—of citizens of the world is revealed.

1. Choose another story and find parallel news article(s) of your own, creating a two-page spread similar to the layout of *Dateline: Troy*. If others are interested, compile your efforts, creating your own classroom book, which will document "civic practices," but not necessarily "civic ideals."
2. Read Paul Fleischman's *Joyful Noise: Poems for Two Voices* (illustrated by Eric Beddows; HarperCollins, 1998, 44 pages, ISBN 0-060-21852-5) for which Fleischman received the Newbery Medal. Choose your favorite part of the story of Troy and write it as a poem for two voices. Find a partner and read your work to the class or another audience.
3. Winner of the Scott O'Dell Award for historical fiction, Fleischman's *Bull Run* (illustrated by David Frampton; Harper Trophy, 1995, 104 pages, ISBN 0-064-40588-5) could be read aloud as Readers Theater. After doing so, have a class discussion that identifies parallels between the Civil War presented here and the battles in Troy.

THE SECRET OF SARAH REVERE

Ann Rinaldi. (San Diego, Calif.: Gulliver, 1995) 320 pages. ISBN 0-15-200392-4. Performance expectations: a, b.

Thirteen-year-old Sarah ponders one issue throughout this historical novel: "What matters? The truth? Or what people think?" Living in pre-Revolutionary War days, Sarah is surrounded by Patriots. She is constantly forced to confront the issues of the day, all revolving around questions of individual human dignity, liberty, justice, equality, and the rule of law. She knows that her father and his best friend believe in this "new order," and yet she worries for their safety as events escalate.

1. Read aloud "Paul Revere's Ride" by Henry Wadsworth Longfellow, perhaps the illustrated version by Ted Rand (Puffin, 1996, 40 pages, ISBN 0-140-55612-5). After reading both the novel and the poem, decide how "historically accurate" you believe the poem is.

2. Imagine you attended a meeting of the Long Room Club with Revere and Warren. If they had had a written agenda, what issues would have been listed on it? List these, and then recreate the conversation the sixteen members might have had.

3. Read one or more of the other historical novels by Ann Rinaldi that also deal with this time period: *The Fifth of March: The Story of the Boston Massacre* (Gulliver, 1994, 335 pages, ISBN 0-15-22751-77), *A Ride into Morning: The Story of Tempe Wicke* (Gulliver, 1995, 289 pages, ISBN 0-15-20067-37), and *Finishing Becca: The Story of Benedict Arnold and Peggy Shippen* (Gulliver, 1994, 362 pages, ISBN 0-15-20087-99).

SECOND DAUGHTER: THE STORY OF A SLAVE GIRL

Mildred Pitts Walter. (New York: Scholastic, 1996) 176 pages. ISBN 0-590-48282-3. Performance expectations: a, b, c, d, f, g, h, i, j.

Living just before the Revolutionary War, Aissa and her older sister Bett are slaves, but Bett listens carefully to the talk of freedom and comes to believe, that when those around her talk about "all men are created equal," that this phrase applies equally to her—despite the fact that she is both a slave and a female. Mildred Pitts Walter based this artfully woven, passionate story of moral courage on the 1781 case of Mum Bett, a slave who sued her owner for her freedom under the Massachusetts Constitution . . . and won.

1. At the close of the novel, Aissa states, "Say no to bondage and no one can keep you a slave. And I have now learned that no one can set you free. Freedom is living with realities in a way that they don't overcome you." Do you agree? Can a person be a slave in body and free in spirit? Write an essay sharing your position.

2. Similarly, also in the epilog, Aissa says that Sarah gave her the most wonderful gift, "the secret treasure of words." What did these words do for Aissa? Do you think students of today value words in the same way? Should they? Would it make a difference in the quality of their life if they did? Is the "secret treasure of words" critical to an informed citizenry?

CAT RUNNING

Zilpha Snyder. (New York: Dell Yearling, 1996) 168 pages. ISBN 0-440-41152-1. Performance expectations: a, b, e, f, g.

In this story, set in a small town in California during the Great Depression, Snyder presents a heartwarming story of one girl's compassion and virtue. Catherine, "Cat," Kinsey is the fastest runner in Brownwood School—until Zane Perkins, another sixth grader and an "Okie," shows up. Because of her father's religious beliefs, Cat is not permitted to wear slacks—even on race day—and so she decides not to run at all. But that does not mean that she never runs with Zane. In fact, one afternoon, they run from Okietown to Cat's house where they telephone the doctor and plead with him to see Zane's little sister, Sammy. If they had not, Sammy would have died. Despite her family's and the townspeople's warning to stay away from "those people," Cat comes to know Sammy, by sharing her secret hideaway in the canyon, and her brothers, by studying with them in school.

1. Who in this story seems to understand his or her responsibilities to others? Who appears not to understand this? Write a short paper acknowledging these "truths."

2. Find out more about "Okies." Write a Readers Theater production, sharing the "voices" of "Okies," letting each tell his or her story of what it was like to have to travel around the country to survive during these challenging years.

3. Do a short newscast about the Great Depression. Explain what caused it and what the effects of that event were.

4. During the Great Depression, what options did people have to help others? Write a story that describes how people survived by helping one another.

UNDER THE BLOOD-RED SUN

Graham Salisbury. (New York: Yearling, 1995) 246 pages. ISBN 0-440-41139-4. Performance expectations: a, b, d, e, j.

Set in Hawaii, this historical novel provides a glimpse into the treatment of Japanese Americans on the islands versus their treatment on the mainland. In this confusing time, Tomi has great difficulty understanding where his loyalty should be. Should he side with his grandfather, who is having a hard time reconciling the attack of Pearl Harbor with the values of his homeland? Should he resent his current country for incarcerating his father? How can he best help his mother and still discover what he believes?

1. After reading the book, in a short paper, answer the three questions stated above as you believe Tomi would.

2. At time of the bombing of Pearl Harbor, about 150,000 people of Japanese ancestry lived in Hawaii—more than were interned on the mainland. The Hawaiians, those closest to feeling the attack of Pearl Harbor and those who would seemingly feel the most threatened in the future, were nevertheless the most reasonable in addressing the fears people had of people with Japanese backgrounds. Read *Pearl Harbor Child* by Dorinda Makanaonalani Nicholson (illustrated by Larry Nicholson; Arizona Memorial Museum Association, 1998, 64 pages, ISBN 0-963-13886-3). Find out more about how Japanese Americans in Hawaii, and on the mainland, were treated.

3. Read Graham Salisbury's earlier book, *Blue Skin of the Sea* (Dell, 1994, 224 pages, ISBN 0-440-21905-1). Choose one of the eleven stories and retell it to the class. Afterwards, explain why you chose that particular story and what you learned about Hawaiian culture.

4. Read Graham Salisbury's later work, *Shark Bait* (Laurel Leaf, 1999, 151 pages, ISBN 0-440-22803-4). What do Mokes's decisions have to do with civic responsibility?

5. Or read Graham Salisbury's *Jungle Dogs* (Bantam, 1999, 192 pages, ISBN 0-440-41573-X). Should Damon be running with a gang? How does the concept of a gang relate with "civic ideals and practices"? Is it Damon's right to do as he pleases?

THE WATSONS GO TO BIRMINGHAM-1963

Christopher Paul Curtis. (New York: Delacorte Press, 1995) 210 pages. 0-385-32175-9. Performance expectations: a, e, h.

This 1996 Newbery and Coretta Scott King Honor book certainly deserves these awards. In prose that is relaxed and entertaining, Curtis tells a sometimes amusing and sometimes provocative story of a family. Kenny, the middle child of three, narrates the story of his Momma, Dad, little sister Joetta, and thirteen-year-old brother Byron, who seems to be headed for delinquency. Consequently, the whole family packs up the Ultra Glide to escort Byron from Flint, Michigan, to Birmingham, Alabama, where Grandma is supposed to "straighten Byron out." The ending, the bombing of a church, takes everyone by surprise, including the reader. Kenny, especially, has difficulty reconciling this event with the previous peacefulness of his life.

1. Discover who the girls were who Curtis says the book is "In memory of." Describe the event that cost them their lives. Decide what an appropriate monument to them would be; then write an "In Memoriam" speech to dedicate such a monument.

2. Before the Civil Rights amendment was passed, what was life like in the South? Write a journal entry comparing everyday life in the South now with previous ways of life there.

3. Compare and contrast the bombings of the churches in the sixties and the church burnings of the 1990s. Write a position paper calling for an end to such violence.

4. Read one of the other Coretta Scott King Honor books for 1996: *The Notebooks of Melanin Sun* by Jacqueline Woodson (Point, 1997, 160 pages, ISBN 0-590-45881-7) or *Like Sisters on the Homefront* by Rita Williams-Garcia (Puffin, 1998, 176 pages, ISBN 0-140-38561-4).

EAGLE SONG

Joseph Bruchac. Illustrated by Dan Anderson. (New York: Dial Books, 1997) 80 pages. ISBN 0-8037-1918-3. Performance expectations: a, b, c, j.

"It takes a lot more courage to make a friend sometimes than it does to make an enemy." Danny, an Iroquois Indian, is the son of a steel worker and a social worker. The family moves away from the reservation to the city for employment. The boy resents the decision because he is the only Indian in his school, and a classmate teases him because of his heritage. His father visits the school and tells how the Founding Fathers were inspired by the Iroquois League. Danny realizes he must confront his tormentor. He does so, and acceptance follows. This is a good read aloud for the lower middle grades.

1. Survey the class. Discover how many of your classmates have had to move to a new school. Prepare a "newcomers" book from advice they give about how to make friends in a new school.

2. Make an acrostic honoring the Iroquois. Write the key word (in this case, *Iroquois*) vertically and place a symbol (such as a pine tree) around the word. Think of words that describe the person and that include a letter in the key word. Place blanks, as appropriate, to the left or right, or on both sides of the letter. For each word, write a clue.

THE RIFLE

Gary Paulsen. (New York: Laurel Leaf, 1997) 105 pages. ISBN 0-440-21920-5. Performance expectations: a, b, c, e, g, i, j.

The book jacket proclaims, "This powerful short novel, with deadly accuracy, takes aim at the notion that 'Guns don't kill people, people kill people.'" In 1768, gunsmith Cornish McManus creates a masterpiece, a "sweet" rifle, which he eventually sells to another man, John Byam, who also treasures it. From generation to generation, the gun changes hands until one day it is placed above a fireplace . . . and it discharges. Teachers may need to prompt students into a discussion of civic rights and responsibilities, but the resulting dialog will probably be intense.

1. Find out what the National Rifle Association's position on handguns is. Find out what your state's policy is concerning citizens' rights and the owning of firearms. Decide whether you are in favor of the current laws or whether you would prefer that they were changed. Write an editorial stating your opinion.

2. As you read the text, keep a list of each owner's uses for the rifle. Then create a timeline for the rifle, listing each use below each date. Finally, write a short paper noting any patterns you discover.

HOPE WAS HERE

Joan Bauer. (New York: G. P. Putnam's Sons, 2000) 186 pages. ISBN 0-399-23142-0. Performance expectations: a, b, e, f, g, h, i, j.

The great news, actually, is that Hope is here, and that this treasure of a book can remain with its reader for a lifetime. Sixteen-year-old Hope and her Aunt Addie, "diner cook extraordinaire," have traveled the country, and their latest roost is in rural Wisconsin. The Welcome Stairways diner, with its regular patrons, along with plenty of new ones who come to enjoy Addie's fine cooking, is the center for a tale that is entirely believable and heartwarming, although not sentimental or predictable. A main theme is the importance of voting in the democratic process. In this story, citizens expose and weed out all kinds of political shenanigans.

1. The youth in the novel believe that "getting the vote out" is critical to their candidate's success. What "plan" did they have to motivate voters? What ideas would you borrow from this novel if you were campaigning for student council?

2. Choose a character and make a two-column chart to explain how he or she lives out "civic ideals" through his or her "practices." In the column on the left, write different "civic ideals," and in the column on the right, write the specific action of the character that shows this characteristic.

3. Read another of Bauer's books, *Backwater* (Puffin, 2000, 240 pages, ISBN 0-698-11865-0), the story of another sixteen-year-old, Ivy Breedlove. Her passion is history, particularly her family's and that of her Aunt Josephine, who lives as a hermit in the mountains. This memorable book shares the importance of recording family stories and remembering, "You can't pursue history without finding hope" (p. 185).

THE LANDRY NEWS

Andrew Clements. (New York: Simon & Schuster, 1999) 123 pages. ISBN 0-689-81817-3. Performance expectations: a, b, c, d e, f, g, h.

Once upon a time and three years running, fifth grade teacher Mr. Larson is named "Teacher of the Year." But as time goes on, Mr. Larson becomes less and less of a teacher and more and more of a room-sitter, allowing his students "to learn independently, as well as from each other." So Cara Landry writes an editorial in *The Landry News* and posts it one Friday, asking why Mr. Larson is earning a salary if she and her classmates are doing all the teaching. Mr. Larson reconsiders his position over the weekend and gives the students an assignment, which at first turns into a class newspaper, and then becomes a lesson in interpreting the Constitution, particularly its guarantee of free speech. Nearly suspended by the school board for allowing students to have total ownership of the newspaper, Mr. Larson is "saved" by his students' understanding of the Bill of Rights and the difference between news articles and editorials. Clements has created a believable scenario for important discussions about censorship and authority.

1. Is there a relationship between citizenship and censorship? How? What does it mean for each citizen? Write several paragraphs exploring this relationship.
2. Research instances in which school authorities censored school newspapers or literary magazines. After reading and analyzing all that you can find, what conclusions can you draw?
3. Does your school district have a written policy about school publications? If so, get a copy and read it. How would Mr. Larson's case have been handled in your district?
4. If your district does not have a written policy, write to local districts (or look on the Internet) asking if they could send a copy of theirs to you. Then draft a policy for your district.
5. Recreate Mr. Larson's disciplinary hearing, with various students taking on the roles of Mr. Larson, the principal, the school board president, and Michael, whose work is the central reason Mr. Larson is at the hearing. Is your dramatization "better" than the book's version. Why or why not?

SHILOH

Phyllis Reynolds Naylor. (New York: Yearling, 1991) 144 pages. ISBN 0-440-40752-4. Performance expectations: a, b, c, d, e, f, h, j.

Walking past the old Shiloh schoolhouse one day, eleven-year-old Marty finds a young beagle that he names after the school. Shiloh follows him home. Marty pleads with his parents to let him keep the dog, but they insist he return the dog to his owner, Judd. The problem is that Judd mistreats his dogs, including Shiloh, and Marty is adamant about protecting him. Ultimately, Marty becomes the rightful owner of Shiloh, but the path is difficult.

1. Marty argues with his father that he should be allowed to keep Shiloh because Judd abuses him. He argues that abused children are not allowed to remain in their parents' home and that this is the same principle. His father does not accept this argument. He says that the law must be upheld. What do you think? Is there a higher law than civil law? Find someone who agrees with you and two who do not, and lead a discussion with your class.
2. To accomplish his goal, did Marty have any other options? Brainstorm alternative paths that Marty could have taken.
3. Read the sequels: *Saving Shiloh* (Aladdin, 1999, 137 pages, ISBN 0-689-81461-5) and *Shiloh Season* (Aladdin, 1998, 120 pages, ISBN 0-689-80646-9).

Poetry

MUSIC AND DRUM: VOICES OF WAR AND PEACE, HOPE AND DREAMS

Laura Robb. Illustrated by Ed Young and Debra Lill. (New York: Philomel, 1997) 32 pages. ISBN 0-399-22024-0. Performance expectations: b, d, e.

Over the past decade, and even earlier, social studies educators have acknowledged and promoted the use of literature to teach citizenship. All writers, especially poets, help us understand what it means to be human. This book is further evidence of that belief. It is admittedly an anti-war work. The authors include notable poets such as Langston Hughes and Carl Sandburg, and noted children's authors Lucille Clifton and Eve Merriam, as well as a sixteen-year-old writer from Northern Ireland and children from Israel and Jordan.

1. After reading these poems, use either war or violence as a theme and write a poem expressing your thoughts. Consider an alphabet poem in which one adds a new word with the same first letter to each succeeding line.

    For example: War / Wrongful War / Wrongful Woeful War.
2. With a friend, write a variation of a cinquain poem. The format is as follows: Line one is a one-word title. Line two consists of two words to describe the title. Line three is three words that describe a feeling related to the title. Line four uses four words to describe the title. Line five is one word that refers to the title or is a synonym of it. For example: War / Violent, Wrong / Painful, Scary, Lonely / Families torn apart forever / Battle.
3. A poem that is useful for describing opposites is a *diamante* (diamond). The poem begins by describing the first concept, such as war, and at the middle of the poem, the center of the diamond, the poem begins to describe an opposite such as peace. This is the format: Line one is a noun. Line two has two adjectives that describe the noun. Line three has three participles about line one.

    Line four has two nouns that describe line one and then, after a space, two more nouns that describe the opposite of line one. Line five has three participles that describe the last line. Line six has two adjectives that describe the last line. Line seven is a noun that is the opposite of the first line. For example: War / Awful, Thunderous / Shooting, Bombing, Killing / Bloodshed, Enemy, Friendship, Accord / Singing, Praying, Rejoicing / Awesome, Quiet / Peace.

Notes

1. National Council for the Social Studies, *Expectations of Excellence: Curriculum Standards for Social Studies* (Washington, D.C.: Author, 1994), 105.

► BOOK TITLE INDEX

This index includes the titles of childrens's books that are annotated or recommended in Part Two, as well as books for which authors offer teaching suggestions in Part One.

▶ SUBJECT INDEX

This index lists the places, authors and subjects of the works of children's literature that are annotated, discussed, or incorporated in teaching suggestions in this book. Social studies disciplines are not listed in this index and readers interested in identifying books suitable for a particular discipline should refer to the chapter dealing with the appropriate strand of the social studies standards. For example, for books with historical themes, the reader should consult chapter 4, which deals with the strand of Time, Continuity, and Change.